Ailish Johnson
EUROPEAN WELFARE STATES AND SUPRANATIONAL GOVERNANCE OF
SOCIAL POLICY

Archie Brown (*editor*)
THE DEMISE OF MARXISM-LENINISM IN RUSSIA

Thomas Boghardt
SPIES OF THE KAISER
German Covert Operations in Great Britain during the First World War Era

Ulf Schmidt
JUSTICE AT NUREMBERG
Leo Alexander and the Nazi Doctors' Trial

Steve Tsang (*editor*)
PEACE AND SECURITY ACROSS THE TAIWAN STRAIT

C. W. Braddick
JAPAN AND THE SINO-SOVIET ALLIANCE, 1950–1964
In the Shadow of the Monolith

Isao Miyaoka
LEGITIMACY IN INTERNATIONAL SOCIETY
Japan's Reaction to Global Wildlife Preservation

Neil J. Melvin
SOVIET POWER AND THE COUNTRYSIDE
Policy Innovation and Institutional Decay

Julie M. Newton
RUSSIA, FRANCE AND THE IDEA OF EUROPE

Juhana Aunesluoma
BRITAIN, SWEDEN AND THE COLD WAR, 1945–54
Understanding Neutrality

George Pagoulatos
GREECE'S NEW POLITICAL ECONOMY
State, Finance and Growth from Postwar to EMU

St Antony's Series
Series Standing Order ISBN 0–333–71109–2
(*outside North America only*)

You can receive future titles in this series as they are published by placing a standing order.
Please contact your bookseller or, in case of difficulty, write to us at the address below with
your name and address, the title of the series and the ISBN quoted above.

Customer Services Department, Macmillan Disribution Ltd, Houndmills, Basingstoke,
Hampshire RG21 6XS, England

Local Governance in Central and Eastern Europe

Comparing Performance in the Czech Republic, Hungary, Poland and Russia

Tomila V. Lankina
De Montfort University

Anneke Hudalla
Independent Scholar and Journalist

with
Hellmut Wollmann
Humboldt University

In Association with
St Antony's College, Oxford

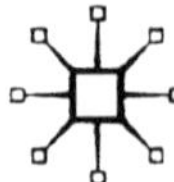

First published 2008 by
PALGRAVE MACMILLAN
Houndmills, Basingstoke, Hampshire RG21 6XS and
175 Fifth Avenue, New York, N.Y. 10010
Companies and representatives throughout the world.

PALGRAVE MACMILLAN is the global academic imprint of the Palgrave Macmillan division of St. Martin's Press, LLC and of Palgrave Macmillan Ltd. Macmillan® is a registered trademark in the United States, United Kingdom and other countries. Palgrave is a registered trademark in the European Union and other countries.

ISBN-13: 978–0–230–50036–5 hardback
ISBN-10: 0–230–50036–6   hardback

This book is printed on paper suitable for recycling and made from fully managed and sustained forest sources. Logging, pulping and manufacturing processes are expected to conform to the environmental regulations of the country of origin.

A catalogue record for this book is available from the British Library.

A catalog record for this book is available from the Library of Congress.

10 9 8 7 6 5 4 3 2 1
17 16 15 14 13 12 11 10 09 08

Printed and bound in Great Britain by
CPI Antony Rowe, Chippenham and Eastbourne

Contents

List of Tables

Notes on Authors

Tomila V. Lankina is Research Fellow at the Local Governance Research Unit of De Montfort University in Leicester. She received her D.Phil. from the University of Oxford in England. She is the author of *Governing the Locals: Local Self-Government and Ethnic Mobilization in Russia* (2004), and of numerous articles and book chapters on local and regional politics in Central and Eastern Europe.

Anneke Hudalla is a scholar specializing in the politics of the Czech Republic. She received her doctorate from Humboldt University in Berlin, where she also worked as Senior Research Fellow. She is the author of several articles on Central and Eastern European politics, and the book *Außenpolitik in den Zeiten der Transformation: Die Europapolitik der Tschechischen Republik 1993–2001* (2003) [Foreign policy in the time of transition: European policy of the Czech Republic, 1993–2001].

Hellmut Wollmann is Emeritus Professor of Public Administration and Public Policy at the Institute for the Social Sciences of Humboldt University, Berlin, Germany. He has done research on comparative government with a focus on local government in European countries, including Central and Eastern European countries and Russia. Among his many publications, he is coeditor (with Harald Baldersheim and Michal Illner) of *Local Democracy in Post-Communist Europe* (2003) and co-author (with Vesselin Dimitrov and Klaus H. Goetz) of *Governing after Communism: Institutions and Policy-making* (2006).

Preface

This book is the product of a collective effort. Hellmut Wollmann provided overall project administrative management and guidance. Tomila V. Lankina is the principal author of the study. She wrote Chapters 1, 4, 6 and 7, carried out research in Hungary and Russia, and revised and rewrote the original research project manuscript for publication as a book. Anneke Hudalla wrote Chapters 2, 3 and 5 and conducted research in the Czech Republic and Poland. Sections of chapters authored by one scholar incorporate research conducted by both scholars in the respective countries. We are extremely grateful to the German Public Science Foundation for providing generous funding for the research project. We would like to thank Judit Keller for her outstanding research support in Hungary, Alexander Belousov for his research in Berlin, and Magdalena Szaniawska and Jacqueline Kuehn for their excellent research assistance. We are also very grateful to the anonymous referee for his thoughtful comments and suggestions for improvement of the manuscript. Finally, we express our gratitude to local officials, members of civil society organisations, businesses and civic activists in the cities of Staraya Russa, Balashov, Jelenia Góra, Biała Podlaska, Ústí nad Labem, Karviná, Szolnok and Sopron who provided valuable insights for our study and facilitated our research. Any errors are of course solely our own.

Hellmut Wollmann

1
Methodology and Case Selection

When we set out on our research voyage to explore municipal performance in Central and Eastern Europe, we were struck by enormous within-country variation in local outcomes. These patterns defied conventional wisdom about the role of the structural 'givens' and broader national or regional institutional frameworks in charting a town's developmental trajectory.

The cities of Sopron and Szolnok are, for example, both Hungarian towns, and yet Szolnok is more comparable to the backward towns in the less well-off post-communist east. Sopron has suffered from many of the same economic and social problems as Szolnok, but local decision-making patterns are vastly different in the two towns. In Sopron, decision-making is politicised, but there is greater continuity of administrative personnel. Here businesses and civic activists pool resources to help the local government out in times of crisis, and there are regular meetings between the civic and municipal actors. A purely local political party with strong local roots helps keep the political balance when things get too heated in national elections and threaten to spill over into the local party-political arena. In Szolnok, a massive purge of administrative personnel accompanies the election of a new mayor; decision-making is highly conflictual; there are no strong local parties; and a local 'civic culture' of cooperation among local government and civil society is all but absent.

Likewise, the Russian cities of Balashov and Staraya Russa share little in common beyond past literary fame. Both served as prototypes for towns in two masterpieces of Russian literature: Pasternak's *Doctor Zhivago*, and Dostoevsky's *The Brothers Karamazov*. Here, however, the similarity ends.

Once a charming provincial town immortalised in Pasternak's poetry, Balashov is now a monstrous sight of crumbling roads and drab buildings.

In winter, the snow lies for weeks on the main roads without any sign of clearing, and in summer the weeds proliferate through the omnipresent cracks in the drab facades. And the *Profilaktoriy* (resort), the city's pride, threatens to crush the occasional visitor with a door loosely hanging on one hinge.

In Staraya Russa one relives the charm of Dostoevsky's beloved spa city. The streets are clean, the plants trimmed, and historical monuments and churches carefully preserved. The visitor-friendly city dwellers share a pride in the past and a confidence in the future of their city.

Although both are Russian towns, Balashov is in fact more similar to Szolnok, and Staraya Russa is more similar to the success-story cities in Central Europe, struggling against and overcoming the communist legacies of central planning, the socialist architecture that scarred their faces, and the immense social costs of change. What then explains the stark differences, however impressionistic, in the paths that these cities have taken?

To date, most studies of local government in Central and Eastern Europe have focused on cross-national variations in local institution-building and performance. This study seeks to explain both cross-national and *within*-national variations in local outcomes. In other words, it aims to understand not only why post-communist states have differed markedly in their local government developments, but also why they have had such contrasts between their cities even though they have ostensibly created broadly similar local government institutional frameworks. To the extent that cases are drawn from states in both Central and Eastern Europe – both some that have acceded to the European Union (EU), namely Poland, Hungary and the Czech Republic, and one that has no such prospect, namely Russia – the study also differs from many other works on post-communist local institution-building. In fact, we show how individual cities within Central Europe may have more in common with their counterparts across national borders and with those in less developed countries of Eastern Europe than with their next-door neighbours within the same state. The following sections identify and briefly discuss the theoretical and methodological approaches that have been advanced to explain local performance in various national settings.

Theoretical approaches

Socio-economic contexts

The most straightforward set of explanations for variations in local performance may be loosely grouped under the label of socio-economic contexts. It refers to both the narrower, locality-specific structural endowments, and the broader social-economic structures of the larger area. The locality-specific factors may be the availability of or proximity to roads or other transportation arteries. They may also include structures inherited from the communist or even pre-communist periods, such as giant industrial enterprises or tourist resorts, or the degree of economic concentration and constellation of industries (Stoner-Weiss 1997).

Structures of the larger area have also been referred to as the 'ecology' of place or location.[1] The localities, according to such approaches, are parts of broader socio-economic environments which significantly affect the local socio-economic structures and development (Friedland and Bielby 1981: 140). As Paul Peterson suggests, because cities, unlike states, are 'open systems', they are particularly sensitive to contextual socio-economic changes, such as labour flows. While states have a variety of instruments for protecting themselves against potentially negative external influences, cities are legally constrained in the choice of the relevant defensive mechanisms (Peterson 1981: 69).

The 'ecology' of the locality has been particularly salient in post-communist settings, considering the persisting legacies of the 'company town' syndrome with its high industrial concentration and large mono-structures. Not only does the nature and constellation of local industries per se have an impact on general developmental outcomes, but it has also been suggested that it influences local elite constellations, their propensity to cooperate and economic decision-making. One study found, for example, that a small number of larger industries and a limited number of key economic players are associated with better performance outcomes than a more 'dispersed' and conflictual constellation of industrial versus agricultural players. The dispersion of economic power, it is suggested, leads to the dispersion of political power, leading to conflicts and bad decision-making (Stoner-Weiss 1997).

Other scholars of transitional economies have likewise suggested that 'an economy with highly concentrated assets offers greater potential for elite enrichment, while dispersed assets offer fewer such opportunities'. Scholars have also specified the assets that are particularly likely to lead to successful efforts in elite capture. They are oil, minerals and large real estate, that is, resources already under government control and organised in 'corporate form' (Walder 2003). Alternatively, examples of dispersed assets would be small-holding agriculture or a small-scale entrepreneurial economy with manufacturing and services carried out by small private or household firms. While unattractive to the old elite, these assets might be highly attractive to elite newcomers; such an economic structure is therefore more conducive to the influx of new forces. These structural inheritances arguably continue to influence efforts to transform the post-socialist economies and the overall well-being of localities (Grabher and Stark 1997: 16–18). Accordingly, our inferences about performance variations should take these factors into account.

Another example of the contextual influences on smaller localities is the variable of the 'spillover' effect of regional collective goods (Bennett 1990: 231). While national collective goods may be evenly distributed across all territories, regional collective goods may vary substantially depending on the broader region-specific economic or structural factors, or the fiscal policies of a given region. This factor should play a strong role in countries where regional economic disparities are very pronounced, and/or where regions – or in federations, federal constituent units – are endowed with substantial powers to devise their own fiscal policies.

A crucial 'ecology' factor is also what we might call the east–west effect. Not only are there wide economic disparities at a sub-national level in the countries we are investigating, but there is also a pronounced east–west dimension observed in some aspects of post-communist development. For example, scholars have shown that civil society is more likely to be developed in more western locations than in eastern ones, even within one national setting. The more western located countries of the post-communist world were also shown to be more likely to pursue democratic political reform. The very pattern of democratization – from the Central European countries that have now acceded to the EU, to the subsequent Rose and Orange Revolutions in Georgia and Ukraine – would suggest a sequencing of democratisation patterns that has a west-east dimension (Kopstein and Reilly 2000; Lankina forthcoming 2007; Fish 1999; Bunce 2003; Kubik 2005).

'Historical legacies' and patterns of imperial incorporation of the various territories have been commonly advanced to explain these current disparities (Fish 1999). For example, whether a locality had been part of the Austro-Hungarian and Russian Empires or Prussia arguably impacted on patterns of the development of bourgeoisie, property rights or local autonomy. Long-term religious tradition, Protestant, Orthodox or Catholic, which also has a pronounced geographic dimension, may likewise influence contemporary political outcomes in terms of political authority patterns. Finally, institutional legacies, more versus less bureaucratic or centralist, likewise related to imperial rule over certain territories, may have an impact on current institutional choices and practices.

Recently scholars have proposed a complementary explanatory framework for analysing the impact of geographic location on political or economic performance. The framework, while not discounting the role of legacies, incorporates current patterns of geographic diffusion conceptualised as 'flows', as well as prospects for EU accession and EU developmental efforts, as key factors in explaining post-communist developmental outcomes. The theory, advanced by Jeffrey Kopstein and David Reilly, draws on political geography and globalization literature. In the diffusion analysis framework, 'flows' refer to exchanges of information, ideas, technologies, trade and commerce through human interaction and facilitated by the geographic proximity or contiguity of one country to another. In addition, EU accession prospects are powerful stimulants for elites in formerly communist countries to pursue political reform (2000). In another study, the authors of this book have refined the Kopstein and Reilly framework to include sub-national territories (Lankina forthcoming 2007). It is argued that sub-national territories are likewise experiencing the variable effects of these flows, alongside the targeted efforts of Western donors, such as the EU. This results in 'geographically incremental' patterns of development and reform proceeding from the west eastwards.

For the purposes of this study, if such patterns do exist, then a more western location would be more propitious for better performance outcomes. In some settings, such as Poland, a west versus east location might overlap with the variable historical legacies of belonging in such distinct entities as the Russian Empire, Prussia or Austro-Hungary. Even in Russia, there are areas which boast a historical legacy of engagement with the West going back to the Middle Ages and contrasting with the legacy of isolation characteristic of other, more eastern located areas.

Contemporary geographically conditioned factors are also extremely important for local outcomes. Local governments in more western locations, we may surmise, are more likely to experience the positive spillover effects coming from their western neighbours. Examples of such effects would be foreign investment or tourism that would facilitate their developmental efforts, or progressive ideas about social service delivery that would be diffused through interaction with EU donors.

Accordingly, in an effort to account for the possible impact of contextual factors on local performance we consider such factors as the geographic location of a given town and historical legacies of imperial incorporation; the density of local transport infrastructure networks; the structures of local economies; the degree of their diversity at the outset of post-communist economic transformations; and broader regional economic variations. We examine the possible impact of the structural factors in Chapter 4, as well as in the sections on regional finance in Chapter 5.

The impact of historical legacies on politics and performance in the various locations is explored in Chapter 6.

Institutions

In the last two decades, a large body of literature has explored the role of institutions in accounting for cross-national variations in political outcomes (March and Olsen 1989; North 1990; Evans, Rueschmeyer and Skocpol 1985; Ostrom 1990). Institutions are understood both as formal structures and as 'rules of the game' affecting the incentives and behaviour of political actors (Przeworski 1991). Scholars have suggested various ways of manipulating local actor incentive structures through institutional design by imposing more or less centralist arrangements, changing the size of municipalities (Keating 1995: 117–34), changing local electoral legislation, or the formal relationships between the representative and the executive bodies, to name just a few (Jones 1995: 85).[2]

A starting point for institutional debates on local government is whether decentralisation is a desirable goal in itself. Broadly defined, decentralisation refers to a dispersion of authority to smaller sub-national units, as opposed to concentration of political decision-making in the central government (Wolman 1990: 30). There is much agreement on the *normative* desirability of local government as one that is close to local communities and that can best engage, represent and serve the grassroots (De Tocqueville 1994; Stoker 1996). There is much less consensus as to whether greater local autonomy always in practice matches expectations with regard to both its representative and service aspects. That local government bodies are often unrepresentative of the relevant communities or not very responsive to their needs, even in advanced Western democracies, is a fact well documented in numerous studies (Newton 1976; Bachrach and Baratz 1962; Schattschneider 1960). Much less straightforward and methodologically more complicated is an assessment of local government performance in more versus less autonomous local governments. For example, more autonomous local governments may be more responsive to the local populations and may serve them better, but they may also be subject to local corruption that, if left unchecked by the central or regional authority, may significantly damage the interests of the local population.

If the degree of institutional autonomy from the central state matters for local performance, we need to outline some basic criteria for comparing institutional variations in our respective states. Following an established tradition in public administration and social science we use several yardsticks to assess the degree of local autonomy vis-à-vis the central state (Goldsmith and Newton 1988; Page and Goldsmith 1987). The first yardstick is the nature and scope of local functions. The second is the mechanisms of judicial and/or state supervision and control over local government. The third set of measures relates to the fiscal aspects of local government: the degree to which local governments rely on own sources of revenue; the amounts they spend in proportion to over-all state expenditures; the amount of central grants and other central funding; and the conditions attached to such funding. The assumption is that central funding with strings attached can increase the likelihood of national state intervention into local expenditure decision-making (Oates 1990). Another simple formula for distinguishing between more and less centralised systems is whether the central state endows munici-palities with general competence powers allowing actions not explicitly prohibited (more decentralised) or whether only activities explicitly authorised by the national government are permitted (more centralised) (Wolman 1990). The impact of the variable institutional arrangements on local performance is discussed in Chapters 5 and 6.

The politics of local performance: leadership, values, and partisanship

A related set of variables could be grouped under the label 'politics of local performance', which have a particularly rich tradition in urban policy analysis. Classical studies of community decision-making in American cities from those of Robert Dahl, to Nelson Polsby, Floyd Hunter and Kenneth Newton's work on Birmingham have examined the political aspects of local governance (Dahl 1966; Polsby 1963; Hunter 1968, 1980; Newton 1976). The primary concern of these studies has been an identification of 'who rules', and the related question of 'who benefits', which is distinct from the question of 'with what effects', that is, performance. Thus, scholars would explore the social, economic, ethnic, racial or gender characteristics of the local 'power elite', as well as 'leadership' or other qualities of local actors (Moyser and Parry 1989; Meadcroft 2001; Newton 1976; Szuks 1998).

The question of 'who rules' has been the preoccupation of the first generation of scholarship on newly decentralising post-communist states. For example, scholars analysed party-political affiliations of local councillors in an effort to ascertain the proportion of communist 'old-timers' versus newcomers in the local bodies, and the values associ-ated with the respective backgrounds (Gel'man et al. 2000; Matsuzato 1999; Friedgut and Hahn 1994; Le Huérou 1999; Lallemand 1998; Lankina 2001, 2002, 2004a; McAuley 1992, 1997; Mendras 1998, 1999;

Young 1994; Baldersheim et al. 1996; Horváth 2000). The effects of the composition of the ruling groups on local performance, other than allocation ones (who benefits) have been secondary to much of the above analyses, however.

Such a focus is distinct from the more recent Western urban studies and decentralisation literature, which has experienced a shift from the question of 'who rules' to 'with what effects', in both theory and empiricism (Judge, Stoker and Wolman 1995; Bachrach and Baratz 1962; Banfield and Wilson 1963; Clark 1973; Dahl 1966; Hunter 1968, 1980; Mabileau 1989; Newton 1976; Polsby 1963; Schattschneider 1960). Moreover, there has been a much greater emphasis on contextual – institutional or other – factors affecting political actor preferences and behaviour, and ultimately local outputs. This shift of focus to performance has been less felt in the scholarship on post-communist local settings, perhaps understandably so considering that those 'who rule' have had little time to study 'with what effects'. Moreover, in defence of the above studies one may say that local government reforms continue to be at the implementation stage and local bodies weakly institutionalised, complicating an assessment of the longer term impact of institutional factors on actor preferences (Horváth 2000).

In terms of effects on governance, Robert Putnam's work on 'social capital' in particular has sensitised us to the importance of a set of historically conditioned values and traditions in accounting for local government performance variations.[3] Putnam defines social capital as 'features of social life – networks, norms, and trust – that enable participants to act together more effectively to pursue shared objectives' (Putnam 1995). Social capital arguably affects the orientations and decision-making patterns of local officials and their relationships with the local constituencies. It might affect the degree of tolerance of alternative views and positions, and actors' propensity to cooperate, or alternatively, pursue conflictual modes of decision-making. Communities with greater levels of social capital of a 'bridging' kind are characterised by horizontal relations of 'reciprocity and cooperation', not 'vertical relations of authority and dependency'. This in turn ensures active participation in public affairs by the broader citizenry, likewise affecting local performance. Civic associations are crucial for social capital because cross-cutting membership in local associations serves to instil in members 'habits of cooperation' (Putnam 1993).

In its stress on value systems social capital is similar to what other scholars conceptualise as political culture (Almond and Verba 1963). Generally, political culture refers to 'the *subjective understanding of politics* and is concerned with people's *values*, their *perceptions* of history – as distinct from history *per se* – and with their *foci of identification*' (Brown 2005: 182). These cognitive patterns in turn affect 'dispositions of actors to act in certain ways in sets of situations'. According to Harry Eckstein, culturalist theory is postulated on 'oriented action', whereby 'actors do not respond directly to "situations", but respond to them through mediating "orientations" ' (Eckstein 1988: 790). Social capital and political culture have proved to be powerful explanatory frameworks accounting for various political outcomes, from institutional choices to the durability and stability of political institutions, and to the quality of governance.

The post-communist contexts we are investigating should make us particularly sensitive to the importance of cultural values of the local administrative personnel and other actors influencing local performance (Lamentowicz 1990). In circumstances of uncertainty, legal vacuum, institutional change and weak institutionalisation of local government rules and procedures, culture is bound to play a strong role. Cultural orientations have been in particular juxtaposed to 'rational' calculations when there is great uncertainty about decision-making outcomes. As Nicolai Petro writes, 'the greater the degree of socio-economic turmoil, the less people will believe that decisions should be made on the basis of what worked in the past'. It is during such times in particular that 'people turn to culture for meaning' (Petro 2004: 96). At the same time, while cultural orientations are durable, they do change (Eckstein 1988; Hahn 2005). It has been suggested that 'fundamental normative orientations' might be more important during the early phases of post-communist transformation, while more instrumentalist actions would be associated with later periods when people will have had more experience with post-communist settings and would be able to make more informed cost-benefit calculations, or indeed ones based on changing value orientations. Cultural orientations might be important for the kinds of institutional choices that are made at a local level – for example, a stress on strong executive rule versus strong council – or policy preferences (for example, social welfarism versus market liberalism) (Whitefield 2005). At the same time, people's self-identifications are likely to influence their attitudes to the non-post-communist West and their receptivity to external economic reform and democratic institution-building programmes. This would be particularly relevant for our EU accession candidate states, Poland, Hungary and the Czech Republic, but also Russia, which is not a candidate, but has been a recipient of a large volume of EU aid (Lankina forthcoming 2007).

While culture may be an important explanatory factor for local performance during the first post-communist decade, we here concur with Archie Brown that it is 'just one of the elements to be explored in political analysis, alongside institutions, interests, leadership, power, and ideas. The centrality of one or other of these components to an explanation of *particular* political change or continuity will vary greatly from case to case' (Brown 2005: 180; Rose et al. 1996; Rose 1994, 1997).

Accordingly, while sensitive to the role of normative and other qualities of individual leaders and other local actors in discussing the politics of local performance we largely focus on the explanatory factors that our own field research suggested to be most powerful, namely party political factors. These variables have been in fact linked to performance in a tradition that goes back to Dahl and Polsby, and continues with the neo-institutionalist stress on institutional engineering as a determinant of performance. There is a large body of local government scholarship that distinguishes between partisanship and non-partisanship. Partisanship refers to electoral arrangements placing parties at the centre of local electoral politics, while non-partisanship is a 'system of elections ... in which no candidate is identified on the ballot by party affiliation' (Banfield and Wilson 1963: 151; Tarrow 1977). The idea that partisanship can be damaging to local efficiency and performance is part of a century-long debate rooted in American history and practice. The notorious machine politics of the late nineteenth and early twentieth centuries generated a reform or 'progressivist' movement which sought to make local government more service oriented and less partisan and politicised, the latter seen as damaging to its efficient operation. A radical reform of local government institutions was seen as crucial to reducing local conflict and improving local administration. The key aspects of the reform involved setting up more professional and managerial local executive structures, and an electoral system to the local councils based on largely non-party based elections. Although the theory and practice of depoliticised 'reform' local governments are rooted in the American and, to a lesser extent, West European contexts, their implications are wide ranging for various national settings.

Central to the definition of partisanship are political parties. While their role is marginal in smaller townships, they become more important in larger urban settings, which are the focus of this study. Local government institutional design and the nature of the party system in a given country are seen as key determinants of whether parties will play a strong role in local decision-making, or whether their role will be marginal or non-existent (Gottdiener 1987; Banfield 1961, 1985; Lineberry and Fowler 1967; Domhoff 1998; Eisinger 1973; Leif and Clark 1972). Some yardsticks for establishing cross-national variation in local government institutional structures are the mechanisms for election or appointment of the key local executive and his or her administration; and the way the local council is elected, in particular, whether any mechanisms exist, electoral or other, for the representation of political parties.

In discussing the role of formal institutional arrangements, we also consider the role of leadership (Stone 1995), social capital and political culture discussed earlier in this section. As Putnam's study reminds us, when institutions are put into place, the variable leadership qualities, value systems and behavioural styles of individuals operating within these institutions might result in quite different outcomes even if, say, electoral arrangements and party systems are identical in two different settings. Harry Eckstein's concept of 'congruence' likewise sensitises us to the link between authority patterns at social and political institutional levels (1988). No matter how good the institutions, they might be dysfunctional if they are not supported by appropriate cultural patterns at a broader social level. Social capital or political culture might therefore be important, if not central, to the way parties operate and the degree of partisanship and conflict in local councils. Our chapter on the politics of local performance, while focusing on parties, seeks to take all of these factors into account. The impact of party political factors on performance in settings with variable institutional arrangements and levels of party institutionalisation, from the highly party-competitive Hungarian case, to Russia, where parties have played a negligible role in local politics during the period we are investigating, is discussed in detail in Chapter 6.

Evaluating performance

This study seeks to explain variation in institutional performance, our key dependent variable. Local government performance may be defined as the ability to address local social needs and improve the well being of the locality as a whole. Evaluating and measuring performance has been the thorniest issue of local government studies (Clark and Ferguson 1981; Bish and Ostrom 1973).

Scholars have argued that public services measurement instruments designed for a particular urban setting may be inappropriate in others and may yield unreliable or even distorted results. For example, the same production inputs may result in different outputs in an area with different characteristics, such as a sewage system which may be much more costly in hilly as opposed to flat areas (Bish and Ostrom 1973: 26). Likewise, corporate style benchmarking of local performance may not be an appropriate evaluation tool: different municipalities may provide a similar array of services, but their quality may vary substantially. Moreover, even if service quality may be assessed as good, for example in the area of healthcare using the criteria of the number of hospitals, many residents may not have access to these healthcare facilities, which makes measurement of service quality difficult (Gottdiener 1987).

Another example of measurement complexities is trying to evaluate the effects of variable fiscal policy choices, which might be assessed quite differently depending on the positions and preferences of various social groups, or indeed the political position of a scholar studying local government. Redistributive policies or the imposition of overly protective social safety nets may positively affect the needy, but may drive businesses out of the city, which might ultimately negatively affect the local economy (Peterson 1981).

An important consideration, as Paul Peterson stressed in his classic study of urban governance, is also that cities *do* have limits. To the extent that they are parts of the wider regional and national political, institutional and socio-economic contexts, their shortcomings or failures may to a greater or lesser extent also depend on these broader structural or political factors outside of their control (1981). A nuanced examination of local performance should therefore be sensitive to the variable locality-specific or contextual environments in which local governments operate, and the complexity of the local policy choices that they are faced with.

Three methodological approaches to assessing performance may be identified. The first one is studying local public opinion with regard to the level of satisfaction with local government, most notably with the degree of its responsiveness. Responsiveness has been defined as 'the capacity of governmental organization to satisfy the preferences of citizens'. The approach is justified on the grounds that local populations are the main consumers of local services, moreover, that they are the 'best judges of their own interests' (Bish and Ostrom 1973: 22). The shortcomings associated with this approach, however, would be that local public opinion may not be a reliable source for evaluating local government performance. Studies have shown, for example, that local governments are often blamed for poor services even if they have no authority over the particular service in question, which may be actually performed by the central state or the regional government. Focus group studies with representative samples of local populations have also revealed that citizens often express opinions regarding municipalities based more on common sense or prejudice than on actual awareness of local policies (Startsev 1999; Lowndes, Pratchett and Stoker 2002).

A second approach would be to study levels of consumer satisfaction using a much smaller sample of respondents from particular institutions that are either recipients or deliverers of local government services or both, be these public or private agencies. This could also include an investigation of local government personnel's satisfaction with their own work and their view of the issues facilitating or hampering local performance. The consumers of economic development programmes would be the managers and employees of small, medium-sized or large enterprises, while the consumers and deliverers of social policies would be the staffs and clients of homeless shelters, foster homes or NGOs. The local administration respondents would be staffs in the relevant departments charged with the respective service provision.

One study, for example, examined service delivery by police, social workers, teachers and small traders by interviewing three sets of actors: service providers, such as the police and schools; citizens who were consumers of the respective services; and city leaders.[4] This and similar studies suggest that if the particular policy area is within the scope of local government authority, local performance in the narrow field would be a reliable indicator of that of local government as a whole. Even though a particular agency or an NGO may be separate from the public agency of the local government, it may be integrated into the local government policy-making process. This is because local government decision-making regarding service provision, that is, deciding on the availability of a service and arranging for its delivery, affects the actual production of the service by the respective non-local government agencies (Hawkins). A consumer and provider satisfaction approach to particular institutions would also allow for a nuanced understanding of the various factors affecting local service provision and delivery, which may not be evident from the more large scale population surveys. Research on urban politics in other settings has suggested that in fact 'reasonably reliable' data could be obtained from interviewing a dozen, or even fewer informants (Clark et al. 1981).

A third and related approach, which should complement the latter, would be to devise evaluation criteria for local government 'outputs', as 'consumer satisfaction' alone may not be a reliable indicator of local performance. We use the latter two approaches in assessing local government performance. At this point it is important to identify the precise policy fields of investigation. The number and scope of these fields, as indeed the concrete sub-policy areas, are of necessity to be narrowed down considering the evaluation complexities involved in such a task.[5]

Social services

As objects of study we chose to focus on two areas of local government work: social service provision and economic promotion/development. Social service provision is a responsibility of local governments in various national settings. It is performed by local governments in the highly autonomous Scandinavian group of countries, as well as those with more centralised Napoleonic systems like France (Bennett 1993). Social service provision, which refers to decision-making over the availability of a service and the arrangement for its provision is distinguished from delivery, which refers to the actual production of the service (Higgins 1989: 95). Even though local government is now seldom the sole deliverer of services with co-providing and contracting out (Warren, Rosentraub and Weschler 1985: 74; Higgins 1989: 95–96) a fashionable prescription of the new public management or public choice school (Bish and Ostrom 1973: 1; Keating 1991: 3), it is still a coordinator, a decision-maker and/or financer of local services. This is because social services are public goods, that is, those that are available to and can be enjoyed by all members of the community. Such goods are subject to the classic 'free rider' dilemma, which makes it difficult to finance them through voluntary effort. Local government therefore becomes a crucial agency in organising and enforcing the distribution of services (Bish and Ostrom 1973: 19).

Many social services address the needs of small segments of the local populations, such as drug addicts or victims of family abuse. Others, such as aid to the elderly, serve increasingly large groups of people, particularly in the developed post-industrial world with its ageing population structures. Such services to the socially unproductive populations by definition generate no profit, and are costly and burdensome. How well the social services are performed in these areas can be a good indicator of local government performance.

Comparative service evaluation is a complicated task, however, because service-providing systems are different in each country. In one state a given service area may be the exclusive responsibility of local government, while in others it may be shared between different levels, or is the exclusive task of the meso, regional, level, or the central government. Moreover, in recent years many countries have experienced a decentralist shift not just between different levels of public authority, but also between the public, on the one hand, and the private, or not-for-profit sectors, on the other. This is also true for the settings that we are investigating. In some Central European countries, such as Hungary, the relevant central ministry even requires NGOs to have formal contracts with municipalities as a precondition for giving aid to the former. As a result, the degree of cooperation and the nature of relations between the public and the private agency become crucial determinants of the availability of central funding, and ultimately the quality of local social service provision (Osborne and Kaposvári 1998: 10, 17–18).[6] NGO support may also take many other forms, however, including those that require minimum or no financial inputs. Examples include the provision of free premises and the creation of 'not-for-profit centres'; the creation of public databases on local NGOs to stimulate cooperation among them; the publication of free newspapers and newsletters with information about local NGO activities; and the provision of legal or other advice to NGOs. In addition, local government officials' membership of various non-profit organisations may encourage cooperative public–private interactions (Csóka 2000).

Contracting out is another important local government practice, which may vary across different settings, but may likewise affect local government performance. In this area municipalities in post-communist states have been given discretionary authority. In Russia, although federal legislation mandates the provision of certain social services to vulnerable social categories, such as victims of domestic violence, it has allowed much freedom in the forms that their administering can take (Chagin). Here, as in most other states of the Commonwealth of Independent States (CIS), local governments may choose between several types of service delivery, namely directly by municipalities, through contracting out, or through grant provision to non-profit organisations. This is also the case in Central European states. Empirical studies have shown that the practice of contracting out often produces positive results because local administrations are overburdened with the provision of legally mandated services in which the central authorities play a marginal role. Contracting out also sometimes applies to non-mandated, but essential social services. Although contracting out is now being practiced in some Central European municipalities, it is not very widespread. One study of Hungary found that only 11 per cent of local governments have contracted out social service provision to NGOs despite the potential benefits of such cooperation (Csóka 2000.[7] A study of Russia also found the record to be low, with municipalities maintaining service provision 'monopolies' in most cases (Chagin 2005: 9).

The above discussion illustrates the complexities involved in comparative analysis of social services delivery as in different states or even municipalities within one national setting the degree of public versus non-public agency involvement may be different (Chagin 2005: 8; Bennett 1994: 11; Hatry 1994; Sevic 2003: 21). Another consideration that is important to bear in mind is that an evaluation of one service area may tell us little about the overall performance of local government. Municipalities often have to balance between several distinct groups of policy choices, such as development, redistribution and routine local services (Wong 1989: 219). An over-stress on one set of policy areas might be at the expense of quality performance in others.

The above challenges of comparative evaluation often merit a choice of research instruments which make evaluations across the diverse national, regional, municipal and administrative settings and policy areas feasible. In view of these considerations, we devised several qualitative yardsticks for evaluating social services performance. These yardsticks allowed us to obtain 'soft', but comparable data, while also allowing us to be sensitive to locality or country-specific variations affecting local outcomes. First, we examined the nature of internal organisational decision-making within the local administration, such as the record of comprehensive policy formulation and planning. Second, we sought to determine whether there is close cooperation between various administrative levels: local, regional and national/federal government and that between the local government on the one hand, and the non-governmental agencies on the other. In particular, in the area of local government–NGO cooperation, we sought to determine whether there were regular meetings between the local government and NGOs. We also sought to establish whether the local government supported local NGOs directly and/or also actively assisted them in their fundraising from external sources. In addition, we sought to determine whether there are regular mechanisms for obtaining information on the local social situation and service demand. Finally, we examined the quality of the services provided and the record of service innovations, if any, in the policy fields we are investigating.

Economic promotion

The second policy area that we chose to study is economic promotion or development, which has come to occupy an increasingly important place in municipal activities in various national settings. Robert Bennett defined local economic development as 'sub-national action, usually sub-state and sub-regional, taking place within the context of a labour market, and often covering an area greater than one local-government area, but with activity focused on specific sites and needs for development or regeneration' (1990: 222). Another scholar defined it as 'special activities, undertaken by public or private groups, to promote economic development' (Bartik 2002: 2). Although a multitude of actors may be involved, such as private sector agencies, training organisations, universities, NGOs, chambers of commerce, utility companies, and regional and federal agencies, local government plays an important role in the process of stimulating, coordinating, or channelling local economic activity (Bennett 1990: 222–3; Bartik 2002: 39). Scholars have argued that this role has increased in recent years with city officials in advanced democracies identifying economic development as their 'major responsibility' (Bartik 2002: 1–2).

In a tradition that goes back to Charles Tiebout (1956), public choice theorists have even likened cities to private firms, which compete with one another in the efficient use of local resources and in attracting capital and high quality labour force (Peterson 1981: 29). Municipalities are seen as producers of goods and services, and local residents as consumers, with the urban setting regarded as a 'market analogue'. The localities arguably try to outbid other towns in offering tax incentives to individuals, and the latter opt to move to a locality that offers the best tax package (Judge et al. 1995: 7).

It is generally recognised, however, that the picture is much more complex in the real world. Local economic promotion and development is concerned with both wealth creation and employment and redistribution (Bennett 1990: 222). On the one hand, like social services, it generates 'indivisible' public goods, which may be enjoyed by all (Clark 1985: 1; Bish and Ostrom 1973: 18–19). On the other hand, it may also be seen to provide 'separable' goods benefiting much narrower groups, such as business contractors or the local elites. Moreover, policies that may be considered efficient from an economic point of view may conflict with the redistributive needs and pressures of marginalised social groups (Peterson 1981: 38).

As with social services, economic development activities can be performed by a wide range of other, non-local government actors, including private companies and the central state (Bennett 1990: 222). However, local government has an important, if not a decisive, role in the choice of a given course of action with regard to development, in competing with other cities to make the city more attractive to investors, and in determining which groups will benefit from its policies in the long and shorter terms (Wong 1989: 218–9).

Studies have shown that influencing investment decisions is possible even in the absence of substantial resources or local authority over the choice of legal or tax stimulants. Even such 'intangible' assistance to businesses as providing quick and reliable information on sites and cutting bureaucratic red tape can have an impact on corporate decisions to locate a business in a given area. Subsequent 'business visitations' by local officials to inform themselves of the potential issues a given business is facing and to try to address them may likewise positively affect the decision of a business to stay. Lobbying regional or central state bodies for developmental funds or for investing in local universities, training, research or high tech centres is another cost-effective possibility for encouraging local economic development (Bartik 2002: 15, 21, 32). The municipalities may also foster 'good citizenship' policies among local entrepreneurs, such as donations or gifts for local charity causes or the formation of ad hoc 'percent clubs' aimed at solving broader community issues; investment in more disadvantaged areas; or voluntary involvement in public affairs and other 'community affairs activities'. These creative measures do not require substantial resources, but can do much to foster a sense of responsibility and an interest in the welfare of the locality as a whole among local businesses (Bennett 1990: 224–5).

The new post-communist local governments are no exception in viewing economic promotion as one of their key priority areas. These attitudes were revealed as early as in 1991 in a survey of local officials in Central and Eastern Europe conducted by Harald Baldersheim and his collaborators. Significantly, the enthusiasm surrounding the new possibilities for local development that greater local autonomy offered to democratically elected municipal actors did not subside in the subsequent years of economic turmoil and local budget constraints. A survey conducted as recently as 2003 in the Czech Republic, Poland and Hungary has shown that activities associated with economic development continue to rank very high on mayors' lists of priorities (Baldersheim et al. 1996: 168–70; Swianiewicz, Herbst and Lukomska 2004: 6). Moreover, in some countries, such as Poland, mayors even admitted to laying greater stress on local economic efficiency than on values related to democracy and autonomy (Swianiewicz, Herbst and Lukomska 2004: 19).

As our key yardsticks for assessing economic performance we chose to look at the ability of local governments to agree on a long-term economic development strategy, and their success or failure in implementing its key aspects within the set time frame. As with social services, we also look at internal organisational decision-making within the local administration with regard to long-term developmental planning; and the record of cooperation between various administrative levels – local, regional and national/federal government – and that between the local government on the one hand, and businesses and other relevant non-governmental agencies, on the other. Such yardsticks allow us to obtain comparable material across the eight cases. Because we focus on local government efforts that do not require substantial resources, they also allow us to isolate broader contextual socio-economic factors that may account for higher levels of economic development of some towns, but do not per se explain the performance of local government.

Our research was conducted between June 2001 and July 2004 on two trips to each of the case study cities. In the course of the field trips we carried out in-depth interviews with several groups of respondents. In order to study local performance in the social sphere, we interviewed the social department chiefs and staffs of the respective municipalities, and the heads and senior staffs of the respective social facilities. We also administered closed end questionnaires to staffs in the above local departments and institutions, as well as to consumers of the relevant services. In order to examine performance in the area of economic promotion, we conducted interviews with economic department heads and staffs in each municipality, as well as with 'consumers' of the department services, that is, senior executives of key large businesses, and a group of small and medium-sized enterprises. Closed end questionnaires were also administered to these three sets or respondents. We analysed the interviews and questionnaire results together with other materials gathered during field trips, such as the structures of local decision-making, including the record of cooperation with NGOs and private businesses, local budgets and local political and electoral processes. A more detailed discussion of our methods is contained in Chapters 2 and 3, where we evaluate the performance of the eight case study towns in the areas of social policy and economic promotion.

Case selection

The glamour of the showcase cities of Budapest, Moscow or Prague illustrates the triumphs of the post-communist states in shedding their communist pasts. Showcases, by definition, are not an accurate reflection of the life of the populations of the countries at large. Although admittedly the capital cities concentrate large populations, the overwhelming majority of people live outside the respective national capitals. Many, of course, also live in small towns and villages, but most people reside in medium-sized cities. The towns and villages too congregate around urban centres, which provide employment, wealth and infrastructure for the surrounding localities. These 'medium-sized' cities are a logical choice for a study of governance affecting the average populations in the post-communist states. What is, however, a 'medium-sized' city?

According to Louis Wirth's classic definition, a city is 'a relatively large, dense, and permanent settlement of socially heterogeneous individuals' (cited in Smith and Klemanski 1990: 89). The *Urban Politics Dictionary* refers to it as an 'imprecise term that describes a permanent human settlement large enough to house strangers, support a diverse and complex economic base, and serve as a communication centre' (ibid.).

It is well known that in the industrialised world the vast majority of citizens live in cities. What is less known is that most of these cities are medium in size. The narrow definition of a city as confined to its administrative borders would of course include many small settlements. For example, the US demarcation for a city threshold is a settlement consisting of 2500 inhabitants. But urban centres usually serve much larger surrounding areas, providing jobs, social services and trade, and forming a 'single economically integrated community'. These larger settlements have also been described as 'urbanized areas', in the US defined as 'a central place and adjacent area with a population of 50,000 or more' (Smith and Klemanski 1990: 88–9). In many national contexts, cities of approximately this size are formally classified as medium cities. We define a medium-sized city as an urbanised area with a population of 50,000 to 100,000 people.

The medium city is an ideal place to start for evaluating local government performance because *much can be done at this level*. In his famous address to the American Political Science Association, Robert Dahl advocated the 'all-round optimum size' for a contemporary US city as one with between 50,000 and 200,000 inhabitants. Such a unit, he maintained, 'can and must be clothed with great powers, if it is to manage its problems, and yet can be small enough so that citizens can participate extensively in determining the ways in which the great power will be used' (1967: 965–6).

Although Dahl lamented the rise of the monstrous and impersonal metropolis, in many advanced countries, large proportions, if not a majority of the population live in medium cities of the kind that he advocated. Our countries of investigation, which are in this respect not much different from other industrialised nations, illustrate the central place of the medium city. In Hungary, the number of larger towns is much smaller than that of tiny rural settlements. Yet these towns concentrate disproportionately large populations, with 29.4 per cent of people living in settlements with populations of 10,000–100,000, and 29.4 per cent living in large settlements with over 100,000 people. In Russia, the legislation defines a city as a settlement with a population of over 12,000 people.[8] Of the country's approximately 8,000 local government formations existing in the period we are investigating, only 2.36 per cent of municipalities had between 50,000 and 100,000 voters, and 0.60 per cent between 100,000 and 200,000 (Goryunov et al. 1999: 12). The highest proportion of the country's cities, 68.4 per cent, however, had up to 50,000 people, and 15.7 per cent of the cities had populations of between 50,000 and 99,000 (Lappo 1998: 5). And in the Czech Republic, although only seventeen municipalities have between 50,000 and 99,999 people, and only five more than 100,000, almost 34 per cent of the population lives in towns with between 10,000 and 100,000 people, and approximately 21 per cent in cities with over 100,000 people. Thus, the medium cities are home to very large percentages of the local populations.

Two medium-sized cities were chosen in each of the four countries. Aside from the medium city baseline similarity, we sought maximum variation in the cities. First, in order to see how space and legacy factors might affect local performance, we sought to identify cities in various geographic locations. Second, we used a 'rich-versus-poor' criterion. Third, within the broad 'medium' criterion, we also sought to identify cities varying in size.

Assessing the possible importance of the east versus west geographic location is a very straightforward matter for most of our cases. The better off neighbours in all four states are located in the west, and the worse off in the east. The west–east neighbour distinctions also tend to overlap with variable historical-imperial incorporation legacies. The worse off neighbour for the Czech Republic is Slovakia, for Hungary it is Romania, and for Poland, it is Belarus, Ukraine and Russia. Poland and the Czech Republic have Germany in the West, and Hungary has Austria. Russia is a less straightforward case, considering that two of its immediate western neighbours, Belarus and, at least until the December 2004 Orange Revolution, Ukraine, have been weak performers in terms of both democratic and economic development. In its northwest, however, there is a concentration of well off neighbours, the Scandinavian countries, and the Baltic nations, now European Union members. The choice of the two cases in each country corresponds to the east–west criterion.

The degree of economic well being of the locality as a whole may be considered a straightforward explanation of the level of local government performance. After all, it may seem natural that the well offs have more money to perform better. Comparative urban studies, however, often indicate that the explanation of performance variations is much less straightforward than that. The extent to which the locality profits from the well being of its environment may be a matter of local politics or local policy choices. Accordingly, in order to assess the possible role of this factor we tried to choose cities in one relatively well off larger region, and in a less economically advanced one.

Finally, we tried to choose cities that also vary in size, with a contrast between those with around 50,000 and those with approximately 100,000 people. We hoped that this contrast, although quite small, may help us to assess the impact of city size on performance.

Admittedly, there is enormous variation in localities in all the four countries. This makes it difficult to draw broader inferences from the eight towns to other municipalities. We hope, however, that our case selection will allow us to make broader generalisations about the determinants of performance, and that the conclusions would stand up in other towns as well. Despite the variations in size, location and patterns of historical incorporation and development, the eight cases are fairly typical of the more versus less structurally advantaged post-communist municipalities of their countries, and of the issues that they confront in social-service delivery and economic promotion.

Sopron

Sopron is an example of a town with highly advantageous starting structural conditions. It is a medium-sized town with a population of slightly over 50,000 people (53,436 in 1995). It is located in Western Hungary next to the Austrian border. The city is only 70 kilometres from Vienna, and approximately 210 kilometres from Budapest. It is part of the broader Győr-Moson-Sopron county divided into seven towns and 168 villages.

Sopron is one of Hungary's oldest cities, steeped in history and boasting Roman, Medieval and Renaissance architecture. It is here that the composer Franz Liszt performed some of his first concerts as a child prodigy. Sopron was the only city allowed to hold a plebiscite on its status after the 1919 Treaty of Trianon, which virtually dismembered Hungary. The city overwhelmingly voted in favour of remaining part of Hungary, and, due to Hungary's territorial losses, became a border city. It has since been called the *Civitas Fidelissima* or the most faithful city.[9] Sopron's second hour of world fame was on 19 August 1989 when it hosted the so-called Pan-European Picnic allowing the crossing of East German nationals through the Hungarian border into Austria and precipitating the inevitable collapse of the Erich Honecker regime. 'The pulling down of the Berlin Wall began in Sopron', the city's website proudly announces.[10]

In addition to its advanced tourism infrastructure, Sopron has had a relatively developed industry and even in the communist period boasted such modern industries as electronics. It is also home to a forestry university, which was made world famous when its students and alumni emigrated en masse to Western Europe and North America and obtained jobs in universities abroad after the 1956 Hungarian uprising.

Szolnok

The city of Szolnok of county rank is in Jász-Nagykun-Szolnok county. The town's population of 81,000 makes it the eleventh largest city in Hungary. The town was already known in 1030 when it was made centre of the county. In the medieval period it was a centre of the salt and timber trade. During the communist period, Szolnok became a victim of grand industrialisation schemes, although it may not be considered a typical socialist company town built around one single industry.

Szolnok is located 100 kilometres east of Budapest, at the meeting point of the Tisza and Zagyva rivers, and is also a crossing point for the Alföld (Great Plain) railway and other overland routes. The city is part of a county which has a much lower status (17th) in terms of GDP per capita compared to Sopron (2nd place).[11] According to recent figures, the county generates 3.6 per cent of Hungary's total GDP. Per capita GDP is 89 per cent of the counties' average, placing it 14th in the county ranking. The unemployment rate is 8.6 per cent. The two counties of Jász-Nagykun-Szolnok (JNS) and Győr-Moson-Sopron (GMS) also significantly differ along other indicators of development. With comparable population sizes of 419,100 (JNS) and 425,500 (GMS), the latter has almost twice as many private cars, and many more telephone lines.[12] Not only is the town disadvantaged in terms of industrial development, but in contrast to Sopron, tourism development, a potential source of revenue for the local budget, has also been slow as the town boasts few historical monuments or cultural attractions.

Biała Podlaska

The town of Biała Podlaska has a population of approximately 59,000 people. It is located in the east of Poland, near the Polish–Belorussian border. The town's history is closely connected to the Radziwills, one of the most famous Polish noble families. During the fifteenth century, when Biała was mentioned for the first time, the town was owned by another noble family, the Illniczs, and belonged to the Grand Duchy of Lithuania. As a consequence of the Lithuanian–Polish Union of 1569, Biała came under the Polish rule of the Radziwill family, which encouraged town development and built an academy, which in 1633 became a branch of Cracow University. After the late-eighteenth-century partitions of Poland, the town became part of the Russian Empire and remained a provincial capital under Russian rule until 1918.

Despite its importance as a regional centre, the town did not have a developed economy until the interwar years of the twentieth century. After the First World War numerous industrial enterprises were set up there, the most important of which was the Podlasie Airplanes Production Plant. Furniture and textile industries were also developed here after the Second World War. Biała Podlaska's growing importance as an industrial centre was reflected in the administrative reform of 1975, which bestowed the status of a *województwo* capital on the town. The recent administrative reform of 1999 came as a shock to local politicians, as Biała Podlaska lost its *województwo* status and was downgraded to a town of *powiat* status. Moreover, Biała Podlaska was incorporated into the Lublin *województwo* despite the town's historical and cultural identification with the neighbouring Podlasie.

The town was hard hit by the post-communist economic transformation, as many industries stagnated and workers were laid off. Along with the other eastern *województwos* the Lubelskie region remains one of the most backward regions in Poland.

Jelenia Góra

The city of Jelenia Góra has a population of 93,000. In contrast to Biała Podlaska, it has been throughout its long history a major economic and cultural centre. Located in the *województwo* of Lower Silesia close to the Czech and German borders, the city has not only played an important role in trade and industry, but since the nineteenth century it has also been known as a centre of regional tourism. Jelenia Góra is one of Poland's oldest towns. As early as the Middle Ages the inhabitants of Jelenia Góra called themselves 'townsmen', which reflected the town's predominant economic position on the local trade routes.

After the local line of the Piasts, the first Polish dynasty, had died out at the end of the fourteenth century, Jelenia Góra came under Czech rule. However, when at the beginning of the sixteenth century the Jagiellons ascended the Bohemian throne, Jelenia Góra was provided with broad self-governing competences and even the right of own coinage. In the middle of the century, the development of linen production ushered in a golden era, which turned Jelenia Góra into one of the richest cities in Silesia. The golden age was interrupted in 1742 when Prussian troops occupied the city, isolating it from important markets. To make matters worse, machine-produced English linen squeezed out the Polish hand-made textiles from European markets. One century later, however, new production plants and especially the rapidly developing tourism led to a new economic surge.

Jelenia Góra benefited from the administrative reform in 1975 when it was elevated to the rank of a *województwo* capital, and several surrounding settlements were incorporated into it, making it the largest town in Western Sudetenland. Similar to Biała Podlaska, however, as a result of the 1999 *województwo* reform Jelenia Góra lost its former status and was downgraded to a city of *powiat* status.

Karviná

The town of Karviná is located in the northeast of the Czech Republic in the Moravian-Silesian region, which borders on Poland and Slovakia. The region of Northern Moravia has been severely affected by the economic transformation and the breakdown of whole industries. Although in 2000 it contributed the second largest share to Czech GDP,[13] at 10.7 per cent, it also has the second highest rate of unemployment in the region, 15.11 per cent. Within the broader region, the district of Karviná, which comprises the city and surrounding towns and settlements, has the highest rate of unemployment, at 18.6 per cent.[14].

The town itself has slightly over 65,000 inhabitants, occupying the fifteenth place among all Czech settlements. Karviná has a long history as a centre of trade and industry. First mentioned in 1268, Karviná was part of the Tesin principality ruled by the Polish Piast dynasty until the end of the sixteenth century. Due to its geographic location on the trade route from Hungary to Silesia and the Baltic Sea, already in the Middle Ages the town became an important centre of trade and handicrafts. The Thirty Years' War and several fires put an end to economic wealth and urban expansion. In 1776, the discovery of black coal deposits on the town's territory ushered in a new phase in local development. During the nineteenth century several coalmines were opened, which soon led to the development of heavy industry such as steel production. These developments allowed Karviná to play an important role not only within the Austro-Hungarian Monarchy, but also in the Czechoslovak Republic, and led to the bestowing of city status on it in 1923.

In 1938 the city was forcibly integrated into Poland and a year later into the German Third Reich. After the Second World War Karviná and Northern Moravia became buttresses of the communist economy. In 1946 Karviná was the first Czechoslovak town to experience large-scale socialist construction to house coal miners coming from all over the country. This led to the establishment of a reputation for Karviná as the 'iron heart of the republic'. Although coalmining and heavy industry have undoubtedly had a positive impact on the town's economic development and its overall importance in Czechoslovakia, Karviná at present continues to pay a high price for its industrial heritage, mainly in the form of environmental devastation.

Ústí nad Labem

The city of Ústí nad Labem is located in the northwest of the Czech Republic, on the River Elbe near the East German border. With more than 96,000 inhabitants it is not only the ninth largest city in the Czech Republic, but is an administrative and cultural centre of Northern Bohemia and of the recently established *Ústeckí kraj* (Ústí region).

Although Czech national mythology considers the surroundings of Ústí to be the power base of the first Czech prince Premysl, during the Middle Ages the city of Ústí was of minor importance. It is not until the second half of the sixteenth and the beginning of the seventeenth centuries under Habsburg rule that the town gained in economic strength. The Industrial Revolution gave a fresh impetus to the development of the originally small settlement. Over sixty brown-coal mines were opened in the town's environs at this time and handicrafts and small industries were developed. Due to its favourable geographical location on the river and near the railway track from Berlin to Prague and Vienna, Ústí gradually became one of the most important traffic junctions and a major industrial centre of the Habsburg monarchy. At the beginning of the twentieth century, with nearly 40,000 inhabitants Ústí was already one of the largest cities in Bohemia.

While the First World War did not have a particularly negative impact on Ústí's economic development, during the 1920s political and social problems threatened to undermine the north Bohemian success story. Aside from severe environmental pollution caused by the chemical industry and the growing class-consciousness of the numerous factory workers, the 'national question' gained particular salience at this time. From the late sixteenth century onwards Ústí experienced an enormous inflow of German immigrants, who soon formed a majority of the local population. During the inter-war years, Ústí became a microcosm of the overall 'national problems' that destabilised the First Czechoslovak Republic. Under the slogan 'Heim ins Reich!' ('Back home to the

German Reich') the Sudetendeutsche Reichspartei headed by Konrad Henlein won an overwhelming majority of the vote in Ústí in the 1935 general elections. After the Munich agreement of September 1938 Sudetenland, which included Ústí, was incorporated into Germany and two thirds of the town's Czech inhabitants were forced to leave.

In April 1945, the Western allies in an attempt to destroy the Ústí railway connection bombed the town killing more than 500 people. Between 1945 and 1946, up to 53,000 Germans were either massacred by the Czech population or forcibly expelled. In order to remedy the resulting shortage of population in the border regions the Czechoslovak government encouraged Czechs from the inner parts of the country and Slovaks, but also people from the Roma minority and the Soviet Union to settle down in the former Sudetenland. Within a period of two years, the traditional population structure was almost completely changed. Not only did the new inhabitants lack local roots, but most of them were young and professionally unqualified, rendering the 'national project' of reconstructing the borderland more difficult than the Czechoslovak government had expected. The communist government continued to further the region's traditional industries with Northern Bohemia becoming the socialist state's centre of heavy chemical industry and brown-coal mining.

At present, despite major achievements, particularly in the area of environmental control, the city is having a hard time shedding its negative socialist company town image. As a consequence of economic transformation, factories were forced to reduce their production. Although at about 15 per cent the unemployment rate in Ústí is well below the rate in the neighbouring town of Most (22 per cent), the town continues to experience social problems on a large scale.

Staraya Russa

The city of Staraya Russa is located in the Novgorod *oblast* in northwest Russia, which borders on Leningrad *oblast*, among other regions. With a population of 747,000 people, it occupies 55,300 square kilometres. It is divided into twenty-one *rayony* (districts), ten cities and towns, and twenty-two urban-type settlements. The largest towns are Novgorod and Borovichi. The oblast has been ranked 39th in Russia in per capita income, 61st in industrial production and 62nd in agricultural production.[15]

Staraya Russa, which is Novgorod's third largest city, is one of Russia's oldest towns, whose origins date back to the tenth century. From the thirteenth century onwards it became an important trade and commerce centre famous for its salt production and engaged in trade and other relations with Western Europe. By the mid-sixteenth century, Staraya Russa was already Russia's fourth largest town after Moscow, Pskov and Novgorod. In the nineteenth century, the city's niche as the centre of salt production was completely taken over by health tourism following the discovery of salt springs with ostensible healing potential. In 1828, the Russian Tsar authorised the establishment of a spa resort in the city. The Russian writer Fyodor Dostoevsky made Staraya Russa a home for himself and his family in 1872–5 and in 1880. It was at this time that he wrote his masterpiece *The Brothers Karamazov*, many of whose scenes and characters were inspired by Staraya Russa. Dostoyevsky's move to Staraya Russa illustrates the status of the city as a favourite resort for Russian 'society' at the time. During the Soviet period, Staraya Russa gradually lost its fame and image as a tourism and health centre as the Soviet regime sought to industrialise it. It also suffered great losses and destruction during the Second World War and German occupation (9 August 1941–18 February 1944). Staraya Russa is now seeking to revive its image of a historical, environmentally clean health and tourism haven.

Although the city covers a territory of just twenty-four square kilometres, it forms a joint unit with the surrounding *rayon*, with which it was merged in 1968. The combined population of the city and *rayon* is 58,000 people, of whom up to 40,000 live in the city. Staraya Russa has a developed transport and communications infrastructure. Located at a distance of less than a hundred kilometres from the regional capital Novgorod, Staraya Russa also has direct rail routes to Moscow, St Petersburg, Pskov and Riga.

The largest enterprise on the territory of the city is the Federal Aviation Repair Plant, which employs 2,000 people, close to 10 per cent of the city's workforce, and contributes up to 30 per cent to the city's budget. Other large enterprises are the mechanical equipment plant, with 1,500 workers, and the chemical machine building plant, with 800 employees.[16] There are also a number of food processing plants. With the exception of two state enterprises, all have been privatised.

The main attraction of the city is the Staraya Russa resort, a successor to the famous nineteenth-century establishment. It boasts a number of natural healing facilities, such as chloride and natrium water, and sulphide spas, and is considered to be one of the best in Russia for the treatment of many internal and external illnesses.

Balashov

The city of Balashov is located in Saratov *oblast*, which is part of the Volga Federal District. It occupies a territory of 100,200 square kilometres, and has a population of 2,711,000 people.[17] The distance from Moscow to Balashov is 452 miles. Saratov is located on an important transport artery, the Volga River, which runs through the *oblast* from north to south. It is a crucial source of irrigation for the area. Saratov *oblast* is also endowed with such mineral resources as oil, gas and natural gas, rock salt, and building materials. In 1995, the *oblast* ranked 37th in per capita GDP, 23rd in total industrial production and ninth in total agricultural production. The *oblast* is divided into 38 administrative districts and 17 cities and towns. The largest cities are Saratov (899,000), Balakovo (207,000) and Engels (185,000).

Balashov settlement acquired its status of *uezdnyy* (district) town in 1781 at the order of Catherine the Great. By the middle of the nineteenth century Balashov had become one of the main centres for grain trade in the Saratov *guberniya* (region). Balashov takes pride in being mentioned in the poetry of Boris Pasternak of the early 1920s, who is rumoured to have had a muse in the city. It has also been argued that the city served as a prototype for the town of Melyuzeev, portrayed during the Revolution of 1917 in the novel *Doctor Zhivago*.[18]

With a population of 98,000 people, the city of Balashov is now the fourth largest city in Saratov *oblast*. It is located in the western part of the *oblast*, 226 kilometres from the regional capital Saratov, at the intersection of several important rail and automobile connections, and the River Khopyor, a tributary of the Don River. The city has a solid industrial base, with over 20 enterprises, including machine building, textile, light and food industries. The main enterprise is the Balashov Textile Factory, also called Baltex. Since its establishment in 1968, this enterprise has occupied an important niche in the countrywide production of such specialised goods as tents, coats and other waterproof textile products.[19] This and other enterprises, however, have been severely hit by the economic transformation, and their recovery has been slow. Although 58 per cent of tax revenue for the local budget comes from industry, Balashov is still considered to be an agrarian town.[20]

Conclusion

The foregoing discussion indicates that there are many similarities in the historical legacies of the eight towns despite their variable national and regional contexts. All of these towns have at some point in history served as important trading, economic or cultural centres. All, however, have also to various degrees experienced the devastating effects of twentieth-century wars and the experiment with communism. They have much to draw upon in terms of symbols from the historical past on which to build a new future, but also to overcome many of the negative legacies of the past century and of the economically painful period of the recent transition to market economies. How have our cities coped with these issues in the last decade? Have the historical legacies and the 'inherent' socio-economic, structural or geographical features served to predestine these towns to a particular course of development, of stagnation or success? Alternatively, have the new institutional reforms of local government made a difference in each particular case? What was the role of political factors in accounting for variations? Despite the seeming 'smallness' and 'localness' of these towns, using them as cases in our study will help us understand the variable developmental patterns at much wider regional and national levels in post-communist settings.

The following chapters hope to address these broader questions by looking at local government performance in the four countries. Chapters 2 and 3 discuss the performance records of the eight cities in the areas of social services and economic development. Chapters 4, 5 and 6 examine the role of each of the three sets of explanatory factors, namely socio-economic contexts; institutional structures; and local party politics. Chapter 4 examines the socio-economic and structural 'givens' of the respective towns and their surrounding areas in an effort to account for their possible impact on performance. Chapter 5 explores the institutional, particularly the intergovernmental and fiscal factors impacting on performance. Chapter 6 discusses the role of party political variables affecting local outcomes, while also considering the role of political culture and other historically or culturally determined value orientations of local actors. The concluding Chapter 7 summarises the findings of the study.

2
Local Government Performance in Social Policy

The social policy areas that we chose to investigate are families in crisis and childcare services. The social transitions in post-communist settings resulted in a chain reaction of unemployment, poverty, alcoholism, family breakdowns or abuse, and abandoned or neglected children. These problems are not limited to, but are much more widespread in the smaller localities that we are investigating, considering that many local economies remained unreformed and maintain higher rates of unemployment than in the booming capital cities or regional centres. Moreover, the related issues of problem families and neglected or abandoned children are pertinent even in the more prosperous towns, such as the western Hungarian town of Sopron. Here, for example, one observed what may be called the 'rich town social syndrome' with the booming local economy resulting in soaring rents, which push the less well off or unskilled labourers out of the previously subsidised housing into homelessness, substance abuse and further down the social ladder.

These new problems of the modern industrialised world, previously submerged by the socialist nature of the local economies, full employment and safety nets for families and children, also require modern solutions, hitherto not in place in post-communist states, or not as widespread as they are in other Western settings. Examples are the setting up of temporary crisis family shelters with sophisticated psychological therapy services, or child-protection mechanisms, which reflect the latest international child conventions and would be a radical departure from the archaic communist practice of placing a child into an institution until adolescence. The following sections discuss the findings in the area of social services and rank the towns accordingly.

Social policy performance: findings

Ústí

We found that the Czech town of Ústí nad Labem had the best social policy performance record compared to the other towns. Ústí is considered a pioneer in the Czech Republic in social service provision. In 1995, in close cooperation with partners from Great Britain, a local NGO called the Centre for Communal Work and the local government the town initiated a complete re-structuring of local social policy formulation and service provision. Within a few years, the new system of Communal Planning became so successful that, in 2000, the Czech Ministry of Social Affairs launched a programme to support other towns in introducing this model.

According to Helena Herbstova, a committed local activist and official in charge of the social department, the system is based on close cooperation between local governments, social facilities and clients of social services. It is aimed at transforming the inflexible socialist-era practices[1] into a modern system tailored to the particular social needs of the locality. In regular meetings with the local administration, social workers and citizens inform the local authorities about the social situation and their experiences. Eight coordination groups, comprising local government officials and staff of social facilities and their clients, meet regularly to identify the socially vulnerable categories to be targeted. A manager heads each group, who also sits on the social commission of the local executive board. The main responsibility for the development of social services, for drafting and implementing new projects, lies with the coordination groups. These projects range from cooperation with institutions in Germany, through organising special charity events, to setting up new social facilities. Before passing a formal decision on a given project, the local government requires the approval of the relevant coordination group and the social commission. In recent years, the coordination groups have drafted a variety of project proposals, waiting for their realisation in the 'project file'.

Aside from the project file, there are three main results of the system of communal planning. First, in June 2001 a local Plan of Communal Care was published. In this plan, each of the eight coordination groups depicted the local situation with regard to a specific segment of local society, defined the needs of the respective target group, gathered statistical data on the demand for specific social services and identified solutions to the relevant problems. Binding implementation deadlines, as well as a scheme displaying the financial costs of each project were set up to guarantee efficient realisation of the plan.[2] A second feature distinguishing Ústí from our other towns is the publication of annual data-reports by the Department of Social Work. Based on questionnaires administered to all local social facilities, these reports contain information about the number of facilities available, their capacities and demand for their services. Finally, Ústí was the first Czech town to restructure local administration according to functional considerations. While in the other Czech towns one social department is responsible for performing all local tasks, in Ústí, since 1995, the local social department has been divided into one operational division and one responsible for the strategic development of local social services. Moreover, through flyers, radio and press advertisements all local institutions dealing with families in crisis inform the local public about their services.[3]

Ústí also ranks high in terms of its policy implementation record, maintaining a number of facilities for women and children or actively supporting NGOs running them.[4] Ústí has two stationary centres for women, which contrasts with almost all our other towns, where one or no such institutions exist. The first facility is the Home for Mothers with Children. The second facility is the Centre for Crisis Intervention, which is operated by Spirala, an NGO known for being active in fundraising from different financial sources, as well as for networking within and outside the Czech Republic. The Centre offers advisory services, as well as an opportunity to live in the facility for up to one week. Four employees keep the facility open 24 hours a day, while external specialists cooperate with the Centre to provide psychological therapies and counselling services. On average, roughly 80 clients visit the Centre per month, and the number has been rising.[5] As with most Czech NGOs, the Czech Ministry of Social Affairs contributes the lion's share to Spirala's annual budget,[6] however, the local government also contributed a large amount of money for the upkeep of the facility.[7]

There are also advisory services offered by the Centre for Crisis Intervention, the Advisory Centre for Marital and Family Life and Interpersonal Relations, and the Advisory Centre for Women and Girls, which also operate telephone Lines of Trust. The Centre is fully financed by the local government.[8] In 2000, eight full-time employees (social workers, psychologists, a clergyman and a lawyer) served 714 clients, while over 3300 people talked to the Centre staff on the telephone. In the same year, the Advisory Centre for Women and Girls, operated by one person, had 317 clients.

Several local institutions enjoying the active support or involvement of the municipality, offer stationary as well as day-care services to children.

The most comprehensive services are provided in two foster homes located in town. Another local facility specifically deals with children from problem families. The Centre of Volunteers, an NGO founded in 2000, encourages local residents to volunteer in various social projects,[9] in order to build up or enhance their 'civic consciousness'. In a special programme called 5P, socially disadvantaged children are attached to a volunteer who meets them several times a week and engages in 'healthy' leisure activities with him or her. Although the programme is largely dependent on external sources of funding, the local government also makes substantial contributions to its operation.[10]

Staraya Russa

Another example of a town with good performance assessed on the criteria of coordination, policy formulation, data gathering and, most importantly, policy innovations, is Staraya Russa. The town has not suffered from social problems on the scale of Russia's other more depressed provincial towns. However, post-Soviet economic restructuring resulted in lay-offs and related social problems, such as poverty, chronic unemployment, alcoholism, abandoned or abused children and family violence. According to the records of the municipal social department in this town of less than 50,000 people, in 2002 there were 688 children and 2593 families officially registered with the local government social department as requiring special protection.

Staraya Russa has a detailed social and economic plan adopted in 2002 which analyses the social and population structure of the locality and suggests policies that would improve the local employment and welfare situation. Another mechanism for regular solicitation of information on local social demands is the so-called Social Partnership arrangements.[11] They involve public and private agencies and employees. The town is also unique among our cases in that since the mid 1990s it has maintained a sophisticated social-needs computer database. The database relies on experimental software specially developed for the servicing of the social sphere. Records of all socially vulnerable individuals served by the department are put into the database, and regular monitoring is conducted as to the family incomes, budgets and even nutrition of aid recipients.

Staraya Russa demonstrates how the leadership and skills of administrative officials can play a crucial role in affecting the quality of service provision in circumstances of tough budget constraints. Like most Russian localities, the town largely relies on regional funding to cover the costs of social service provision, which consume one third of the local budget, and is not sufficient to cover mandated services. According to the mayor, this constantly forces the local administration to think creatively and 'wisely' about where to get funding and how to spend it.[12] An increasingly important part of local long-term social policy planning is solicitation of funding from external sources. The city official in charge of social services, a quintessential social 'activist', maintains that she sees seeking out funding options and aggressively lobbying in federal ministries as one of her key occupational priorities. 'If need be', she maintained, 'I will personally go to Moscow'. Accordingly, Staraya Russa has been successful in winning many of the federal social targeted grants, which came in the form of equipment for the local social facilities. It also won a Soros Foundation grant to help equip the local social college. Funding is also obtained from local entrepreneurs or 'philanthropists' who are made to feel that contributing to the city's social well being helps build a greater civic consciousness and a sense of responsibility for the locality. 'We do not spare money on paper to write to them', claimed the social department official. Another funding strategy pursued by the social department is to provide the social facilities with incentives to save. If the social facilities save on electricity, they are allowed to keep the money that they have saved and decide on how it is spent. Finally, the town social department pursues innovative, cost-free or cost-effective solutions to the problem of skilled human resources. For example, considering the lack of funding in the municipal budget for training local social workers and social personnel, Staraya Russa proposed to serve as host to training seminars organised by federal or regional agencies provided that the local staff also participates in them.

Staraya Russa has also maintained effective social policy coordination mechanisms with both the higher regional level and the 22 lower-level village administrations, which make up the Staraya Russa city-*rayon* administrative unit. One productive area of cooperation, according to the head of Staraya Russa's social department, is the joint preparation of applications for obtaining funding from federal and other external sources. Considering that municipalities themselves may not be beneficiaries of many external grants, it actively helps local NGOs to seek out funding options and helps them prepare applications.

The town's policy implementation record has also been relatively good, although the crisis family services still lag behind those of our more 'western' towns. The city does not have a stationary home for families in crisis although the head of the social department indicated that there is a strong need for stationary facilities. This issue is particularly pertinent in Russia considering the difficult housing situation. Because of the costs of obtaining housing, as well as tough requirements for local residence registration, many women are forced to continue to live with abusive husbands even after divorce. However, the social department official suggested that a legal vacuum still exists in this area at the regional as well as federal levels, a fact that would complicate obtaining funding for a stationary facility. Even if the municipality were to squeeze out funding from local sources for one year, it would not guarantee that the centre would be maintained consistently for a longer period of time. The only relevant services available in Staraya Russa are the Consultative Centre and a Telephone Hotline, which is part of the broader municipal Social Service Provision Centre. The Centre is staffed with two people and is fully funded by the municipality. It offers psychological and legal aid, as well as other related consultative services. Although the Centre tries to advertise its services as broadly as possible, these efforts often clash with established cultural stereotypes, as well as the reluctance of local press outlets to publish information that is of little or no commercial value.

Cultural factors also account for the very low number of women, no more than two or three per month, who come to use the services and a similar number of complaints filed by women against abusive partners in one year, as against the much higher demand estimated by the Centre staff. While as many as 279 of the 2593 families receiving social help from the local government are registered as 'crisis families', only a fraction of those come to the Centre for legal, psychological or other advice. Thus, the capacity of the Centre as such is not a problem. The Centre, together with municipal officials, however, also regularly engages in preventive measures aimed at identifying problem families. The staff refers to this as *reydy* or raids. These raids are conducted once a week, and involve conversations with neighbours, family members and teachers, as well as local government district administrators. In addition to having a prophylactic intent, the raids are also meant to serve remote localities, whose residents would otherwise have trouble finding transport and money to travel to Staraya Russa, where most of the social facilities are located. The raids, as well as other prophylactic measures, are carried out in cooperation with the police, the local foster home and other concerned institutions.

The legal void at the federal level with regard to the establishment of crisis facilities has not precluded Staraya Russa's social department from looking for innovative solutions to the problem. In the absence of a stationary centre, one possibility considered by the social department is to provide victims of crisis families with holiday camp vouchers that would enable them to leave the city for a certain period of time. The department has already made some concrete steps on the way to implementing this goal. 'We had a summer rest house for kids', maintained the social department head, 'but my dream is to turn it into a rehabilitation centre that will stay open the whole year.' An item in the budget has already been allocated for these purposes, and in 2003 the department was to apply for federal funding for the project, mostly in the form of equipment. The department has also sent its staff for training in the areas of family and childcare social work in the city of Samara, which is known for its progressive social policies. The head of the department also maintained that she hopes to obtain more training for its staff in such 'modern' areas as business communication considering that 'we work with people'.

In the area of childcare, the city pursues innovative policies that stand out even if we compare it with our Central European cases. Childcare in Russia is regulated by several pieces of legislation: the 1996 Law on Additional Guarantees of Social Protection of Foster Children and Those Without Parental Care; the 1995 government's Basic Provision on Educational Facilities for Foster Children; the government's 1995 Basic Provision on Boarding Schools; and a 1996 Government Provision for Specialised Institutions for Children Requiring Social Rehabilitation.[13] In addition to this legislation, special government 'social normative provisions' and 'norms' lay out rigid guidelines for the volume and amount of supplies for the relevant institutions, from the daily ration of bread per child in grams, through clothing, to books, which are funded from federal, regional and local budgets.[14] Thus, most of the legislation continues to reflect the Soviet-era assumption that an *institution* – foster home, boarding school or other – is a solution to the problem of parentless children, or those living with problem families. The above legislation provides a basic framework for sub-national childcare legislation and policies, mandating that regional and local authorities set up the relevant institutions, appoint their directors and supervise their activities.

Against this archaic background, Staraya Russa's approach to childcare may be considered a feat of policy innovation and flexibility. Staraya Russa houses one of Russia's most progressive child facilities, *Nadezhda* (hope). *Nadezhda's* Director Leonid Kirillov is well known throughout Russia, as well as in child welfare communities in Europe.[15] Kirillov illustrates how in circumstances of institutional change and uncertainty, individual leaders may make a decisive impact on local social services, even if the wider federal or regional environment may not be favourable and funding insufficient.

Although much of the city's success in addressing child issues could be attributed to the personality and enthusiasm of Kirillov, there are also generally favourable relations between Kirillov's institution and the municipality. According to Kirillov, the local government supports him in this advocacy of policy and institutional change.[16] Initially under Novgorod regional jurisdiction, in 1996 the home was transferred to the local government's jurisdiction. The transfer was made on the city's own initiative based on the logic that the '*oblast* is too far from the local kids and their problems'. In 1999, in an effort to coordinate work in the area of childcare, *Nadezhda* signed a special tripartite partnership agreement with the local government and an NGO called Christian Solidarity.

Not only are Kirillov's leadership skills and the cooperativeness of the municipality of interest here, but also the value orientations of this activist, which have shaped his vision about childcare services. Scholars writing on the values of post-communist local actors have laid particular stress on the importance of socialisation in a communist setting for shaping an 'old-timer' mentality with welfarist leanings. What might be overlooked in such assessments is the importance of post-communist exposure to other values, which is bound to be magnified over time. The 'other values' in this case stem from exposure to the West, which is more likely in western-located regions of Russia. Like many other Russian local and regional officials, Kirillov has been no stranger to the numerous training seminars and exchange visits massively funded by Western donors. Western donors also presented Kirillov's organization with computer and Internet connectivity, even before such connectivity was available at the Staraya Russa municipality, likewise facilitating exposure to external sources of knowledge.

Our interviews with Kirillov, which lasted several hours on two separate visits, are extremely revealing of how local actors filter experiences from communist-era socialisation through Western lenses. Many of his statements about the merits of the various child welfare systems are backed by examples from Europe and childcare partner institutions there. 'We took as a basis [for our work] the British foster family system', he maintains for example, in discussing his efforts to prevent family break-downs. Much of his work is also influenced through his partnership arrangements with a child welfare institution in the West German city of Celle: 'We have many friends in Celle ... our main goal is to exchange technologies ... we are in the twenty-first century, so we need new technologies of family help', he said.[17] Kirillov's institution proudly displays the German nameplate *Haus der Hoffnung*, a gift from Celle meaning 'house of hope', a more poignant characterisation of his efforts even than the simple title *Nadezhda* (hope). In a symbolic clash of values, local and Western, the local *kraevedy* or patriotic savants and defenders of all things local, were at first openly resentful of the *Haus der Hoffnung* German plate being proudly displayed on what is now one of the nicest buildings in town, renovated partly with Western money. But Kirillov persevered, keeping not only the German plate, but also developing values and practices influenced partly by his Western colleagues. While many Russian childcare institutions continue to function as foster homes, Kirillov has been successful at phasing out the old Soviet-style practices, and has developed *patronat* (host family) partnerships with a 100 per cent rate of child placement. The idea behind these policies is that rather than allocating funding for the archaic institution system, it should be channelled to activities aimed at substituting for blood families, which provide children with a stable and loving family environment. Kirillov has developed these practices in the circumstances of a legal void, as there has been no legislation stressing the need to place a child with a family as opposed to keeping it in an institution. His early efforts even led to an investigation of the home's activities by the procuracy as regards their alleged illegal nature. Kirillov then resorted to lobbying the deputies of the Novgorod *oblast* Duma (legislature). Finally, his ideas became the subject of careful study by the region's education committee, and have been integrated into the Novgorod regional legislation on childcare.[18]

In January 2001, the Novgorod government adopted a special decree on the regional targeted programme Children of Novgorod Region. The decree specifically addressed the issues of the 'reorganisation of Staraya Russa corrective foster home into a *patronat* children's home and the development of *patronat* families in the city of Staraya Russa'. It also mandated the 'publicising and the widest dissemination of information on the experience of the *Nadezhda* home'. Significantly, the decree contained almost no mention of the traditional foster home institutions, focusing almost exclusively on 'experimental' *patronat* family practices, and on prophylactic measures against parentless childhood.[19]

Nadezhda now has 25 staff, which includes university-trained education specialists and psychologists. Although the centre serves only approximately 15 children at a time, in general, 70 children go through it every year. Most of the children stay between one week and six months. As a municipal institution, *Nadezhda* is 100 per cent funded by the local government. In addition, Kirillov maintains personal networks with a host of Western institutions, most notably with that in the city of Celle in Germany, which are also a source of funding and individual donations. But the municipality also plays an active part in the generation of external funding for *Nadezhda* because as a municipal institution it requires the official support of the social department. With local government support, Kirillov has already successfully applied for the federal Children of Russia targeted funding, winning four computers for his facility. In addition to Kirillov's institution, there is another municipal facility for smaller children. The home, which has a staff of 12 people, has a capacity to host 15 toddlers. The children stay in the facility until they reach a certain age, after which, unless they go back to their blood families, they may be transferred to Kirillov's facility.

The municipality is the main agency coordinating child welfare and the work of the relevant institutions. It is the local government guardianship organs (and not the courts), together with the police, that are allowed to take the initial step of withdrawing a child from a family. The child may then be temporarily placed in one of the city's child institutions. The work carried out jointly by the respective institutions is premised on the assumption that no effort should be spared to either return the child to his or her blood family, or to find a new home with substitute parents. Both the local government organs and the respective institutions monitor the progress a family is making in getting back to normality, and assessing whether and when to transfer the child back. Once the child has been registered in the local government database, the social department continues to monitor the child's and the family's welfare, even after their reunion.

Karviná

The performance record of Ústí nad Labem and Staraya Russa contrasts with that of the towns of Karviná, Jelenia Góra, Biała Podlaska and Balashov, although the demand for the relevant social services there is equally high or even greater. In the Czech town of Karviná, as in Ústí, the social situation is characterised by high unemployment, which stems from the peculiarity of the town's economic structure during communism. Since 1990, the Czech national unemployment average has not exceeded 9.2 per cent,[20] however, in the district of Karviná, the figure is as high as 20 per cent. As a result, there are rising numbers of social welfare recipients and soaring crime rates.[21] The demand for crisis family services has been even higher than in Ústí. In 2002, for example, the social department in Ústí registered seven applicants for the women's shelter, while in the same year in Karviná 47 women applied for the service.[22] Our interviews with social workers in town likewise suggested that the demand for crisis family services is particularly high. The Director of one women's facility, for example, maintained that the problem of domestic violence is more urgent in Northern Moravia than in the other parts of the Czech Republic, which is a consequence of high unemployment and related social problems. He maintained:

> In the past, many people came here just because of the jobs in the coal mining industry, they lack local roots. Once they lose their jobs in the coalmines, they face enormous problems. Another factor explaining domestic violence is the high number of alcoholics in this region.

A study conducted by the Moravian-Silesian Institute of Social Analysis revealed that, among several important towns within the region, significant differences existed as to the number of victims of domestic violence. While in the less coal-mining-dominated town of Opava, only 18 per cent of female respondents reported incidents of domestic violence, in Karviná, the figure was as high as 36 per cent.[23]

Karviná contrasts with our other towns with high demand for social services, such as Staraya Russa, where leadership skills helped fill the vacuum in funding. Here high demand for the relevant social services is not fully met by the local administration, and there are no outstanding leaders in the local administration who could lift the town out of its morass of social problems. In personal interviews, many respondents in the municipal social department mentioned the problem of lack of staff to handle the growing demand for social services. This fact was used to justify the generally passive attitude with regard to the issue. 'Either people come here themselves or we get tip offs from schools or neighbours', one official maintained.[24] Moreover, in contrast to Ústí and Staraya Russa, in Karviná cooperation between the administration and social facilities is mainly based on personal contacts rather than on a system of regular consultation or information exchange. While some facilities reported 'very good relations' with the social department, others said they would prefer more regular and more intensive cooperation.

In Karviná, as well as in the broader region in which it is located, there is reportedly the 'densest net of shelter facilities', however, most of these are run by NGOs and are only partly funded by the local government.[25] In addition, although the quality of the services in these facilities is higher, there is little evidence of the local government actively supporting them. Finally, the local government refused to run some of the former municipal institutions and passed on responsibility for their operation to the regional level.

Most of the relevant facilities are either run by NGOs or are partly or fully under the jurisdiction of regional authorities, a fact which in some cases stems from the municipality's unwillingness to take over the provision of certain services. Of the two stationary and several non-stationary facilities for women and children,[26] only one is a local-government-operated-and-funded institution, the Home for Mothers with Children set up in 1994.[27] The quality of the services and the infrastructure in this facility contrasts unfavourably with SARA, another institution providing similar services but run by an NGO. The Protestant Church-linked Silesian Deaconry set up SARA in 1990. In addition to some limited local funding, SARA has also repeatedly obtained grants from the Czech Ministry of Social Affairs.[28] SARA is located in a more modern building, is significantly better equipped than the municipal facility and is known to provide substantially better services.[29] The Silesian Deaconry also recently set up another, non-stationary facility, which provides advisory services for victims of violence, crime, torture and sexual abuse. The local government had formerly run a similar facility, the non-stationary Centre for Psychological Help, set up in 1973 by the then district office of the state administration. In the course of the latest round of administrative reform, however, the local government refused to take over the Centre, and passed the responsibility on to the new regional office.[30]

In the field of childcare, the relevant institutions are likewise largely run either by NGOs or the regional office. The key stationary childcare facility is Camomile, which was founded in 1997 at the initiative of the Director of the DMD and is largely aimed at supporting young women from foster homes.[31] In addition to some limited funding from the local government, the facility is largely funded from external sources, such as the Ministry of Social Affairs.[32] The regional office and the local social administration operate the other support institution, the Pedagogic-Psychological Advisory Centre, jointly.

Jelenia Góra

The social situation in the Polish town of Jelenia Góra is similar to that of the Czech town of Karviná. The *województwo* of Lower Silesia, where the town is located, has been particularly hard hit by unemployment because of the reduction of coal mining. A study on the situation of families in Jelenia Góra conducted by the local Social Work Centre documented a dramatic increase in poverty and related social problems in the region.[33] The study also reported rising alcoholism, family conflicts and violence.[34] In 1998 alone, the police reported 128 cases of domestic violence.[35]

Jelenia Góra's record in identifying local social demand and tailoring social service provision accordingly is mixed, however. As in Karviná, local officials blamed lack of staff, as well as social workers, for the shortcomings in local responsiveness.[36] One official for example, maintained: 'The law on social welfare prescribes a ratio of one social worker to 2,000 residents. Therefore, we are actually supposed to employ 44 social workers, but we have only 26.' This situation arguably negatively affects the morale of the social department staff and social workers, and the quality of the services they offer: 'A social worker has hardly any time to visit his clients at home ... The staffs are on edge, because our building is constantly full of clients.'[37]

There was little evidence, however, of the social department adopting measures that would be cost-effective or cost-free, but would improve both the staff's working conditions and quality. The local social department, for example, contrasts with Ústí in that it neither possesses its own webpage, nor provides citizens with downloadable forms or information materials. This shortcoming is curious considering that the homepage of the local government offers a wide range of information on other topics. As a result, potential clients have to make a personal visit to the local centre for social help even if it entails long distances and substantial transportation costs.

The record of service provision is likewise mixed in this city. Although according to the Law on Social Welfare Jelenia Góra is obliged to set up a Centre for Crisis Intervention, there is no such institution in town, a fact blamed by the local government on lack of funding.[38] The only local stationary facility for abused women is the Centre for Victims of Violence. The Centre is reserved for residents of the town, and the maximum period of stay per client is two weeks.

The non-stationary advisory services that exist in town are operated as part of the alcohol prevention programme, which is nationally mandated rather than being a specifically local initiative. Polish municipalities are not only legally obliged to take measures against alcohol abuse, but alcohol licenses are an important source of local revenues, which must not be spent for purposes other than the prevention of alcoholism.[39] The city's advisory services are partly operated by the local government itself, several are managed by NGOs and financially supported by local authorities.[40] There is also an institution offering counselling to victims of domestic violence. Originally established by the *województwo* author-ities, in 2000 the local government took over the organisational and financial responsibility for maintaining the facility.[41]

In contrast to the limited number of local social facilities for victims of domestic violence, there are several institutions dealing with child protection, including municipal ones, and the quality of their services is relatively high. The two facilities directly operated by the local government are the Adoption Centre and the Centre for Standby Care.[42] As a municipal institution, the Adoption Centre is supposed to be funded by the local government, but the facility to a substantial degree depends on private donations.[43] Children stay in the centre until they are adopted, sent to a foster family, or returned to their own parents. The Centre is very successful in placing children in new or old families. In 2001 for example, out of 57 children, 39 left the OAO for their legal or natural parents.[44] The record is poorer in the Centre for Stand-by Care, which is a transitional institution testing up to 80 teenagers from socially weak families for psychological or other disorders and partially funded by the local government. Besides the two conventional foster homes, there are also four 'family homes' providing small groups of children and teenagers with a surrogate family. There are also two day-care centres operated by the Catholic Church, but partly funded by the Town Hall.[45]

Biała Podlaska

Even greater discrepancies between social service demands on the one hand, and the responsiveness of the social administration on the other, exist in the Eastern Polish town of Biała Podlaska. With a rate of unemployment of close to 20 per cent, which is above the regional average of approximately 15 per cent, and with 11 per cent of the population living below the poverty line, it is one of the most socially disadvantaged towns in Poland.[46] The Director of the local Centre for Social Help described the effects of the social situation on families and children: 'We pay social benefits in order to prevent children from being too hungry to learn. There were cases when children didn't attend school because they didn't have a pair of shoes to go out in.'[47] Another consequence of unemployment and poverty is alcoholism.[48] In a recent study, 26 per cent of local primary school pupils admitted to 'sometimes' or 'frequently' consuming alcohol, and of those 60 per cent 'in order to forget about family problems'.[49] Finally, domestic violence has also been on the rise. Police and court statistics suggest that while in 1999 there were 563 cases of domestic violence attended by the police, by 2001 the number had almost doubled to 1115 cases.[50] Between 1999 and 2001, the number of court decisions constraining parents in their parental rights doubled from 31 to 63 cases.[51] In 2001, 29 children were placed in stationary educational facilities, which represented a 45-per cent increase compared to 2000.[52]

Despite the magnitude of the local social problems, the town has no regular mechanisms for information gathering on social service demand, while the local residents are also not adequately informed about the available social services. The ratio of staff to clients is even worse than in Jelenia Góra. With 14 social workers out of 28 employees, the Local Centre of Social Help, *Miejski Ośrodek Pomocy Społecznej* (MOPS) has approximately 50 per cent of the number of social workers prescribed by the law. According to a recent study of 47 Polish towns, Biała Podlaska was ranked the lowest in terms of the ratio of social workers and local residents.[53] Finally, MOPS does not have a website, and the local government does not offer downloadable forms or information sheets on social services. This may be attributed to the low levels of Internet usage, especially among the socially vulnerable categories, although the municipality also does not actively disseminate information by other means.

The lack of an adequate policy response to local social needs is also reflected in the fact that there is not a single facility offering stationary shelter to victims of domestic violence in the city and clients have to make their way to Rokitno, a small town lying 15 kilometres away from Biała Podlaska. The family help centre there is not operated by the municipality, but by an NGO called Foundation for Family Help, Prevention and Therapy. The location of the facility reportedly poses significant problems considering that most women are dependent on public transport, which is irregular and unreliable. Although the local government contributes limited funding to the operation of the facility, most of the funding for it comes from the *województwo*.[54] The one institution in town specifically targeting domestic violence was set up in 2001 on the initiative of a group of local residents – psychologists, pedagogues, therapists and social workers. The non-stationary Advisory Point offering counselling to victims of domestic violence has received only limited funding from the local government.[55] The municipal administration did devote substantial funding to combating alcoholism, which is seen locally as the root of many family problems. In 2001, for example, it spent an equivalent of roughly 59,000 euros on anti-alcohol activities and services.[56] These services, however, are actually mandated by national legislation rather than being a specifically local initiative. Moreover, national law also prescribes that all local revenue obtained from alcohol licenses must to be spent on alcohol prevention or substance abuse activities.

Similar performance weaknesses are observed in the area of child welfare. In fact, Biała Podlaska even failed to meet its nationally mandated legal obligations in child protection. The town does not have an equivalent of the Centre for Adoption Care, or other stationary facilities for children. The closest foster facilities are located in Lublin, the *województwo* capital. The distant location entails significant difficulties not only for the children committed there, but also for the staff of other child facilities located in Biała Podlaska. One official complained, for example, 'Our cooperation with children and parents would be a lot better if the closest stationary facility were not located in Lublin, because once the child is sent there we lose all contact.'[57] The only local institutions for children from problem families are the six day-care centres, some of which are partly funded from the alcohol prevention programme.[58]

Balashov

The Russian town of Balashov likewise had a mixed performance record. Balashov is situated in a remote eastern agricultural region. It has had to cope with social issues on a scale larger than Staraya Russa. In contrast to Staraya Russa, most of the social facilities are under *oblast* rather than local government control. The local government social department maintains that it has 'supervisory responsibility' over the social facilities. The latter in turn 'report' to the local social department, even though the Ministry of Social Affairs in Saratov maintains formal authority over them.

At the local level, formal meetings involving the relevant local social facilities and the local officials are held twice a week. However, communication between the relevant facilities and the main supervisory bodies at the *oblast* level is infrequent, and the lack of adequate infrastructure and funding exacerbates the problem of coordination further. There is no e-mail connection between the *oblast* and the social facilities, and communication is limited to telephone conversations or visits to the regional capital Saratov. These take place approximately once a week or every two weeks and a report on the local social situation is sent to the *oblast* once a year. Most of the communication with the *oblast* is in fact by telephone. The staff did not mention participating in any training sessions other than those conducted in Saratov. The social department does not have a single computer and the only social database is a paper database.

The town was, however, impressive in its support for the establishment of a family crisis centre. This policy is a response to regional level legislation, and the institution itself is subordinate to regional, rather than local, authorities. The municipality, however, has the general responsibility for coordinating all the relevant services. The *oblast* Law on Social Protection of the Population of January 2001 mandates the establishment of centres for social aid to women, families and children that are to provide social, economic, psychological, medical, pedagogical and rehabilitation services. The law, however, does not specify whether the facility is to be stationary or not. The city maintains a Women's Crisis Service (WCS), which has lawyers and psychologists. The centre was established in accordance with the Saratov decree of 2001, which in turn was a response to a Russian federal government provision. It is fully funded by the *oblast*. In stark contrast to Staraya Russa, there is apparently a much higher demand for the services, and a much higher number of registered applications for aid from the facility. Out of a total of 180 cases and 46 formal complaints of women against abusive partners, in 2002, 40 were related to family violence. In the social department, 570 families are registered as 'problem families' requiring special attention. The divorce rate in the city is also alarmingly high at approximately 72 per cent.

Despite the high demand both for immediate emergency services and prophylactic measures, the city does not have a stationary centre yet, although the social administration staff recognises the need for one. The Director of WCS, for example, maintained that at a training session in Saratov he learned that 'such centres exist in the West'. But the non-stationary services that WCS is able to provide are very impressive considering the generally depressed economic state of the town and its isolation from the regional institutions that maintain formal authority over the relevant facilities in Balashov. The WCS encourages women to come to the facility by advertising through the local mass media and through distributing leaflets, including in surrounding villages. It also conducts prophylactic work with young families by holding training sessions that are supposed to foster a responsible attitude to family and parenthood. Another WCS prophylactic measure is the maintenance of a day-care facility for teenagers aimed at combating teen delinquency.

Underfunding and a lack of infrastructure significantly hamper the work of the facility, however. The WCS is weakly computerised. The Director of the facility does not use the Internet and e-mail. There is no computerised database in the centre. In contrast to Staraya Russa, it is also poorly equipped with other means of communication, which complicates work with clients. For example, the Director maintained that the centre has only one car that is used to cover distances of over 100 miles. While in 2002 the petrol budget was 25,000 roubles WCS received only 6,000 roubles from state or municipal sources.

In the area of childcare, in contrast to Staraya Russa, the Saratov *oblast* legislation does not lay stress on *patronat*-type services to children.

The *oblast* legislation only mandates the setting up of Centres for Aid to Children, which are 'specialised establishment[s] for social adaptation of children providing, together with care-taking organs, the placement of children into families or child institutions based on their psychological and physical state.'[59] The city maintains one traditional Soviet-style childcare institution. In 2002 the home had 99 children, most of whom stay for up to six months, and are then transferred to a traditional foster home in the *oblast*. In contrast to Staraya Russa, no special effort is made to place children with families, and the placement record is very low, at about 10–20 per cent. In a personal interview, the Director of the home did not show awareness of alternative adoptive or *patronat*-type policies, and admitted not having participated in training seminars outside the region.

Sopron

On the face of it, the poor performance of the depressed towns, such as Balashov or Biała Podlaska, could be attributed to lack of funding which prevents the social departments from adequately tackling social issues. Interestingly, however, our westernmost town, Sopron, located on the border with Austria, and generally considered a booming town, maintained a rather modest performance record, even lagging behind such 'eastern' towns as Staraya Russa. The social situation in Sopron is relatively good compared to the other regions of Hungary. We were even told that within the city, the demand for foster care services is quite low. The most serious issue mentioned by many respondents is high rents, which literally force families out into the street and push them down the social ladder. The opening of the border with Austria in the 1990s led to a boom in small business and consumer tourism. This in turn prompted the skyrocketing of the real estate and housing markets.

The one positive aspect of the local policy process in the area of social policies is the active involvement of NGOs and civic actors in social welfare issues. There is currently a special Social Roundtable Forum, set up by the local government, as well as a special Social Fund with a value of three million forints, aimed at providing grants to NGOs. One particular example of NGO-social facilities cooperation is the annual family charity ball. The event is organised jointly by the family centre and various private organisations or individuals. In 2003, the year we conducted the interviews, the 'patron of the ball'[60] was the owner of the local John Bull Pub, a businessman called Tamás Perkovátz, who is also known to everyone in the city as a 'civic activist'. The local government also seeks to foster closer ties with the Church. For example, at the behest of the local government, the town bishop called a meeting of priests of surrounding settlements informing them of the social department's plans to involve the Church in child and family welfare-service provision.

Other aspects of local government internal decision-making, however, are characterised neither by long-term social planning nor inter-institutional coordination nor policy innovativeness. In Sopron, social policy does not appear to be regulated by a long-term social plan. A Social Conception was passed in 1996; however, successive administrations after each local election have tended to produce a new shorter-term social policy paper. We were told that the new administration, elected in 2003, was still working on a new policy plan, which was to be presented to the council by the end of the year.

The main challenge to effective policy coordination and implementation appears to stem from the rigid institutional separation between county and local functions in some key aspects of social welfare. The rigidity of the legislation precludes effective cooperation between the two administrative tiers, ultimately negatively affecting consumers of the relevant services. It also leaves little room for personal initiative and flexibility which would allow individual leadership skills of local officials or civic activists to influence social services.

The area that we are investigating, child welfare issues, is illustrative of this problem. The 1997 Hungarian Law on the Protection of Children and the Administration of the Court of Guardianship states that child protection is the responsibility of both state and municipal organs. The law distinguishes between 'professional' and 'basic' or 'non-professional' child services. Non-professional services refer to the monitoring of child welfare and the provision of day-care services to children and of temporary care. Professional services deal with grave situations where a decision may be made regarding a child's withdrawal from a family and placement with foster parents or foster home. Legally, settlement-level municipalities are mandated to perform 'non-professional' services, while the counties perform 'professional' ones. While seemingly clear-cut, this distinction is more problematic in cities of county rank such as Sopron.[61]

There is no stationary childcare facility in the jurisdiction of the municipal, as opposed to county level. The Act on Child and Family Protection states that a municipality with a population of over 40,000 people is mandated to have a temporary home for children. According to another piece of legislation, by 1 January 2006 all towns of county rank are mandated to have the facility irrespective of their size. According to Sopron's social department head, she has repeatedly put the issue of funding for the centre on the council's agenda.

The council failed to approve the decision based on lack of funding in the city budget.

The rigid division between city 'non-professional' and county 'professional' handling of the child in practice means that once the endangered child is placed into the authority of the county court of guardianship, the municipality is not in any way further involved with the matter. The fact that the 'professional' childcare services continue to be handled by the county and not the city institutions is actually a source of much confusion and frustration for social professionals involved in the system, as well as for recipients of the care. For example, the Director of the county-level foster home for teenagers and young adults aged 18 to 23, located in the centre of Sopron, maintained that he has hardly any contact with the city's social department located at walking distance from his facility. The following quotes illustrate the frustration of the home's staff with lack of coordination between the various local government formations, a fact blamed both on institutional factors and on the failure of the local administration to show initiative and flexibility in addressing this shortcoming:

> The way I see it, there should be much stronger cooperation between the town and county institutions. The only reason that there is any kind of relationship at the moment is that me and [another staff member] sometimes go over to the other side of the road and talk to them, socialize with them. But this is our own initiative. But the same can be said about the town court of guardian, the town social department, etc. ... To put it bluntly, it is like this: everyone is doing his or her own job but there's no contact among the different participants of the child protection system.

> In Mosónmagyaróvár [another town where he worked], we used to have monthly conferences or meetings where we discussed territorial education issues. Here nobody cares about us. I find it strange that I wouldn't know who is sitting in the social department in Sopron, in the court of guardian, etc. ... The reason that I know them now is only due to my own initiative.[62]

The fact that smaller children have to be sent to remote locations simply because the town has no stationary facility is also considered to be traumatic for the child and difficult and costly for its relatives. The LG social services staff members are aware of this problem, though they tie the addressing of it to the passage of the relevant legislation at the national level.[63]

Similar institutional problems and the rigidity of local administration in addressing them exist in the area of crisis family services. In Sopron, according to official statistics, 152 families are registered as 'problem' families. The city maintains one stationary centre for families in crisis. The shelter can accommodate 20 people at a time. On average, 80 to 85 people go through the centre in one year. Most people stay up to six months, and it is very rare that families request the extra maximum of three months allowed by the facility. The staff did mention, however, that some families return to the centre up to three times as they continue to be unable to pay housing rents and get evicted. The centre has three full-time staff with higher education, and four people working with children who have secondary education. The centre has only one computer and no Internet connection. The situation is similar to other social institutions that we visited in town. They had one to three or no computers, and no Internet connection.

In contrast to Staraya Russa, where the city facilities serve the surrounding rural areas, no such service provision exists in Sopron. Moreover, the city has even passed a rigid decree prohibiting the provision of aid to crisis families who do not have a permanent address in the city. Legally, the town could make social provision agreements with smaller towns in neighbouring areas, but the Sopron city administration has refused to do so for financial reasons. At the same time, the smaller towns also lack funding for performing these services for their inhabitants. Many people therefore end up being outside of legal framework that would entitle them to social service provision.[64]

Thus, although the staff would be willing to help, the rigidity of the local legislation prohibits them from exercising the flexibility that individual family cases would require. The only way they could help the non-eligible persons is by going around the law and finding ways for the families to obtain local residence registration.[65] Another serious issue mentioned by the centre staff is the lack of awareness of the demand for the services. The centre personnel feel that it would be the municipality's responsibility to conduct and fund a survey of the locality's social needs. The local government, however, has not taken any initiative in this respect, nor has it shown a willingness to fund such a survey. This contrasts sharply with Staraya Russa, where weekly 'raids' within the town and in the surrounding areas aimed at assessing the need for crisis family service, as well as the upkeep of a computer database tracking the well being of each socially vulnerable family, are considered to be key priorities of the municipal social department.

The centre staff also indicated that they do not receive much help from the municipal social department in preparing applications for external funding aside from obtaining the mandated signature. Lack of modern equipment in the facility was also blamed on the municipality. For example, several staff members mentioned that they see absence of Internet connectivity in the shelter as a significant hindrance, given the importance of 'surfing the net' for finding out about funding opportunities. Even with one computer, the family centre is considered well equipped compared to the town's other social institutions. Thus, a member of the Child Welfare Service maintained: 'For months we have been saying that we need Internet … We aren't well equipped with electronic devices.'

Sopron's social department in turn blamed problems with social provision infrastructure on the general funding situation of the town. The head of the local government social department maintained that as a member of the Western Transdanubian Regional Development Council's social committee, she always keeps her eyes open for possible funding opportunities. According to her, most tenders tend to focus on economic development issues, and there is little EU funding specifically aimed at social issues. In general, the crisis centre appears to have very limited contact with local government. The municipality comes once a year to inspect the facility, and the social staff and local social department officials interact once a year at the annual child protection conference. There is no common computer database.[66]

Szolnok

The eastern town of Szolnok had similar shortcomings in responsiveness and implementation. Szolnok is located in one of Hungary's most economically depressed areas with an extremely high unemployment rate (up to 20 per cent de facto). The most common problem identified by all as a source of crisis is expensive housing and joblessness. Once people are out of a job, they cannot afford to pay rents and are forced out on to the street.

As in Sopron, however, coordination between the agencies involved in social service provision is low, and the rigidity of the division of tasks between the various administrative tiers only exacerbates the problem. The social department within the administration is very lean, and includes only supervisory-level staff, with the key services performed by the municipal social service facility, the Human Centre. Formal contacts between the bodies involved in social service provision occur only once a month, although the social department officials claim that informal contact is 'much more frequent'. The post-election turnover within the administration social department appears to be high, which further hinders the effectiveness of the policy process. For example, the head of the department has been in her position only since January 2003, and had to defer to her junior colleagues to answer some of the interview questions about the local social services.[67]

The local government has sub-contracted the operation of some of the key facilities to NGOs. As the following discussion shows, however, this fact per se is not indicative of the quality of local government performance. Similar to Sopron, there is one stationary centre for women in Szolnok, run by an NGO, but co-financed by the local government, as well as non-stationary facilities providing additional services. As in Sopron, family service provision mandating the performance of such services as psychological and other types of counselling is regulated by the 1993 national legislation. Another piece of legislation mandates the setting up of a stationary temporary home for families in crisis in cities with a population of 50,000 or higher by the end of 2003. The responsibility for taking care of families in crisis is divided between three institutions: the Human Centre, which is a local government institution proper, whose director is approved by the local council; an NGO, the local branch of the nationwide Ecumenical Foundation (EF) whose headquarters are in Budapest; and Contact, a centre for 'mental' health, another NGO.

The EF maintains the only stationary facility for families in crisis, while the other two agencies provide consultative or financial services. The foundation obtained the shelter, a former warehouse, from the local government after it provided charity aid to the town following the 1999 flooding in Szolnok. In May 2001 the local government signed a contract with EF delegating to it authority over crisis family service provision, and in July 2001 the facility formally opened. The local government covers 50 per cent of the facility's operational costs, with the remaining 50 per cent coming from the foundation itself. The EF takes families for periods of up to nine months, has a capacity of 40 people, and has four professional social workers. Unlike in Sopron, the facility provides services to both Szolnok and the surrounding settlements.[68] The shelter is constantly overstretched. 'During these nine months if someone else applies, we can't help, we have no more room,' maintained the Director. The biggest problem generating high demand from people is high rents.

While most of the relevant facilities admitted that local government is financially limited in its capacity to provide funding, there is also little evidence of the municipality's active involvement in assisting NGOs with obtaining external grants. The Director of EF indicated that as the centre looks for and applies for external funding, the local government, while formally supporting the applications, does not conduct such searches. The Director lamented this fact, given that local government's matching funds are essential to obtaining external grants.

Problems of funding, coordination, lack of initiative and even shunning legally mandated responsibilities likewise exist in the area of child welfare. Szolnok maintains a system of childcare almost identical to that of Sopron since it is rigidly regulated by national legislation. The town therefore also replicates both the advantages and the disadvantages associated with the system identified in Sopron. The town maintains a legally mandated Child Welfare Service similar to that in Sopron, which includes the monitoring of child welfare through a network of institutions and individuals – schools, nurses, doctors and neighbours. The county maintains the 'professional' service, which is provided when the child is in serious danger, and when the child has to be withdrawn from the family. As in Sopron, Szolnok has failed to set up a temporary home for children, even though it is legally mandated to do so.

The actual foster system is maintained not by the municipal-level institutions, but by the county Child and Youth Protection Institute (CYPI), a national agency with territorially based bodies across the country. The local government's participation in the system is limited to helping the CYPI and county bodies to find parents that could be trained as foster parents. The foster system actually consists of 'households' of 10 or 12 children attended to by two or three professional caretakers, replacing the giant communist era foster facility where 300 children were housed together. There is also a temporary care system for children whereby children whose parents are in hospital or away for another reason for a short time period can be placed temporarily with substitute parents. The service is maintained by the Human Centre, which has contracts with six households.

The advantage of the system is that it is based on the 1997 Law on Child Protection. The law is based on the United Nations conventions on child welfare, and it ensures that high standards of childcare are observed at all territorial levels. The national legislation, for example, clearly states that the preferred model of childcare is to place a child in a foster family. According to the head of the CYPI, 51.71 per cent of the relevant children in the county are placed with foster parents. The disadvantage of the system is its rigidity and lack of coordination between the various institutional levels of government involved in the childcare system. For example, the CYPI official complained that she is often not informed about the fate of the children once their papers are passed on to another level of authority. Also, rather than working together, the local, county and state guardianship institution representatives often fail to show up to important placement conferences. The head of the CYPI, for example, also maintained that he has virtually no contact with the local government. Another disadvantage is that Szolnok, while having county status, can still avoid taking up county functions in childcare, although like Sopron it will be obliged from 2007 to take over some of the professional functions in childcare. According to the Director of the county CYPI, this creates problems when a situation arises where a child needs to be placed in a facility for just a few weeks.

Inadequate technical facilities and equipment only exacerbates the problem of weak coordination. Says the Director of CYPI:

> I can't really imagine a shared database because they need different data in the municipalities and we need different data here as well. But I could imagine something like a central database, to which everyone would have access and could get all those pieces of information that are important for them. ... If things keep going in this direction, we will get lost in the piles of paper.[69]

By contrast, the municipality-run Human Centre has computers in every room, of which two have an Internet connection. Although it would have been sensible for the various agencies to cooperate, there is very little information-sharing between them.

Conclusion

The foregoing discussion suggests that Ústí may be ranked the highest in terms of social performance, followed by Staraya Russa, Karviná, Jelenia Góra, Sopron and Szolnok, and Balashov and Biała Podlaska. The better performers, such as Ústí and Staraya Russa, have smooth policy processes that result from internal institutional reorganisation and the setting up of coordinating mechanisms in internal decision-making and policy planning, involving a variety of actors from both the municipal and NGO sectors. They have also devised regular mechanisms for informing themselves of local social needs, such as the *reydy* in Staraya Russa or annual data reports in Ústí. These towns also maintain high quality social facilities to the extent that funding permits them. The poorer performers, in contrast, such as Biała Podlaska, Sopron and Szolnok, cannot boast effective internal coordination, data gathering or policy implementation.

These results contradict some widely held assumptions about Central and Eastern Europe. What is most striking is the comparably poor record of the two Hungarian towns. Although both Sopron and Szolnok perform very well as far as women in crisis services are concerned, the respective local governments' lack of efforts to identify the social needs of their localities, as well as their insufficient support for NGOs, justify a less positive evaluation of the two towns' performance. A second interesting finding is the surprisingly high position of Staraya Russa. Although it does not operate a stationary women's shelter, Staraya Russa's local government performed impressively with regard to the remaining evaluation criteria. Finally, we observe a west–east dimension with the more western towns ranking higher than those located further to the east. The exception to this rule is Hungary, where both towns ranked low. Table 2.1 summarises our rankings, with the letters H, M and L standing for high, medium and low performance, respectively.

In all the four countries and the respective cities, we found that what is variously called 'families in crisis' or 'problem families' and 'child protection', or 'child welfare' form distinct parts of the local social policies. The mere existence of services in these areas, however, is as such a weak indicator of social performance considering that they form part of the nationally mandated local obligations. As we discussed earlier, the municipalities enjoy, to a greater or lesser extent, depending on the country, freedom to tailor local services to precise local demands. Our research agenda involved investigating the degree of local government responsiveness to these demands. In this respect, we found significant variations, although the quality of the services was relatively high in all eight cities.

As the foregoing discussion has shown, most of the cities in our sample failed to fulfil one or several important requirements mandated by the respective national legislation. Moreover, where a given task assignment was optional, the local governments tended to be more,

Table 2.1 Performance in social services

	JG	BP	SP	SZ	U	K	SR	B
Responsiveness	M	M	L	L	H	M	H	L
Cooperation, NGOs	M	M	M	M	H	M	H	M
Services, children	H	L	M	M	H	H	H	M
Services, women	M	L	H	H	H	H	L	L

Source: assessments by authors.

rather than less likely to pass it on to other administrative, usually regional/county, levels, even if that entailed negative consequences for the recipients of a given social service. This was particularly true in Hungary, and in one of the Russian towns. However, in some cases, as in Ústí and in Staraya Russa, the municipalities were ahead of the national legislation and their progressive practices were singled out for application in other municipalities. Moreover, as in the case of Staraya Russa, they even voluntarily took over some social welfare institutions from the regional level because it would improve social service delivery.

One striking finding is the relatively developed nature of the NGO sector. NGOs, including church-affiliated ones, are now running, or, co-running with municipalities, most of the relevant social facilities. The country that has the most impressive record of NGO activity is the Czech Republic, followed by Hungary, Poland, and, to a much lesser extent, Russia. The relatively developed nature of the NGO sector, and the existence of formal service contracts between NGOs and local governments, however, is not per se indicative of a high level of local government performance. Indeed, as the foregoing discussion has shown, local governments in some towns fail to actively assist NGOs with seeking out external funds, limiting their support to formal endorsement of applications for funding. Another complaint (with the exception of the Czech Republic, where the national government provides large subsidies to NGOs) that we frequently heard in interviews and personally observed is the stark contrast between the much higher level of equipment with computer, technical or other infrastructure of local government facilities proper, on the one hand, and those run by NGOs, on the other. Not only does the local government equip its facilities better than NGOs that run local government-contracted out services, but inadequate cooperation also often precludes the sharing of the relative infrastructure. This fact is striking considering that NGOs, despite the overstretched nature of their work and underfunding often provide higher quality services than those legally mandated to be performed by local governments, but are shunned by them.

Where local governments do actively support non-local government actors in social service provision, and where effective coordination exists between the various agencies, public and private, this often results in generally higher levels of social policy performance. Leadership skills and activism of outstanding individuals likewise may play an important role, as is demonstrated in Staraya Russa. Still, although actors outside the local administration may initiate policy innovativeness, as was the case with Kirillov, it is the support of the municipality and its responsiveness and willingness to implement these ideas that crucially affects local social policy outcomes.

Another impression is that despite the complaints of understaffing and a lack of funding to support service provision, there appears to be no correspondence between the socio-economic situation of the town and the quality of social services. The well off town of Sopron, for example, ranks quite low in terms of social service provision, while the Russian agrarian town of Balashov performed well in at least one area of service provision, namely families in crisis counselling. What further confirms the general impression that funding is not always decisive for local performance is that while some towns pursued cost-free or cost-effective service mechanisms, such as using the already existing local website to post information on local services, or soliciting donations from local businessmen, others maintained a more passive attitude. Another example is internal reorganisation and restructuring, as well as the passage of innovative legislation, which, while not requiring the hiring of additional staff, may entail positive consequences for service provision.

An east–west dimension does appear to be present in the area of policy innovativeness. The two westernmost countries, the Czech Republic and Hungary, maintained stationary facilities for families in crisis, although their quality varied from town to town. No such stationary facilities are operated in either the Polish or the Russian towns. While in Russia, one explanation for this fact is the lack of appropriate federal-level legislation, the Polish case is puzzling, especially if we consider that the EU, as in the other two central European states, has influenced national frameworks here. At the same time, the more western Russian town of Staraya Russa was more innovative in the area of child welfare services compared to Balashov, its eastern counterpart.

In general, national-level institutional frameworks do not appear to be decisive for the quality of services. The strongest evidence of the impact of national institutional frameworks on local social outcomes comes from the two Hungarian cases. Here the national legislation appears to limit significantly the localities' potential for coordination with county or state level actors in the area of child welfare, and, to a lesser extent, families in crisis. Here too, however, the locality may play a decisive role. It may, for example, decide on the provision of a given service or pass it on to the county level. Alternatively, it may foster informal cooperative arrangements with county institutions, even though the national legislation may not specifically mandate it. The extent to which social-economic, institutional, political and cultural factors may account for these variations is explored further in subsequent chapters.

3
Local Government Performance in Economic Promotion

Three fields of activity feature prominently in the developmental programmes of post-communist municipalities. First, local governments in the post-communist states strive to attract direct investment, national or foreign. The main responsibility for attracting direct investment lies with the national level. Within this general national framework, local governments possess a limited, but tangible set of possibilities for competing against other towns in attracting investment.

A second important aspect of local economic development relates to the promotion of small and medium-sized enterprises (SMEs). Although over the last decade the SME sector has continued to expand in post-communist countries, small private companies continue to be plagued by such problems as lack of capital; limited possibilities to raise additional capital from commercial banks; general lack of business experience; and a lack of awareness of the availability of SME development support programmes at national or international levels, particularly the EU. As in the area of direct investment, it is not the local, but the national government that bears the main responsibility for introducing SME support instruments. Within these broader frameworks, local governments have a range of options that they could pursue in order to promote SME growth. But as will become clear from our detailed description of local government activities, not all localities make good use of the opportunities that their respective national governments offer.

A third crucial aspect of local economic promotion is tourism. This includes the restoration of historical buildings; the arresting of socialist era environmental devastation; and the improvement of local tourist infrastructure, such as the building of accommodation facilities of reasonable quality, the setting up of information centres, and the establishment of culture and sport tourist attractions.

The following sections discuss the performance of the eight towns in the area of economic promotion by focusing on their record of adoption and implementation of long-term economic development strategies aimed at attracting large investors, developing the SME sector and promoting tourism.

Evaluating performance

Karviná

The Czech town of Karviná is the leader among our eight towns in economic promotion activities. The USAID-funded Barents Group drafted the town's economic development strategy. In the area of large investment, the programme called for the setting up of an industrial park.[1] In 1997, the local administration, in cooperation with a private company called Rozvoj (development), identified and purchased appropriate land sites. In the autumn of the same year the local council passed a decree on the selection criteria for potential investors. In 1998, Karviná was one of the first two Czech towns to apply successfully for financial support from the Czech government, and began construction work.[2] The local administration chose the Managing Director of Rozvoj, who was also the regional representative of Czechinvest, to work as a professional project manager. In July 2000, the first Czech investor began production on the industrial park site, followed by four other companies, including from Japan, Belgium and Sweden.[3] It is estimated that these investors will have created over 1700 new jobs by 2006. In 2003, Czechinvest awarded the town a prize for building the 'industrial park producing the biggest social benefit'.[4]

The town's performance in SME promotion was likewise impressive. In 1997, consistent with the goals identified in the Barents strategy, the city opened a business incubator housing the first 12 businesses.[5] The local government also passed a special programme aimed at complementing the Czech government SME support instruments by providing matching funds from the local budget.[6] From 2000 onwards, local residents have been entitled to up to 1700 euros in order to obtain access to business advisory services. These include business analysis, business plan development, assistance with bank negotiations, preparing applications for loans, access to information on national and international support programmes, and help with obtaining quality certificates.[7] In recent years, the local government has also encouraged cooperation among local SMEs, as well as networking with business partners abroad.[8] Between August 2000 and April 2002, the local government spent the equivalent of roughly 125,000 euros on these activities. A final example of local government efforts in SME promotion is its record of close cooperation with the local university. The 1996 strategy had already called for tapping into the existing academic infrastructure for developmental aims. The 2000 SME support programme provided for more concrete measures to enhance the cooperation between business, academia and local government. Examples of this synergy are the Silesian university's research projects on the local SME sector,[9] as well as the setting up of a special Institute of Small and Medium Entrepreneurship.

Similarly impressive was the performance of the town in the area of tourism. Notwithstanding the proximity to the Beskidy Mountains, the town's medicinal spring, and its tradition of spa tourism, the potential for tourism is limited. This stems from Karviná's record of coal-mining and steel and the consequent environmental degradation. According to the local functionary in charge of tourism,[10] 'at the moment, we are struggling to foster the image of Karviná as a tourist destination, because at this stage people would not be willing to come here even for a single day'.[11] The town's industrial heritage has led it to identify 'the improvement of the environmental situation' as one of the key developmental aims in the 1996 Barents Strategy. Besides reducing air pollution, the strategy called for a wide range of measures to enhance the town's attractiveness for tourists and the local labour force.

Between 1996 and 2002, the local government successfully implemented key elements of the strategy dealing with environment and tourism promotion. In particular, it invested substantial funds in the restoration of the historical town centre with the relevant expenditures amounting to an equivalent of roughly 2.2 million euros in 2001 alone.[12] Since 2001 Karviná Days have taken place annually, together with other events, such as balls, summer music festivals and a book fair.[13] The local government also built a new hotel complementing the existing limited supply of accommodation facilities. Karviná University's 2000 study of the quality of life in town revealed that 52 per cent of local respondents felt that the local environmental situation had improved. Moreover, respondents also positively rated the city's efforts to improve the local lifestyle, and to restore the historical town centre.[14]

Jelenia Góra

Another example of successful economic-development efforts is the Polish town of Jelenia Góra. Despite the involvement of a plethora of actors from the political, administrative, economic, cultural and academic spheres, whom in November 1997 the local government invited to participate in the drafting of the economic development strategy, the draft was produced within only six months.[15] In May 1998, the planning group adopted the final draft. The strategy builds on a comprehensive study of the local socio-economic situation, as well as on a 1997 public opinion poll aimed at revealing local attitudes and expectations with regard to economic development. The document, which is meant to serve as a rough guide to economic development until 2010, identifies several priority areas. It also provides for the setting up of a special committee to coordinate and monitor the implementation of the strategy. Since 2001, the committee has published annual monitoring reports adopted by the local council. We draw on these reports to assess the local government's ability to implement the development strategy.

In contrast to most of our other towns, Jelenia Góra's economic program does not provide for the setting up of an industrial park. Considering that the town has been for many decades the seat of chemical industries, it already has an industrial zone with brownfield and greenfield investment sites. However, the chemical industry being the source of significant air pollution, the local government has sought to encourage the development of alternative environmentally friendly industries. In the area of investment promotion, the 1998 strategy identified five key goals that it seeks to attain by 2005. They are the restructuring of municipal companies and businesses; the setting up of a Regional Economic Promotion Centre (REPC); the creation of a system of local pro-investment policy; public investment in existing technical and transport infrastructure; and the construction of department stores.

In addition to the strategy, the local council adopted other documents aimed at attracting investment. A decree adopted in 2000 provided for the setting up of special investment sites, for intensifying economic promotion activities, for bringing local education more into line with employer demand, and for drafting an economic transformation pro-gramme that would make the town eligible for financial support from the European Union.[16] The municipality also sponsored the renovation of the local technical and transport infrastructures, some of which dated back to the pre-Second World War era.[17] By the end of 2000, the Town Hall had spent an equivalent of over 3.5 million euros[18] on repairing and expanding the relevant sewage facilities, paving roads and sidewalks, and building bridges and parking sites.[19] The local government also successfully applied for external funding from the EU. A bypass which relieved the town centre from heavy traffic was to a sig-nificant extent financed from the EU's PHARE funds.[20] In 2002, Jelenia Góra successfully qualified for the EU ISPA funding which will bring the local government 28 million euros in infrastructure development projects.[21]

In evaluating the town's efforts in the area of SME support it is important to note that in Poland, SME promotion is largely the function of the state. The Polish national Agency for Enterprise Development provides enterprises, the unemployed, the state administration and regional and local governments with advisory services on financial support programmes, legal questions and technological innovation. It also organises information and promotion events, conducts business analysis, and co-finances projects with other institutions. At the regional level, the Agency is represented by regional development agencies and at the local level by advisory centres, which offer free services to SMEs.[22] In Jelenia Góra, the advisory centre is a shareholding company with the majority of shares owned by the regional government.[23]

Because SME support is a state or regional task, the local government's 1998 strategy did not provide for concrete measures to promote SMEs. However, the municipality did take some practical measures to stimulate this sector. For example, the department of economic initiatives within the local administration informs beginning entrepreneurs about services offered by the development agencies.[24] In addition, in 2001, the local government together with other institutions established a Regional Fund of Loan Guarantees. The Fund has already made a capital contribution of an equivalent of over 72,000 euros for local SME support.[25] Finally, the local council adopted several decrees concerning SMEs, such as the waiving of registration fees and rent payments, and tax concessions to small businesses.

The local government made more comprehensive efforts in the area of tourism promotion, and its performance in this sector is impressive. One local official highlights the contrast between the paucity of efforts to promote tourism in the early 1990s, and subsequent activities:

> When I started to work in the local administration in 1991, I did not have a single zloty for tourism promotion activities. There was no tourist information centre in town, and the first information booklet was published with money from the department of culture and sports. Today, we have two tourist information centres, we are present at tourism fairs and in the press, and three films about Jelenia Góra were shot and shown on German TV. These are the results of our work.[26]

In furtherance of the long-term goal of making the town a 'regional centre of tourism promotion and development', in 1998, the local development strategy recommended a set of measures to boost local and regional tourism. In particular, it called for promotional activities enhancing the tourist attractiveness of the town and for the restoration of the town centre. In recent years, the town square and the surrounding streets have been turned into showrooms of European architectural history. In 2001 alone, the government spent close to (the equivalent of) 70,000 euros on promotion activities at different national and international tourism fairs.[27] The strategy also provided for the construction of a new hotel in the town centre. By 2002 the construction of a new building was well on the way, and the town also had concrete plans for modernising an existing hotel.[28] In the realm of sports and culture, the local strategy outlined an ambitious programme, including the financing of local cultural projects, the setting up of a consulting forum for culture, outlining a programme for the local spa and building new sports and other leisure facilities.[29] Most of these goals in sports and culture had also been attained. In 1998, the local Fund for Cultural Initiatives was set up aimed at co-financing important cultural activities. Between 1998 and 2001, the local government invested over 125,000 euros in the fund.[30] Finally, the local government set out to build new sports and leisure facilities on the territory of an old socialist housing estate.[31]

Ústí

Much less impressive in the area of economic planning and implementation was the Czech town of Ústí nad Labem. Similar to Karviná, the town became a beneficiary of a USAID-funded Barents Group strategy. Although the local council adopted the strategy in 1996, with the exception of some minor elements it did not start implementing the document until 1998. According to a local functionary in charge of economic development, 'very little happened ... roughly one fourth or one third of all projects suggested by the Barents Group were implemented, and in most cases it was the cheaper projects that were realized, that is, primarily projects of administrative re-organization.'[32]

The Barents strategy called for the setting up of an industrial park in order to attract large investment. The local government made the first step in implementing this task by identifying and purchasing an appropriate site. However, by 2002 based on alleged lack of funding, the municipality still failed to set up the required technical infrastructure and to carry out promotional activities to attract investors.[33] The town did apply for funding from the Czech government, but was unsuccessful. Only in the second half of 2002, after it had filed applications with the Czech government and the European Union, did infrastructure development funds become available.[34] This record may be contrasted with the success of the broader Ústí region, which has in the last years attracted a growing share of foreign direct investment to the Czech Republic.[35]

Ústí was more pro-active in SME promotion; but its performance record in this area has also been mixed. The town identified SMEs[36] as the local economy's priority sector. In 1998, the local government charged the local Chamber of Industry and Commerce[37] with preparing an SME support programme, and in late 1999 the first draft appeared.[38] However, a significant hindrance to SME development has been the lack of a Regional Advisory and Information Centre (RAIC), which contrasts with Karviná, where the RAIC has been operational for over a decade. Only in 2002 was the town included in the national network of RPICs, which made it eligible for financial support from the Ministry of Industry and Trade.[39] Recently, the local government did make significant financial contributions to the drafting of projects with which SMEs successfully applied for funding from financial support programmes. These subsidies, in 2002 alone, helped local SMEs to obtain close to 150,000 euros from various external sources.[40] The municipality also offers legal aid to SMEs,[41] and has supported local companies in their applications for public tenders.[42]

In the area of tourism Ústí faced challenges that are similar to the other Czech town, Karviná. But it does not match the latter's impressive record in seeking to mitigate the impact of negative environmental or other tourism-unfriendly factors. Despite the proximity of the river Elbe, the town is not considered to be a popular tourist destination. Destroyed by allied bombing in 1945, the historical town centre was never fully restored and was replaced with socialist architecture. Ústí, however, has done little to improve the town's outward appearance. It also failed to improve the offer of local accommodation although local officials admit that the quality of existing facilities is very low.[43] Finally, while the municipality invested an equivalent of roughly 27 million euros in building an extravagant bridge across the river Elbe,[44] it neglected existing monuments and the town square, provoking strong public criticism.[45]

Similarly weak was the city's performance in the area of culture and sports tourism promotion. In a local opinion poll only 35 per cent of respondents expressed satisfaction with the local provision of sports and cultural facilities, while 53 per cent complained about a lack of relevant facilities and events.[46] As a result, although the number of visitors to the town is growing, in 2002 Ústí ranked only fourth among the seven most important towns in the region. Moreover, with regard to the number of nights that visitors spent in a given town, Ústí even ranked the lowest.[47]

Biała Podlaska

In contrast to the other Polish town of Jelenia Góra, the Biała Podlaska council experienced significant delays in drafting and adopting an economic development strategy. In January 1997, the councillors agreed on the need for the document, but the final version of the paper was only adopted in September 2000.[48] The document prioritised attracting direct investment and creating new job opportunities, and suggested several instruments, such as the establishment of an industrial park, a system of tax concessions and other promotional activities. In addition, the strategy called for the improvement of technical and transport infrastructure.

Although the strategy covers the period until 2010, it is possible to examine the steps already taken to implement it. In 2001, the locality successfully applied for external funding from the EU and received over 2 million euros to start building and equipping the industrial park. By mid-2003, potential investors had been offered a variety of greenfield and brownfield investment opportunities in the park. A special section of the local government website helped promote the sites.[49] In 1999, a new department was set up within the local administration, the main task of which is to promote the town, develop new projects and prepare applications for external funding.[50] In the following year the city agreed on tax concessions to investors.[51]

There were visible signs of modernisation of local infrastructure, which we witnessed during field visits. During our first field visit in April 2002 there were many unpaved muddy roads and shabby housing estates. On our second visit in December 2002 in the winter we observed that roads had been paved, houses renovated and new playgrounds set up. According to a local government progress report, between 1999 and 2002 close to ten million euros were invested in modernising sewage systems, water pipes, roads, pavements and parking sites.[52]

The local government was not very active, however, in SME promotion. The Head of the Department of Economic Development, for example, maintained: 'In the area of SMEs, the local situation is far from perfect. To date, there is no strategy, no operational programme ... There is no document explicitly targeting SME development.'[53] The 2000 strategy did envisage some instruments for SME promotion, such as the setting up of a business incubator by the end of 2002; intensifying cooperation between the local government and business associations; and setting up

SME support institutions.[54] By the end of 2002, however, there was little evidence of the implementation of these plans. The incubator had not been set up, and there were no major changes in the development of SME support networks. Moreover, as late as 2002 Biała Podlaska still failed to participate in the national government institutional frameworks designed to assist SMEs. While in Jelenia Góra, local businesses benefit from advisory services, training courses and loan guarantees provided by institutions located in the town, in Biała Podlaska, the SMEs have to travel to the *województwo* capital of Lublin to obtain similar services, and very few SMEs actually make the effort.[55] Moreover, hardly any communication between the local government and local SMEs appears to exist and there is no centralised information point for businesses. According to a local functionary, 'whenever someone turns to me, I provide him with Internet addresses and information and tell him which steps to take. But there is no systematic way of informing businesses about these things. Since SMEs often do not even have access to email and the Internet, sending around emails is not a realistic alternative.'[56]

In the area of tourism the strategy suggested the modernisation of existing sports facilities, the development of water tourism, the setting up of a tourist information centre, and the revitalisation of local cultural life.[57] However, to date only one project has been completed. In 2001, a historical building was transformed into a tourist information centre.[58] The strategy's other provisions have not been implemented, such as the setting up of a boat station or the building of bicycle lanes. Moreover, although the local government in the strategy committed itself to co-financing cultural activities with the equivalent of roughly 12,500 euros annually, according to one functionary, 'very little money has been invested in tourism.'[59]

Staraya Russa

The Russian town of Staraya Russa has an ambitious economic development strategy, solicited from, and prepared by, external consultants in May 2001. It was funded by a Soros Foundation Small Cities of Russia grant for which the city administration applied and which it won in competition against 35 or so medium-sized Russian cities. The city awarded the contract for preparing the economic strategy to the Bauman Technical University in Moscow. The product of the university's work was a very detailed analysis of the structure of local economy, environment and potential, and a series of concrete proposals for economic growth. The strategy's key recommendations to reduce Staraya Russa's employment and tax revenue dependence on one large enterprise, the Aviation Repair Plant by diversifying the local economy; to develop SMEs; to promote tourism development and infrastructure by building new hotel facilities; to promote the city's image in Russia and abroad; and to promote modern education and encourage qualified workers to stay in the city. Although the town's largest enterprise, the state aviation plant is now subordinate to the federal Ministry of Defence, it provides employment to approximately 2000 of the city and surrounding areas work force of around 23,000 people. Moreover, revenues from the plant amount to approximately 60 per cent of the city's industrial production and 30 per cent of the overall local budget, while all the other enterprises combined account for only 14 per cent. According to the logic of the strategy, not only would diversifying the local economy reduce the risks for the local labour force should the plant's performance falter, but increasing the number and viability of smaller service-sector, particularly tourism-oriented businesses would also help foster a more environmentally and tourism-friendly image of the city. The report saw a strong potential for developing this particular area of the local economy by creating 'clusters' of service and catering businesses. In pre-Soviet times a famous spa town attracting the Russian nobility to its famed medicinal springs, Staraya Russa, it was argued, could capitalise on this by promoting small business development in tourism service areas. The 'progressive' initiative to participate in the Soros competition and the choice of external consultants itself reflected the outlook and efforts of the local Mayor and key officials in charge of economic development. Nikolay Zanin, the young Deputy Head of Administration in charge of the economy who we interviewed, used to be a lecturer at Novgorod University. He is a passionate believer in what knowledge, Western exposure and modern technology could potentially do for his city. By the winter of 2003 there was some indication that the local government sought to implement aspects of the strategy related to SME promotion. According to Zanin, businesses are encouraged to move into the ground floors of downtown buildings as part of a broader plan to revive the historical part of the city and make it attractive to tourists. Interviews with small businesses confirm that there is very little red tape involved in setting up a business, and the local officials are generally business friendly. This also applies to foreign investors. Zanin told us that each investor is assigned a local government official who is held personally responsible for ensuring the fastest and smoothest possible registration process for that firm.[60]

As an example of the success of this strategy local officials like to point out the German-owned fish processing plant, built and made operative within a period of nine months. The company, which employs 60 people, brought the city an investment of one million US dollars, and has a turnover of approximately twelve million roubles per year, exporting much of its production to Europe. By way of comparison, Staraya Russa's Soviet-era machinery building enterprise, with 1600 employees, has a turnover of only 9.6 million roubles per year. According to the local administration, it is also unprecedented for the region that a foreign firm classified as small to medium-sized, as opposed to large, has decided to set up an enterprise in the locality. In what is further indicative of a generally more investor-friendly climate, the firm first thought of operating in the neighbouring region of Pskov, but after some red tape incidents, decided in favour of Novgorod's Staraya Russa.

Local efforts in SME promotion were also evident in the setting up of the Centre for Support of Women's Entrepreneurship, Uspekh (success). The organisation, which also plans to open a business school for women, is aimed at addressing the issues of female unemployment by facilitating the setting up of small businesses.[61] The result of the pro-active efforts at diversifying the local economy has been the gradual reduction of jobs in the Soviet-era large enterprises, and the increase in the numbers of those employed in service and other small and medium-sized business sectors. Approximately 300 employees have flowed from the large enterprise facilities to the SME sector in recent years.

The local government also carried out activities aimed at implementing another key recommendation of the long-term economic strategy, namely 'promotion of the city' and of its administration as 'progressive' and 'visitor-friendly' in order to attract investors and tourists. The strategy recommended various ways of achieving this, including by developing modern and fast forms of communication. Zanin boasts that earlier than many other Russian provincial cities, Staraya Russa acquired cell and GSM forms of communication, and supported companies building Internet cable networks. The fish-processing company is alleged to have found out about Staraya Russa and its investment opportunities through the city's Internet website. The authors of this project during early stages of research were also blessed with the availability of general information about the city on its Internet web page, while also having no trouble obtaining additional required information from the economic department, and setting up interviews with the Mayor and other staff. By contrast, in our other Russian city of Balashov, the Soviet style atmosphere of secrecy and closeness prevailed: in 2002 the city lacked an informative website, its staff denied us meetings and interviews, and we had to rely on personal connections in order set up meetings with some more junior staff members, but not the Mayor himself.

Staraya Russa's record in implementing the other significant aspect of the strategy, tourism development, has been mixed, however. Staraya Russa made progress in one area auxiliary to tourism promotion, which has been identified in the economic development strategy, namely the creation of an environmentally friendly image of the town. The administration blocked the setting up of large industries that would damage the city's image of a quaint tourist town. In an effort to prevent large vehicles carrying wood from Staraya Russa's wood-processing facilities, with investment from Russian and Finnish companies, it also started construction of terminals in a location more remote from the city centre.

Overall, however, the city administration made no consistent efforts aimed at tourism promotion. The city's key claim to tourist potential is the Staraya Russa Resort, or spa medical and recreational facility. In the Soviet times a federal-government-owned enterprise, the spa was privatised in the 1990s and made into a shareholding enterprise, with a capacity for over 1000 patients.[62] The facility boasts not only patients from all over Russia and the former USSR, but also from Western Europe. However, the success of the Staraya Russa resort largely rests outside the influence of the local administration, although the strategy has specifically recommended that by cooperating more closely with the spa, the administration could obtain more benefits for the city. Although the city government also owns shares in the enterprise, their value is negligible, and the management and strategic development decision-making rests with the spa's private owners. The spa's Director did admit that the spa has a good relationship with the spa administration and that the Mayor invites the enterprise management to participate in delegations to Western cities in order to encourage Western clients to visit the resort facilities. The Mayor also said that the city had applied for and obtained a TACIS grant to train spa medical personnel in Germany.

The major source of disappointment both for the spa and for other concerned parties has been the city's remarkable failure to make progress in areas auxiliary to the resort business, namely tourism and tourism infrastructure development. Although tourism was named as one of the key goals in the economic strategy, in 2003 the city administration had no department or even a single official in charge of tourism. In what is very illustrative of a general lack of interest in this area, the official in charge of public relations in the city hall was herself confused as to who may be even marginally responsible for tourism in the administration. Accordingly, when asked about tourism statistics, one official in charge of culture development referred the authors to a private tourism agency and the resort, suggesting that 'they might help you better'. Similarly, when asked if the city publishes fliers describing its tourism potential, we were referred to a non-governmental cultural association that publishes a journal about Staraya Russa's culture and history.

Little evidence of progress was observed in hotel business development, the city maintaining only one Soviet-era hotel. In his interview in 2001 the Mayor, echoing what had been outlined in the strategy, admitted that building a new hotel to replace the only existing one (aside from the rooms of the resort enterprise), a crumbling Soviet style building, was the city's highest priority. In a similar vein, the official in charge of economic development maintained that as one of his main goals he sees the development of a culture of 'family businesses' in hotel services and the introduction of 'bed and breakfast' type services hitherto unavailable in the town.[63] But by the beginning of 2003 no new hotel had been built or even slated for construction in the budget and no small family hotel business facilities set up.

Sopron

Sopron does not have a long-term economic plan, as successive local administrations tend to produce new economic programmes without much consistency with those of the previous administration. City officials blame longer term economic planning on financial constraints, which came as a result of the Town Hall's speculative financial operation, known as the 'Globex affair'. The affair dates back to the Hungarian government's privatisation and decentralisation efforts of the mid-1990s when local governments found themselves with large portfolios of shares. Due to their lack of experience in managing the shares, most local governments in fact ended up immediately selling them without waiting for their value to go up.

Sopron instead chose to invest the funds in a high-risk enterprise. The relevant portfolio of assets that Sopron received in 1997 included shares in privatised companies, such as EGAZ, totalling approximately 1.3 billion forints. The city possessed an additional 1.2 billion in state securities. An initial decision by the mayor's office was to set up a portfolio manager organisation and to invest the shares in government bonds. In an open tender to select a professional portfolio manager, several foreign and local companies applied. The contract, however, was awarded to a lesser known Hungarian company Globex amid speculation about corruption in the mayor's office and council. Critics of the affair maintained that very little information was gathered about the banks involved before awarding the contract. No expert familiar with the banking sector was hired to assess the merits of the various applicants. Finally, no independent study of the experience of other local governments in handling shares was conducted. Shortly after the investment, Globex, which turned out to be a classic pyramid scheme, collapsed. As a result of the deal, most of the city's transferable assets were lost, leaving Sopron with a budget deficit of six billion forints and mounting legal bills; the town can hope to recover only one fifth of the assets' original value (Szuly).

Another illustration of Sopron's weak record of economic performance is the failure to push through the setting up of an industrial park. In 1997, an 'industrial park' title was awarded to an area of 60 hectares located only four kilometres from the Austrian border and three kilometres from the Sopron town centre. Fully owned and operated by the local government, the Park was to begin selling and renting plots by the first half of 2000.[64] As part of the park, the municipality also planned to build an Incubator House including an Innovation Centre with services for investors, laboratories and research hubs. The project aimed to further the image of the town as an environmentally friendly centre of high tech innovation utilising and building upon the intellectual potential of Sopron University. The stress was on small environmentally friendly innovative companies, such as those in electronics, high technology, trade and logistics.

Several factors boded well for the success of the park. To begin with, Sopron received a PHARE cross-border cooperation (CBC) grant amounting to 1.6 million euros to build the park.[65] Second, the timing of the setting up of the park was favourable: according to a survey of Hungary's industrial parks, the most effective, fastest growing and export oriented multinational companies settled in parks which obtained the title in 1997.[66] Although it is widely believed that industrial parks require a period of seven to ten years of 'maturation', the country-wide average investment efficiency of the parks, even in the four years between 1997 and 2001, exceeded that of average industrial growth by over 1.5 times, and national economic output by over 2.5 times. Third, as an entirely greenfield industrial park, it did not have the disadvantages of parks built on former industrial territories whose infrastructure needed major renovation, demolition, or whose layout had limitations for businesses. Finally, Western Hungary was at the outset the strongest magnet for investors in industrial parks. With their potential to connect to global and European markets, many investors chose to settle in parks along the motorway M1 in Győr-Moson-Sopron and Komárom-Esztergom counties.[67]

Six years after the title had been awarded the implementation of the park project was showing mixed results, although the record of inhabitation of the park was higher than in Szolnok. By fall 2002, infrastructure had been completed on 18 hectares of the park, while 42 hectares remained inoperative because of a lack of interest on the part of the investors. The five enterprises that did settle in are a large Hungarian-Austrian construction company; a smaller Hungarian surveying and planning company; and three smaller Hungarian enterprises in various areas.

According to officials of the park, lack of substantial investment stems from stringent criteria imposed by concerns about preserving the environmentally friendly tourist image of the city. But critics of the local administration maintained that there might be other reasons that may have hindered the successful inhabiting of the park. According to them, the PHARE grant was compromised when the city failed to produce the required matching funds in a timely fashion. The election of a new local administration in 2003 put the development of the park on hold further as the new leaders scrutinised the business practices of the previous administration.

A similar lack of sustained policy implementation was observed in the area of SME promotion. The relaxation of the border with Austria in the early 1990s led to a boom in consumer tourism from the rich European neighbour. As a result, there was a marked growth of such services as dentistry, coiffeurs and beauty salons, aimed at satisfying the demands of Austrian consumers for cheaper prices across the border. In dentistry in particular the growth was phenomenal, with the city boasting over 400 dentists by the end of the 1990s. The local administration therefore did not face the problem of SME development faced by other towns under investigation, and the booming SME sector could not be an adequate yardstick for measuring local performance. An indication of the city's performance, however, could be the ability of the city to profit from the growth in the SME sector or to regulate it.

The impression one acquires from interviewing local functionaries is that the city passively observed the spontaneous growth of small businesses without pursuing sensible taxation policies and channelling tax profits from the more profitable and developed areas to those that needed support. Many respondents gave dentistry as an example of policy weakness. The national legislation allows for tax reductions for services in the medical sphere. The municipality, however, did not lobby for changing the national legislation, leaving the dental clinics virtually untaxed. In addition, the local government failed to monitor the dentistry practices officially registered in Budapest, but providing services in Sopron, and hence avoiding paying local taxes. The result was a 'poor city of rich people'.[68]

Tourism development may likewise give a misleadingly positive impression of Sopron's economic performance. The official tourism statistics are impressive. In 2001, the city boasted 19,543 tourists. In 2002 the figure was higher, at 21,420 tourists, the lion's share of whom came from such European states as Germany (26 per cent), Austria (24 per cent), the UK (10 per cent), France (8 per cent), Holland (6 per cent) and Italy (6 per cent). But tourism statistics alone would be a poor yardstick for measuring the city's performance in tourism promotion. Of the eight cities under investigation, it has traditionally been the greatest tourist destination, even during the Soviet period. Sopron is a well-preserved medieval town with an impressive cultural and historical heritage. With 240 historic buildings of Baroque, Gothic and other architectural styles, it is Hungary's second 'most historic town' after Budapest.[69]

Successive local administrations have outlined plans for capitalising on the city's tourism potential. A brochure produced by the city administration called attention to the need for greater emphasis on 'cultural tourism'. It hinted at the commercial rather than the cultural nature of visits by Western tourists, lamenting the 'unfavourable' structure of local tourism, a decrease of visitors to cultural events offered by the city, the underutilised hotel facilities, and the low number of nights tourists actually spend in the town. The town did take steps to change the local tourism structure. With EU funding, it built a new conference centre in the historical part of Sopron. Many of the other cultural tourism projects remained on paper, however, such as the Liszt music festivals. Moreover, even the less complex measures which do not require substantial investment, such as extending the opening hours of the town's museums and keeping them open throughout the year, have not been carried through.

Local actors almost unanimously blame most of the economic failures, such as the lack of an agreement among the various political factions in the council on a long-term economic plan, on 'politics'. At the same time, good managerial and firm leadership skills are regarded as essential to reversing the city's poor economic performance. For example, many interviewees placed high hopes in the newly elected Mayor, a businessman. His socialist credentials (he is a member of the socialist party MSZP) do not seem to deter people, including local entrepreneurs, from supporting him because of the high hopes associated with his business experience and his 'entrepreneurial spirit' and that of 'other young men' surrounding him.[70] According to one entrepreneur and local government official, 'the new local government is very young and what is even better, they are all positive, very intelligent and success oriented young people.

Instead of looking back, they concentrate on the future.' Thankfully, maintained one businessman, the new Mayor 'does not consider party lines'.[71] The interviewees contrasted these credentials with those of the previous Mayor, who is alleged to have lacked 'management thinking', exercised weak leadership and been easily swayed by political interests and business lobbyists, hence the string of bad economic decisions – from the disastrous Globex affair to the failure to tax prosperous dentists. Still, our interviews were conducted very shortly after the elections and it is difficult to judge the extent to which the new Mayor will be able to exercise firm leadership and depoliticise local decision-making. The paralysing impact of excessive party politicisation of local decision-making on economic development in our view is highlighted even further by the fact that Sopron boasts a very active and engaged business and NGO community. The predominantly industrial structure of the economy would suggest higher performance levels. In fact, evidence from Sopron does not support the contention of some studies of regional and local politics in other post-communist settings that such a constellation of economic interests and their involvement in local decision-making should result in better per-formance outcomes (Stoner-Weiss 1997). Likewise, local political culture and social capital, as indeed good leadership skills, may offset the negative effects of excessive politicisation of local decision-making, but the weight of party political factors might still be decisive in the overall developmental outcomes. These factors are discussed in detail in Chapter 6.

Balashov

Balashov does not have a long-term economic development strategy. When asked if the town has an economic strategy, the official in charge of the economy indicated that an 'economic plan' is adopted every five years. In what is illustrative of the city's lack of a modern vision, the Head of the Economic Department, who had been with the local government since Soviet times, refused to provide the authors with a copy of the plan. Judging from the interview, however, the plan appears to be more of a Soviet style forecasting of agriculture and industrial yields, rather than a consistent effort aimed at adapting the local economy to the changing post-Soviet realities. Balashov also does not have a single foreign investor or a joint venture with foreign capital, nor has it applied for or won an external grant for devising an economic plan. The city provides no tax concessions to businesses or foreign investors, or pursues other efforts to bring in businesses.

Senior executives of the town's largest enterprises complained that the local administration does not assist them with identifying potential foreign investors or with other measures aimed at easing their transition to a market economy. The Balashov textile plant, Baltex, which is now a private shareholding enterprise, illustrates this point. The plant is Balashov's main enterprise. Since its establishment in 1968, this enterprise has occupied an important niche in the countrywide production of tents, coats and other waterproof textile products.[72] The plant has not done very well since the transition to a market economy, but remains Balashov's most important enterprise in terms of employment. Although the city to a large extent depends on the plant, according to its Director, the local administration has done nothing to support the enterprise, or to make the town more attractive for workers. When the city administration officials conducted a trip to China they did not invite officials from the town's largest enterprise into the delegation or to identify potential Chinese partners in textiles who could exchange know-how with their Balashov counterparts. The management of other enterprises also indicated that they have limited contact with the city administration.

Szolnok

The Eastern Hungarian town of Szolnok does not have a long-term economic strategy. As in Sopron, each new administration tends to produce a new strategy, while dismissing that of the previous government. For example, the new official in charge of the economy admitted that he 'cannot name a single ongoing project from that time', that is, from the previous administration. In addition to the lack of long-term policy continuity, there is also a low level of policy implementation even within the time span of one administration.

Szolnok has been remarkably slow at attracting foreign direct investment even compared to the other towns in the depressed Great Plain region. The fate of the local industrial park illustrates this point. In January 1999 the local government purchased the land area of the prospective industrial park and in March 2000 it was awarded the Industrial Park title by the Ministry of Economic Affairs. In 2001 the town won a PHARE grant for the development of the park. In furtherance of the plan, a Szolnok Industrial Park and Logistics Servicing company, fully owned by the municipal government, was established. The park covers an area of 154.8 hectares, which includes 124 hectares of new, unsettled areas, and the rest covering pre-existing industrial infrastructure and enterprises. The project activity was to start in August 2002, and was to be completed by December 2003. By the end of the project it was to generate 16,000 new jobs.

When the authors of this project contacted the park management in July 2003, work on setting up the park infrastructure had just begun, with the time schedule for completion of infrastructure, and hence the beginning of the settlement of enterprises, moved to August 2004. According to the representative of the Park, negotiations with potential investors – six to eight small to medium-sized enterprises in services, rather than production areas, such as transport and storage – were already taking place, and they 'looked very promising'. But we were given no concrete evidence of a firm commitment by the companies to establish their presence in the park. In this case lack of sufficient local funding that may have hindered project implementation was just one side of the story. The previous local government administration did not slate 'matching funds' in the local budget, which served to undermine the city's chances of success in applying for PHARE and other external funds.

Moreover, the local administration also did not make available full information on the park to potential investors. According to the manager of one of the town's leading companies, an agricultural machinery enterprise with warehouses in the vicinity of the park, no approaches were made to the local businesses informing them about opportunities and potential gains from the business park. 'I don't know whom they want to see go there if they don't talk to those companies that already have premises in the neighbourhood. That would be the most sensible thing to do', the company manager maintained.[73] The company, which is one of the five largest taxpayers in town, also lamented that its Director did not personally know the Mayor, and that successive mayors failed to establish contacts with its management.

Similar performance weaknesses were observed in the area of SME promotion. The staff of the local government responsible for the economy maintained that SME development has been remarkably slow considering that potential businesses suffer from lack of starting capital. But interviews with small businesses also suggest that there has been very little initiative on the part of the local government to facilitate SME development. The new staff responsible for economic development in the city administration admitted: 'At this moment we can't mention any ongoing projects where the town and SMEs would work together.'[74] There are no regular consultative meetings, and contacts between businesses and the local government staff are largely limited to the early registration and license application phase. Contacts that go beyond this are usually informal and ad hoc in nature.

Finally, tourism has likewise suffered from the local government's remarkable lack of initiative and policy consistency. Szolnok's location at the estuary of the Tisza and Zagyva rivers in the socialist period made it one of the most attractive spots for water tourism, but in 2000 a cyanide spill from a gold mine in Romania led to contamination of the Tisza. This accident significantly undermined the town's attraction as a tourist destination. Our respondents in the area of tourist services, however, indicated that Szolnok's objective disadvantages were but one aspect of the lack of tourism development. Many respondents blamed lack of cooperation with local government, or downright passivity and lack of interest on the part of local administration in tourism promotion. Says the owner of one of the best hotels in Szolnok: 'I have to say that the local government hasn't been helping local tourism businesses at all. Many times we had to act completely on our own, although the results of our enterprise work might be fruitful for the town as well.'[75]

The local government's institutional structure is also illustrative of the low priority accorded to tourism development, and of a failure to foster cooperative decision-making that would involve various interested parties. Until recently, there was no special department within the administration dealing with tourism. Only in 2002 did the local administration set up a committee for tourism promotion. Even then, the main criterion for selecting the businesses to sit on the committee was their party affiliation. The businesses also blamed the local government for its failure to create a positive 'block view' of the town, which is damaging for both individual businesses involved in tourism, as well as the image of the town as a whole. Instead, such basic local services as street cleaning and road maintenance are very poorly performed, and are dependent on ad hoc personal connections and networks. For example, the owner of a hotel maintained that the fact that snow had been cleaned in front of the hotel is a result of his own 'good contact' with the municipal cleaning company, rather than of a consistent and regular performance of cleaning services by the local government.[76]

Conclusion

The foregoing analysis reveals substantial economic performance variations. By 2003, out of the eight towns, only four – Jelenia Góra, Biała Podlaska, Karviná and Staraya Russa – had passed a long-term economic development strategy. At the same time, between these four towns, major differences exist with regard to the timing of the passage of the strategy and the way in which the localities conceived the document.

Karviná was the first to pass a strategy of economic development (1996), followed by Jelenia Góra (1998), Biała Podlaska (2000) and Staraya Russa (2001). While Karviná and Staraya Russa solicited their strategies from national or international professional consultants, the two Polish towns designed their strategies without external assistance, although Jelenia Góra also included a broad range of local and regional actors in the planning process. In the remaining four towns, for various reasons economic policy was based on short-term political documents rather than on a complex strategy of economic development. In the two Hungarian towns, strategic plans were repeatedly abolished as soon as new political leadership was elected. The Russian town of Balashov appears not to have entirely abandoned the socialist practice of following five-year plans. Finally, the Czech town of Ústí decided to abandon a strategy it had adopted in 1996, while failing to produce a new one.

Similar variations exist in the local governments' implementation capacities. Only Jelenia Góra and Karviná were able to implement their strategies. Despite its convenient geographic location close to the Czech–German border Ústí has so far failed to attract substantial foreign investment, not least due to delays in the construction of its industrial park. Until recently, SMEs were also not provided with the advisory services available in the other Czech town of Karviná. Finally, the local government has only recently started to tackle the problem of its negative socialist town outward appearance that had hitherto turned off potential tourists. A similar case is Biała Podlaska. During much of the 1990s, the local government failed to make systematic efforts to overcome the deteriorating economic situation, but over the last few years, some important improvements in the city's performance can be observed. Although there has been little direct investment, the municipality has made efforts to modernise the local technical and transport infrastructure. An industrial park is now under construction after the local government successfully applied for a PHARE grant. It has also promoted investment sites on its web site. Although at this time tourism does not play a significant role in the local economy, the recently renovated old town may help attract tourists in the future. The Hungarian town of Sopron has likewise showed a mixed performance record. It has partially implemented longer-term developmental goals, such as the setting up of an industrial park and attracting foreign investors, as well as building a conference centre in order to enhance its tourism potential. For a variety of reasons, however, it has not been able to agree on a comprehensive long-term developmental strategy that can survive successive local administrations.

Finally, Balashov and Szolnok may be considered failures in stimulating local economic development. Despite efforts to establish an industrial park, the Hungarian town of Szolnok has not been able to attract substantial large direct investment. The local government does not seem to have an easy time finding potential investors and communicating with traditional local industry. The local government's lack of vision and long-term planning is particularly illustrative in the area of SME promotion, and there does not seem to be any programme at all in this regard. Finally, despite the potential for tourism, the local government has largely neglected this aspect of the local economy.

Our last case, the Russian town of Balashov, does not seem to pursue any economic policy at all, despite the fact that in terms of foreign direct investment Saratov *oblast*, where Balashov is located, is one of the more attractive regions of the Russian Federation. Moreover, the local government has also failed to support the existing industry or to facilitate the establishment of business contacts abroad.

Table 3.1 contains a rough ranking of the economic performance of the eight cities, with H, M and L standing for high, medium and low performance, respectively. This evaluation suggests that Karviná and Jelenia Góra rank highest, followed by Staraya Russa, Ústí and Biała Podlaska, Sopron, and Szolnok and Balashov.

This ranking runs counter to several commonly held expectations with regard to local government performance in post-communist settings. Although, compared to the other post-communist states of Central and Eastern Europe, Hungary is often praised for its economic stability and attractiveness to foreign direct investment, both our Hungarian towns are at the lower end of our ranking list. Conversely, despite the well known problems plaguing Russia, Staraya Russa has left behind several towns located in the more advanced Central European countries. A second interesting finding is that the size of the town does not appear to have an impact on performance. Among the five high-ranking towns we find three smaller and two larger towns. The one observable pattern is related

Table 3.1   Performance in economic promotion

	JG	BP	SP	SZ	U	K	SR	B
Goal agreement/adopting strategy	H	M	L	L	M	H	H	L
Strategy implementation	H	M	M	L	M	H	M	L

Source: Assessments by authors.

to the east versus west location of the eight towns. With the exception of the Czech Republic, in all countries the more western town exhibits a better performance than its eastern counterpart. Even when performance is not very high in a western town, as is the case with Sopron, the negative aspects of local decision-making and policy might be offset by such factors as greater levels of civil society development or civic activism, which are less pronounced in the more eastern towns. The following chapters discuss in greater detail the possible impact of contextual socio-economic, institutional, political and cultural factors in accounting for the above variations.

4
Socioeconomic Contexts

The eight cities have variable structural conditions and regional development disparities. These range from their geographic location, through the proximity of dynamic urban centres, to the availability of transportation links, and the economic infrastructures and industries inherited from the Soviet period. Although on the face of it, the high rate of socio-economic development and variable levels of social welfare needs of some towns in the post-communist period may be explained with reference to the above structural 'givens', a more nuanced examination of variations in development patterns suggests that this would be a facile explanation. Many towns, while having relatively similar structural conditions, in fact display divergent performance levels, while those like Sopron or Ústí nad Labem perform less satisfactorily *in spite of* the generally favourable geographic or other economic factors. The following sections discuss this in greater detail and suggest alternative explanations, which will be explored in the subsequent chapters. We focus in particular on three factors: (1) the socio-economic starting conditions, such as the structure of the local economy; (2) the 'east versus west' geographic location of the respective towns; and (3) the level of development of their transport and communications infrastructures.

Hungary

The variation in the structural 'givens', the socio-economic conditions of the two towns reflects Hungary's significant regional disparities. The most basic distinction that is usually made is the east–west variation in regional developmental trajectories. The fault lines between east and west were present in pre-communist times, but intensified in the communist and post-communist periods. During the communist period, the eastern areas of Hungary, including those in the northern Great Plain, were singled out for grand industrialisation projects. New cities were built entirely from scratch, and centring on the servicing of one particular industry. The so-called modernisation projects actually favoured outdated industries, while discouraging those in such more modern and promising areas as electronics. Much of the industrial output was oriented towards the servicing of the communist states' Council for Mutual Economic Assistance (COMECON) market. The fall of communism therefore served to under-privilege these areas in several important ways. The collapse of the COMECON market resulted in the degeneration of company towns previously considered developed. In addition, their traditional orientation to markets in the east, in countries that became losers of the transformation process, such as Romania and Ukraine, did little to transform these areas into boom-zones. The lack of diversification of local industries complicated the adaptation of these areas to new economic realities.

By contrast, the western areas of Hungary emerged as winners in the transformation process. To begin with, under socialism they were never targeted for grand industrialisation projects, and their economies were more diversified as a result. During the first two decades of socialism, western areas of Hungary were separated from their west European neighbour Austria by the Cold War political boundaries. In the context of the Kádár era political and economic liberalisation, however, a significant relaxation of the border regime occurred. Already in the 1970s, Hungarians enjoyed a relative freedom of travel both within the COMECON member states and, significantly, in non-socialist countries, to a degree unprecedented for other socialist regimes. There was also relative openness with regard to admission of foreign tourists in Hungary. The western areas of Hungary in particular benefited from liberalisation of the travel regime. Western Hungary became a popular destination for tourists from Western Europe, many of whom travelled with the aim of obtaining cheaper goods and services in the frontier areas. Consumer tourism boomed, and so did the border towns offering a wide variety of services to Western customers.

Not surprisingly, these more developed areas also became a magnet for tourism and investment in the post-socialist period. Spontaneous consumer tourism boomed in the 1990s, with the local economies in towns such as Sopron profiting enormously from the influx of Austrian day tourists looking for a cheap haircut or a tooth filling. The reverse process also affected the local economy. Thousands of western Hungarians commute to the neighbouring Austrian region of Burgenland daily where they find employment, legally or illegally. Although the employment committee of the border regional council reports that this fact has served to increase the labour shortage in Hungarian western border regions, it also has significant positive effects on local income structures, and accounts for lower levels of unemployment than the Hungarian average. Large businesses from Austria, Germany and other west European countries also preferred to invest in these areas. Geographic proximity was just one factor affecting their decisions. Western Hungary is an area with a highly educated and skilled workforce and with diverse and more modern local economic structures. The EU PHARE cross-border cooperation (CBC) programme that was initiated in 1995 and the respective funding for fostering cross-border cooperation between the Austrian region of Burgenland and the Győr-Moson-Sopron county provided further impetus for the dynamism of this region (Rechnitzer 2001: 375).

The east–west economic disparities thus only intensified in the course of the 1990s as a result of the above processes of social and economic diffusion. The basic economic development and socio-economic statistics of regional developmental variations speak for themselves. The western counties emerge as the leaders in foreign direct investment per capita; in the rate of industrial growth; and in personal incomes. Hungary's most important industrial zone is now considered to be in this area along the western border with Austria with 19.2 per cent of all investments made outside Budapest coming from the border Vas and Győr-Moson-Sopron counties, and 16 per cent of companies selecting this region as the Hungarian base (Rechnitzer 2001).[1] Eastern Hungary, by contrast, 'boasts' some of the lowest rates of foreign investment and growth, and some of the highest rates of unemployment.

Hungarian economic geographers also note significant spatial disparities in unemployment, which stabilised around 1990 and have remained pronounced despite changes in unemployment rates. In July 1999, for example, the unemployment rate in Budapest, at 4.5 per cent, was half the national average. By contrast, the rate was 16.8 per cent in Northern Hungary and 15.8 per cent in the northern Great Plain (Dövenyi 2001: 216–17).

On the face of it, these structural conditions related to socialist developmental legacies and the favourable geographic location of western areas near to developed European neighbours, and the less favourable one for those further to the east, would seem to account for much of the variation in local government performance in the respective cities. Nevertheless, there is an important caveat that indicates the oversimplistic nature of such assumptions. Even within the broad east–west regional constellations, there are tangible developmental variations.

Economic analyses focusing on specific counties or smaller within-county areas have revealed substantial differences. In the area of employment, for example, scholars have noted that county-level statistics provide a distorted and inaccurate picture of *within*-county employment variations in micro-regions. These variations are a reflection of the efforts of individual towns and areas to adapt to economic transformation and to come up with innovative strategies to boost local economies (Dövenyi 2001).

Another factor that we need to keep in mind as we pursue our analysis is that our aim is to evaluate *local government performance*, rather than explain the broader socioeconomic variations of the respective areas. As Robert Putnam reminds us, in evaluating performance, scholars must be careful about attributing to governments credit or blame for matters beyond their control. He makes a crucial policy analysis distinction between *outputs* and *outcomes*, between specific policies, and such broader factors as demographic or economic characteristics of a given locality (1993: 66). With this distinction in mind, it is only logical for us to ask, for example, to what extent the prosperity of the town of Sopron is an outcome of the performance of its post-communist local government? If Sopron was already a paradise of developed tourism even under the centrally planned, centralised, and state-administered government, can we attribute its impressive tourism and development indicators to the success of its now autonomous local government? Or would it be perhaps more appropriate to examine the town's specific policies and outputs that had a direct impact on the local economy, all things considered?

With these assumptions in mind, we now turn from the discussion of the broader regional or county level variations to an examination of the narrower structural conditions peculiar to the two cities under investigation. Although Szolnok is located in an area that has been less privileged, even during the communist period, and which has been particularly hard hit during economic transformation, it is nonetheless not characterised by disadvantages faced by many other socialist cities. Szolnok was not a typical socialist company town built from scratch and centring on one industry. Even during the Soviet period, its economy was relatively diversified. Szolnok therefore does not fit the description of a town with a high concentration of assets that might have led to elite capture by old managerial forces, clientism and corruption, a scenario we discussed in Chapter 1. The town's industrial facilities ranged from agricultural machinery production, to food processing, rolling stock repair, chemical and pharmaceutical industries and paper production. Also, none of these industries were particularly hard hit in the 1990s on a scale similar to the decline associated with coal mining industries or textiles in all the post-communist states.

As a town with several higher educational establishments and boasting a reputation of being a 'student town' it has a significant advantage considering that the educational level of the workforce has affected the employment structure in Hungarian towns. Szolnok has two higher educational establishments, the Air Force Institution of the Miklós Zrinyi National Defence University and the College of Szolnok. The latter offers courses in commerce and economy, and the former offers mechanical and electrical engineering, among other subjects. The significant disadvantage mentioned by respondents in the business community is the unfavourable transport infrastructure. Szolnok is connected to a motorway traversing Hungary from east to west and going through Budapest. Unfortunately, there is no modern high-speed highway linking the town to Budapest and other important centres, and businessmen complain of the low quality of the motorway. The town, however, is the meeting point of four major railway lines linking east and west and north and south Hungary. In addition, from the communist period Szolnok has inherited a 200-hectare grass airfield suitable for small planes.

Still, by any estimate, Sopron would rank significantly higher in terms of inherited structural advantages. Not only was the town's economy diversified even during the Soviet period, but it also boasted such modern and sophisticated industries as electronics. Sopron was also a developed centre of education and is home to a forestry school of international renown, the University of Forestry and Wood Sciences.[2] In addition, Sopron is advantageously located on the western border with Austria, but it also has a developed road and railway communications network. The Sopron rail company, in the pre-communist period a joint Hungarian-Austrian enterprise, re-established this status in the 1990s. The railway is an important connection linking Budapest and east Hungary with Western Europe. Finally, with its developed tourism and service industries going back to communist times, it approximates more closely a dispersed asset economy than one with a high degree of asset concentration, factors likewise considered by some scholars important for better performance outcomes (Walder 2003).

The foregoing analysis indicates that economic, structural and other contextual variations would be an inadequate explanation of performance differences in the towns. Although on the face of it, the east–west location, the proximity of one town to the Austrian border, and the relatively remote and peripheral location of the other one would seem to provide an explanation of performance outputs, a look at the city-specific socioeconomic features reveals a more complex picture. Both towns appear to have starting conditions more favourable than those of many of Hungary's other towns. Sopron enjoys unquestionable predominance in this respect, while Szolnok's starting conditions could be assessed as being medium. Moreover, the nature of the local economic concentration and asset diversity are likewise quite favourable in Sopron and Szolnok. Such an angle fails to explain the performance variations of the two Hungarian towns discussed in the previous two chapters.

Russia

Russia, the only federation among our cases, has particularly pronounced regional disparities. Philip Hanson suggests that the level of disparities among Russian regions greatly exceeds that of the EU level-2 regions, that is, those with similar average population sizes. For example, in these regions (excluding the overseas territories of some of the EU member states), the ratio of the per capita GDP of the richest region, Hamburg, to the poorest one, Epirius in Greece, was estimated to be 4.4:1. By way of comparison, in the Russian republic of Ingushetiya, per capita production was one fifth of Russia's average in 1998, while in the oil-rich Tyumen' region it was 3.8 times the country's average, a variation substantially larger than in the EU level-2 regions.[3]

At the same time, it is less appropriate to talk about east–west developmental disparities here than in the case of Hungary. Economic geographers suggest that many of the more dynamic regions are in the border areas, both east and west, with those in the west profiting from proximity to Scandinavian countries, and those in the east, to Japan and other advanced Asian states. At the same time, the European parts of Russia have many backward regions, while many areas east of the Urals and central Russia also have islands of dynamism.

The Novgorod *oblast*, where Staraya Russa is located, is one of the most dynamic regions, a factor attributed to its favourable geographical location. The region is located in the northwest of European Russia and borders on Vologda, Leningrad, Pskov and Tver *oblasti*, and is 302 miles from Moscow. Novgorod is linked to the Moscow–St Petersburg rail line and is part of a transportation hub connecting Moscow, St Petersburg and the Baltic countries.[4] The town Staraya Russa is located approximately 500 kilometres northwest of Moscow and 300 kilometres south of St Petersburg. The town lies adjacent to the south coast of Lake Il'men, and the intersection of the three rivers Snezh, Polist' and Porus'e. In the spring, as the ice on the lake melts and the water level rises, the river waterways open up to the Caspian, Black and Baltic seas. This convenient location accounts for the historical record of one of Russia's oldest towns as a link on the route *ot varyag v greki*, or from the north to the Mediterranean sea which played a crucial role in the ancient Russian principalities' trade with Europe. Although the significance of the ancient trade routes has long declined, the natural geography even at the present time would allow for river-based cargo transportation to Finland, Sweden, Poland, Norway and the Baltic states.

The Saratov *oblast*'s more remote location would appear to be a considerable disadvantage, but many of the regions on the Volga have also been developing dynamically in the last decade. Saratov *oblast* is located in the northern Volga area. The Volga River traverses it from north to south. The *oblast* borders on Kazakhstan, Volgograd, Voronezh, Orenburg, Penza, Samara and Tambov *oblasti*. The city of Balashov is located in the western part of the *oblast*, 226 kilometres from Saratov city, at the intersection of several important rail and automobile connections, and the river Khopyor, a tributary of the Don River.

There are also important structural features inherited from the Soviet period that we have to keep in mind in discussing the variable developmental trajectories of the areas. Saratov has traditionally been an agrarian region, a factor which would appear to under-privilege it considering the dire situation of Russian agriculture. In the 1990s the region ranked ninth in Russia in total agricultural production.[5] Novgorod has a more mixed economy, but agriculture has also been traditionally more developed here at the expense of industry (Table 4.1). The fact that both regions now rate relatively high on many indicators of economic development irrespective of the structural disadvantages has been attributed to the policies of the respective regional governments headed by the 'young

Table 4.1   Regional economies, 2002

Region	Population	Employment structure, %	Industrial production as % of RF production	Foreign investment (millions of roubles)
Saratov	2,669,000	Industry: 19.8 Agriculture: 19.4	1.3	2001.2
Novgorod	695,000	Industry: 27 Agriculture: 9.8	0.3	1382.6

Source: *Regiony Rossii: osnovnye kharakteristkii sub'ektov federatsii, 2003* (Moscow: Goskomstat, 2003).

reformer' Mihail Prusak in Novgorod and, at the time of our research, the charismatic Dmitry Ayatskov in Saratov. While in Hungary an evaluation of local performance is complicated by the inherent east–west developmental differences, in Russia it is complicated by the fact that the regional level may be seen to play a decisive role in affecting local development. Even a brief look at our specific towns, however, merits a more complex explanation. It would be inappropriate, for example, to regard Staraya Russa as a passive beneficiary of developmental and social policies pursued at the regional level. Instead, even within the region it has been singled out for its innovative policies in the social and economic sphere. By contrast, the town of Balashov does not reflect the dynamism of the region as a whole, its agriculture and industry lagging behind the innovative policies pursued at a regional level.

In the two towns, the inherited structures of the local economies appear to provide both developmental advantages and disadvantages. In 1989, that is, on the eve of the dissolution of the USSR, Staraya Russa was regarded as Novgorod region's key agricultural base, accounting for 13 per cent of the *oblast*'s agricultural production and boasting the largest number of horned cattle among the region's other administrative areas. It was also one of the largest producers of linen. Over the last decade, however, agricultural production has steadily declined and the town gave up its leading position to other areas of the Novgorod *oblast*. Balashov has traditionally been an agrarian town, by the mid-nineteenth century becoming one of the key grain trading centres in Saratov *guberniya*. Most of the town's larger industrial enterprises inherited from the Soviet period have also been oriented towards servicing agriculture, such as the Pritsep agricultural machinery plant, or food processing enterprises such as the Kombikorm plant or the Yantar' sunflower oil producing plant.

Both towns have a dependence on one large enterprise, the textile plant in Balashov and the aviation plant in Staraya Russa, respectively. The Balashov textile plant was founded in 1968 and became one of the USSR's leading producers of textiles, such as materials for tents, rucksacks and waterproof coats. By the time of the collapse of the Soviet system, the plant employed 7500 workers, while the larger social infrastructure built around it included 30,000 people compactly residing in one micro-district. The transition period brought the plant to a state of near collapse and led to lay-offs of hundreds of workers, while those who continued to work would at times get their wages in the form of cloth produced at the factory.[6] In 1997, when the failing enterprise was finally taken over by a new director and a new management team, it had only

1200 workers. Balashov's dependence on the textile plant may be seen to be a particular disadvantage considering that the textile industry was hard hit by the transformation process in all post-communist contexts, as was light industry in general. But even in Staraya Russa an independent economic consultancy audit warned of significant risks associated with the over-dependence on the aviation plant. Although Staraya Russa could not be considered a 'mono town' in the sense that it has a 'city-forming' enterprise similar to the textile plant in Balashov, during the Soviet period this one enterprise accounted for a disproportionately large share of the city's employment and budget revenues, and this remains the case.

Czech Republic

The previous chapters have demonstrated that the more advantageous economic starting conditions of Ústí did not result in spectacular developmental achievements, with the comparatively disadvantaged Karviná outperforming the other town. Likewise, the inherited structural features and social welfare needs resulting from transition do not provide an adequate explanation of performance in the area of social services. Karviná's difficult socioeconomic situation did not encourage innovative or effective solutions to social problems, in contrast to Ústí, which became a national pioneer in local social service provision.

In the early 1990s, the two Czech towns faced similar social and economic problems. For more than a century they had been dominated by heavy industry. Since the eighteenth century, the name Karviná has been associated with coal mining and the steel industry. The communist regime reinforced this image with the region of Ostrava and Karviná becoming the 'iron backbone of Czechoslovakia'. Ústí followed a similar trajectory, in the nineteenth century becoming an important site of coal mining and the chemical industry. During the two world wars, the largest chemical plant located in Ústí held a dominant position on European markets. After the fall of communism, it became obvious that the inherited structural features of the two towns would represent a burden rather than an asset. Both Karviná and Ústí had been heavily affected by environmental devastation and noxious air pollution. In Karviná coal mining transformed the town's surroundings into a moonscape. As mining activities moved ever closer to residential areas, families had to move out in order to avoid being buried by their collapsing houses. The situation was even worse in Ústí where air pollution reached devastating proportions and was manifested in annual winter smog alarms and deforestation of large parts of the Czech–German mountain range.

Another consequence of the predominance of heavy industry in both towns is the human capital problem. In the communist period, the towns attracted large numbers of unskilled workers willing to stand up to the hardships of coal mining and chemical industry production. Accordingly, at the beginning of the post-communist economic transformation, the two towns found themselves with a workforce characterised by low levels of education and lacking modern qualifications. At the same time, under socialism, the predominance of the working class in the local population led to the development of living standards well above the national average. In order to attract workers willing to risk their health or even lives in the coalmines and chemical plants, factories lured their employees not only with high wages, but also with additional props such as modern residential opportunities and exclusive health care. From the outset of the economic transformation process, the privileged position enjoyed by a high proportion of the local population therefore represented a psychological hindrance to quick economic restructuring. Rather than adapting themselves to the market, the workers, particularly miners, resented the new system that demoted them from their position of spearheads of society to those of bottlenecks to the economy.

Finally, the predominance of heavy industry led to high proportions of non-Czech ethnic groups exceeding the Czech national average. While the main reason why many Polish and Slovak workers had come to Karviná was high salaries paid by the mining factories, in Ústí an additional factor encouraged the influx of thousands of Roma families. After the expulsion of the German population from the Czech-German border region in 1945 and 1946, the former Sudetenland became a deserted area, with many abandoned houses and settlements. It did not take too long before the borderlands were populated by people from the inner regions of Czechoslovakia, many of whom were unskilled workers looking for jobs and economic prosperity. Since this natural migration did not suffice to replace the former German population and to revitalise the economically important region, the socialist government encouraged people from all over the country to move to Northern Bohemia.

To summarise, in the early 1990s Ústí and Karviná were in a similar situation, with both towns having to grapple with environmental issues and a workforce largely consisting of unskilled, but well-paid workers, many of whom were non-Czechs. These similarities notwithstanding, one should not overlook a crucial difference between the two towns that, until the mid-1990s, entailed important consequences for their over-all socioeconomic situation, namely the diversity of the local economy. Until the mid-1990s, the local mining company, the Ostravsko-Karvinske

Doly (OKD), controlled Karviná. The OKD not only provided jobs to a large proportion of the local population, but it often had a decisive voice in local affairs. Since the town was heavily dependent on the OKD both politically and economically, any changes in the coal mining and steel sector of the Czech economy would have a direct impact on the local situation. After the fall of communism, the Czechoslovak government sought to restructure coal mining. In December 1992, it adopted a comprehensive restructuring programme providing for reorganisation and privatisation of the mining sector, which also included the closing down or contraction of several mines operated by the OKD.[7] These measures had an immediate impact in Karviná, where unemployment skyrocketed. In 1996, at a rate of 7.75 per cent,[8] unemployment in the Karviná district was twice as high as the Czech national average. Even compared to the rest of the Moravskoslezsky region, Karviná exceeded the average rate by roughly 50 per cent.

In Ústí, although coal mining traditionally played an important role, the local economy did not depend on it to the same extent as Karviná, with several chemical, oil or energy producing companies generating additional jobs in the 1990s. While the government's decision to reduce coal mining negatively affected the local labour market, it did not completely destroy it. By the end of 1996, the local unemployment rate reached 4.5 per cent.[9] While this rate exceeded the national average, it was well below the figures registered in Karviná, and was also lower than that in the broader Ústí region (7.05 per cent). The presence of assets, such as oil, would suggest that we should expect negative performance outcomes in Ústí because of the implications for elite capture and corruption by the old managerial elite. But the proximity-to-the-West factor, which encourages Western investment and therefore also greater transparency in local economic decision-making, would suggest other-wise. As our discussion of the politics of performance in Chapter 6 shows, there has also in fact been more, rather than less, political turnover in Ústí. Geographic location and transport infrastructure like-wise do not fully account for performance variations discussed in the previous two chapters. The Ústí region is located on the border with Germany and at the intersection of several transport arteries. Besides the river Labe, the region is crossed by the high-speed train connection link-ing Hamburg, Berlin, and Dresden to Prague, Vienna and Budapest. The Prague international airport is reachable within 90 minutes, while a new highway connection between Prague and Berlin was also due to open in 2005. The developed transport infrastructure led to the region becoming one of the most attractive areas for foreign direct investment in the

Czech Republic. According to one investor, 'We chose [a town in Northern Bohemia] for its well prepared industrial zone as well as for its excellent location with good access to both our current and future customers in Germany and Central and Eastern Europe.'[10]

The situation is different in the Moravian-Silesian *kraj*. Bordering on Poland and Slovakia, the region is more suitable for companies oriented towards the eastern rather than western European markets. Train trips to Germany take six to seven hours and require changes in either Prague or the Polish city of Katowice. A comparably dense network of roads covers the region, but plans to build a national highway to Prague have repeatedly been delayed due to financial problems. The regional capital Ostrava has a small cargo airport, but as is the case with railway connections, all passenger flights involve stopovers in Prague. Unsurprisingly, Northern Moravia has received little foreign direct investment in the last decade. Although, according to the general director of Czechinvest, 'the interest of investors in the Moravia-Silesia region has recently increased substantially',[11] the region lags behind other parts of the Czech Republic, especially the Ústí and the Central Bohemian *kraj*.[12]

In addition to infrastructural advantages, Northern Bohemia derived other benefits from its geographic location. Throughout the 1990s, one of the most important EU instruments of financial support for candidate countries was the PHARE-CBC programme. Between 1995 and 1999, 50 per cent of all funds allocated to the Czech Republic, totalling 170 million euros, came from this programme. This money, however, was made available only to projects that included at least one EU member state. Only in 1999 was the CBC programme extended to regions sharing borders with other EU candidate states, such as Moravia-Silesia. However, in 2000–2, the Czech Republic received only 57 million euros for PHARE CBC-projects.[13]

Thus, Karviná was confronted with socioeconomic problems on a scale far larger than anywhere else in the Czech Republic. The economic inheritance of coal mining represented an extremely heavy burden in terms of environmental devastation, and the coal mining company OKD did not make matters better. By 1996, the local economy was in deep crisis with high rates of unemployment of a structural rather than a temporary character. The town's remote geographic location served to reinforce concerns as to further local development, since neither the transport infrastructure nor the large distance from western borders fuelled hopes of becoming a major destination for foreign direct investment or EU money.

By contrast, Ústí had every reason to consider itself to be in a favourable situation. From both national and regional perspectives, economic indicators gave no reason for major concerns. Especially compared to other towns of the same region, Ústí stood out for its relatively diversified economy that appeared to be resilient to shocks caused by economic transformation. The well-developed transport infrastructure and convenient geographic location, with the German border only a stone's throw away, must have added to the conviction that, in terms of economic and social development, Ústí was on the safe side. The puzzle of Ústí's weak economic performance levels is summarised in the pessimistic observation of the director of a local NGO: 'At the beginning of the 1990s, Ústí ranked second after Prague, as far as tax revenues were concerned. Today, these revenues are quite low. This means that, a few years ago, we were comparably well-off and now we decline, while other towns might have witnessed the opposite trend in development.'[14]

Compounding this puzzle is the record of massive central funding for both the regions in which the two towns are located. Considering that both the Ústí and the Moravskoslezsky *kraj* suffer from similar economic and social problems, for several years the two regions were at the centre of the Czech government's targeted programmes. The national Strategy of Regional Development, adopted in July 2000, identified both regions as 'heavily marked by the negative consequences of industrial restructuring after 1990, of the phasing out of mining activities and significant environmental damages'.[15] Following a resolution passed by the Czech government in April 2000, the Czech Ministry for Local Development sought to stimulate development in the two regions[16] by implementing special programmes of financial support, for which only north-western and north-eastern regions were eligible. Potential recipients were local governments, large companies or SMEs, depending on the respective programme. Table 4.2 demonstrates that there were no significant differences as to the volume of support allocated to Ústí and Northern Moravia.

Generally, in contrast to other countries of Central and Eastern Europe, the Czech Republic is characterised by relative homogeneity, with only Prague standing out for its significantly higher degree of economic prosperity. The Bohemian lands underwent industrialisation comparably early, so that between the two world wars Czechoslovakia was one of the leading industrial powers worldwide. Considering the large economic disparities between the Czech and Slovak parts of the country, from the interwar period onwards the central government sought to reduce economic disparities. When the communists seized power in 1948, active support for the more backward regions had been already practiced for two decades. The one exception to the rule of the

Table 4.2   Czech local economies

	Severozápad (Ústecký kraj)	Ùstí nad Labem (town)	Ostravsko (Moravskoslezský kraj)	Karviná (town)
Regional development support programme 1999–2003	16,292,156 euros	337,034 euros	15,588,567 euros	594,100 euros
Economic support programme 1999–2003	18,573,500 euros	0 euros	27,579,800 euros	595,833 euros
Support programmes for SMEs[17] 1998–2001	(Ústecký kraj) 9,673,334 euros	(Ústí district) 896,667 euros	(Moravskoslezský kraj) 17,716,667 euros	(district) 3,880,000 euros
Programme for development of industrial parks (1998–mid 2002)	Ústecký kraj 6,297,700 euros	Ústí town 0 euros	Moravskoslezský kraj 6,913,700 euros	Karviná town 1,499,167 euros

Source: *Strategie regionálního rozvoje České republiky*, Prague, July 2000, available from the website of the Czech Ministry of Local Development at www.mmr.cz.

relative developmental homogeneity is the city of Prague. Not only was Prague a leader in terms of economic growth and incomes at the time of communist collapse, but the gap between the capital and other cities has only widened since.

In terms of GDP per capita, in 2002 Prague exceeded the Czech average by almost 120 per cent. On the other hand, apart from Prague, the country is characterised by developmental homogeneity. This is especially true with regard to GDP per capita and salaries. Here, both the lowest and the highest value achieved by individual regions do not deviate from the average by more than 13 per cent. Moreover, between 1996 and 2002, the difference between the remaining regions, including where our two cases are located, has somewhat diminished.[18]

Poland

The extent of Poland's east–west regional disparities, which intensified during the post-communist period, is similar to Hungary. On the face of it, scholars have noted that statistics may suggest that these variations are not as pronounced. For example, the ratio of the GDP per resident of the poorest (Lubielskie) and the wealthiest (Mazowieckie) region approximates 1:2.2, which is lower than in Italy or Spain. These statistics, however, do not reflect the structural variations of the economies of the various regions, which complicate efforts to reduce developmental disparities. The poorest regions, such as Podlaskie, Lubelskie and Podkarpackie, are located in Eastern Poland, while some of the most economically advanced regions, such as Wielkopolskie, Zachodnio-Pomorskie, Dolnośląskie and Lubuskie regions, are located on Poland's western border. Not only have the western regions benefited from proximity to more developed EU neighbours, such as Germany, but historically they have maintained more advanced and modern industries and a better qualified workforce. By contrast, those in the east had greater concentrations of old socialist industries, or, like the region of Śląskie, were largely dependent on the coal and steel industries. Moreover, the economies of some of the eastern peripheral regions are heavily skewed towards agriculture, and have a large share of employment in agriculture and agriculture related sectors (Lobatch).

Because of these regional disparities, Jelenia Góra's geography may appear to be significantly more advantageous than that of Biała Podlaska. In Poland, proximity to the western border is seen to be a key asset not only in terms of attractiveness for investors, but also in obtaining funding from the European Union. By contrast, Biała Podlaska may appear to lack the advantages normally associated with a western location. It is situated in a border region close to Belarus and Ukraine, an area interspersed by woods and steppe. From an inner-Polish perspective, however, the location of Biała Podlaska is not considered to be remote. Biała is located relatively close to the national capital Warsaw and its international airport, and has a dense road network, connecting it to the capital. The Mazowieckie region, where the capital city is located, remains the wealthiest of all Polish regions. This pattern is typical for Central and Eastern Europe, where economic activity has been and remains to a large extent concentrated in and around the capital cities (Lobatch).

Moreover, in recent years due to its location on a direct west–east route linking Berlin to Warsaw and Minsk, Kiev and Moscow in the East, Biała Podlaska has profited substantially from the Polish government's measures to improve the national transport infrastructure. While Jelenia Góra is still waiting for the motorway built by the German Nazi government during the 1930s to be repaired, Biała Podlaska is directly connected to what is known as Poland's best highway, the A2.

There are important similarities in the structures of the local economies and employment. During communism, both towns housed military bases, which Warsaw only closed down in the first half of the 1990s, which led to severe unemployment. A second factor that affected the social and economic situation in both towns in an even more dramatic way was the administrative reform that went into effect in January 1999. Until that time, both Jelenia Góra and Biała Podlaska held the status of *województwo* capitals, which endowed them with a range of administrative and political institutions providing jobs to a significant share of the local populations. Not only did the administrative changes lead to a decline in job opportunities, but more importantly, the loss of status represented a severe threat to further local development, since companies ceased to consider the towns to be attractive.

The key difference in the economies of the two towns is the less diverse nature of Biała's economy compared to that of Jelenia Góra. In the Jelenia Góra sub-region, 22.6 per cent of the population make their living in agriculture, which is a low figure for Poland, while 35.7 per cent work in industry and more than 40 per cent are in the service sector.[19] By contrast, in Biała, at the onset of the transformation process in 1990, aside from a local, state-owned company producing radar equipment for the Soviet market, most of the industries were related to wood processing and cloth manufacturing. The difference in the structure of the local economies lends credibility to the argument that it might reflect on local performance. Before we draw our conclusions about the explanatory power of economic concentration factors, however, we weigh them against other possible influences on local performance discussed in the following chapters.

Conclusion

The foregoing discussion indicates that, despite regional and geographic disparities providing variable developmental contexts for our eight towns, they enjoy a number of comparable structural advantages and disadvantages. The advantages are relatively developed transport links facilitating external trade and the attracting of investors and relatively diverse local economies despite a dependence on large Soviet industrial giants, the restructuring or closing down of which was bound to hurt the local employment force and economy. The disadvantages are the over-reliance of local economies on one industry or industrial facility in some towns, or the legacy of environmental degradation in others. These broad similarities suggest that socioeconomic and structural contexts alone would fail to account for variations in social policy and economic promotion, with the less structurally advantaged towns in some cases outperforming those with greater advantages. Other explanatory factors, namely institutional, political and historical-cultural, facilitating or constraining local choices and strategies and possibly impacting on economic and social performance, are discussed in the following chapters.

5
Intergovernmental Setting and Local Performance

In Chapters 2 and 3 we have demonstrated that there are considerable local government performance variations in Central and Eastern Europe. Not only are there significant differences between countries, but also between towns located in the same state. Moreover, even within one municipality there may be discrepancies between the quality of economic promotion and social services.

An established body of scholarship identifies the intergovernmental institutional setting and relations between various levels of government as crucial explanatory variables. According to this line of thought, local government performance is determined to a large extent by the broader legal, institutional and fiscal environments in which they operate. First, it is argued that local governments perform better or worse depending on the resources allocated to them, as well as the constraints imposed upon their activities by the legal frameworks they are embedded in. This is because local competences, rights, duties and financial resources are regulated by the constitution and other legal norms. Second, apart from delimiting the boundaries of local governments' rights and responsibilities, institutions shape the incentive structures of the relevant local actors, and 'define the rules of the game'. Finally, the long-term implication of institutions is that as actors accept the rules constraining their choices and internalise them, the rules become *institutionalised*. *Institutionalisation* usually implies a de-personalisation of social practices or organisation. Goals are achieved or norms observed independently of the persons that happen to fill the social positions on which the realisation of goals or maintenance of practices depends (Baldersheim and Illner 1996: 2). In other words, institutions can make an important contribution to modernising, professionalising and strengthening local governments by replacing the 'capable ruler' with the more reliable 'well-organised office'. Accordingly, the degree to which institutional rules and laws are complied with and internalised by relevant actors may serve as another explanation of performance variations.

It is therefore not surprising that since the fall of communism, institution building has been the focus of much of the scholarship on local government in Central and Eastern Europe. Changing the intergovernmental setting of states that had been for decades dominated by a centralist political ideology rather than local independence, unification rather than diversity, and state paternalism rather than pluralist competition has proved to be a significant political challenge (Illner 1997). From the outset of the 'threefold transformation' (Musil 1992) that was to lead Central and Eastern Europe from communism to democracy and capitalism, the reform of political and administrative structures ranked high on the political agenda. At the same time, it soon became evident that the reforms would be subject to the tug and pull of very different ideas, political interests and practical considerations (Baldersheim, Illner and Wollmann 2003). While proponents of civil society development pleaded for quick and radical decentralisation, those favouring fast and efficient economic reforms hesitated to deprive the central state of its control over the localities. Parties, which politically depended on the support of specific regional strongholds, took a perspective on administrative reform different from that of political groups enjoying popularity throughout the country. Finally, the EU as precondition of membership mandated that Central European states adopt an intergovernmental framework that would enable their participation in EU regional policy. As a result of the above political and other variations, Poland, Hungary, the Czech Republic and Russia had widely diverging reform trajectories and have accordingly ended up with very different intergovernmental arrangements.

Sub-national institutional structures

After several years of debate (Regulski 2000; Kulesza 2001), in 1999 Poland set up a three-tier system of self-government. The former 49 regions (*województwos*) were abolished and combined into 16 new *województwos*, which were now to perform both state administration and self-government tasks. The administrative *województwo* authority is now headed by the *Wojewoda*, a civil servant appointed by the central government, while the *Marszałek*, an official elected by the regional parliament, the *Sejmik*, represents regional self-government. The two-tier local level consists of 2483 municipalities (*gminy*) and 373 districts (*powiaty*)

(Kowalczyk 2000: 246). Depending on the respective settlement structure in a given area, there are administrative distinctions between urban (*powiat miejski*) and rural districts (*powiat ziemski*), while the Polish municipalities are divided into the rural (*gmina wiejska*), rural-urban (*gmina miejsko-wiejska*), and urban municipalities (*gmina miejska*). Both the *gminy* and the *powiaty* perform local self-government tasks proper, as well as those of state administration or delegated tasks. However, between municipalities or the various kinds of *powiaty* there is no further differentiation of competences, finances or other aspects of government. Both our Polish case study towns are *powiaty grodzkie*. As a rule, the territory of this kind of *powiaty* is restricted to towns or cities which tended to be *województwo* capitals before 1999 and were awarded the *powiat* title as a compensation for their loss of status. Although there are limitations with regard to their population numbers, territory and financial resources, these *powiaty grodzkie* are to perform the same tasks as the other types of *powiaty*.

Similar arrangements exist in Hungary. Local government consists of only one tier, and all the 3153 municipalities belong to it, while the regional level consists of 19 counties (Pigey and Kálmán 1999: 10). As in Poland, both levels have to perform state delegated tasks, as well as local ones, and there is no differentiation between types of municipalities or counties as far as their duties or finances are concerned. Hungary is also similar to Poland in that it has towns with a special status, the so-called 'cities of county rank.' In contrast to Poland, however, these towns are not mandated to perform all the tasks that counties perform. But as we shall see later, they differ from the settlements with regard to range of competences as well as their financial resources. Both Sopron and Szolnok have the status of cities of county rank. Although both municipalities and counties have to perform state administrative functions, in 1994 Hungary also set up a network of additional authorities of state administration, one in each county, charged with coordination and legal review functions. The heads of these Public Administration Offices (PAOs) are appointed by the central government (Temesi 2000: 352).

Somewhat differently from Poland and Hungary, Czech legislation divides the 6251 municipalities into three different groups of settlements, depending on the range of mandated state delegated tasks, although there are no differences in local tasks. This division is a consequence of the following developments. After 1990, as in other post-communist countries, a process of hyper-decentralisation began resulting in a sharp increase in the number of extremely small settlements. Considering that at present almost 80 per cent of all Czech municipalities have less than 1000 inhabitants (Illner 2003a: p. 69), this classification is meant to relieve the smallest settlements from the responsibilities they are unable to shoulder. In January 2003 the Czech government abolished the lowest level of territorial state administration and transferred several additional state functions to the larger municipalities, now called 'small districts' (Illner 2003b: 82). Both of our Czech towns belong to this third group of municipalities with extended competences. In 2000,[1] a regional tier was established, comprising fourteen regions (*kraje*). The regions, like the municipalities, possess dual local and state delegated functions.

Russia has the most complicated system of local self-government, although a new law adopted in 2004 is aimed at introducing greater clarity and transparency into municipal and intergovernmental systems (Lankina 2005). In contrast to the other three states, here federal legislation on local government has been very vague. Until recently, most legal provisions regarding such basic issues as the number of local tiers or the assignment of tasks and revenues between different levels of government have been largely regulated by the 89 federal subjects, and not the central government. Hellmut Wollmann and Natalia Butusova (2003: 228) distinguish between three areas in Russia depending on the regions' choice of models of local administration. In most regions, local self-government has been almost completely hollowed out with larger towns and counties *(rayony)* turned into mere administrative units and only small settlements entitled to perform self-government tasks proper. In a second, rather small, group of federal subjects, local self-government is restricted to the counties *(rayony)* and larger towns, while smaller settlements do not possess self-governing competences. Finally, most of the western regions have a two-tier model comprising the *rayony* as well as towns and smaller settlements. Similar to Poland and Hungary, in Russia many larger towns have the combined status of a town and *rayon*. This is the case with both Staraya Russa and Balashov. How do we begin to assess the impact of intergovernmental set-up on local government performance in the four states? In the vast body of scholarship on local government, we may roughly distinguish between three groups of approaches to performance (Baldersheim and Illner 1996: 2). The first body of studies focuses on the degree to which the local populations are provided with opportunities to influence and participate in local policy-making (*democracy*). The second examines the ability of local authorities to solve problems and deliver important services (*efficiency*). The third focuses on the degree of local *autonomy*, that is, local discretion over important decisions and finances. An integrative approach to performance suggests that the three groups of variables are interconnected and each set of factors has the potential to reinforce or, alternatively, weaken the other two. A high degree of local government autonomy might entail a gain or a loss in efficiency. A locality aiming at maximum efficiency may prefer not to involve citizens in local decision-making, which affects its responsiveness and accountability, and ultimately performance. On the other hand, a locality unable to produce results efficiently may have trouble in the longer term in maintaining citizen involvement in local politics.

It is worth noting that in the early 1990s, in its assessment of the process of sub-national institution building in post-communist Europe much of the literature was somewhat biased in favour of local autonomy. The communist experience made many authors share an unspoken assumption that any reform of the intergovernmental system should aim at the highest degree of decentralisation. Few scholars doubted that decentralisation would foster democratisation because it encourages political participation, allows for the formation of new elites, and introduces further checks on the central government. It was also assumed to support local and regional development and to relieve the central level from tasks that can be better performed by the localities themselves (Illner 2003: 9). However, as the reforms progressed and the first outcomes of decentralisation could be observed, it became obvious that local autonomy had to be balanced by state control in order to meet the requirements of efficiency (Horváth 2000; Wollmann and Lankina 2003).

The growing body of research on local institutions in post-communist Europe suggests that municipalities there possess roughly similar competences. Local governments are responsible for local economic development, maintenance of public roads, public transport, nurseries, administering institutions of preschool and primary education, basic health care, social housing, waste disposal and local supply of water, electricity, and gas (Horváth 2000; Munteanu and Popa 2001). In the area of economic promotion, local governments in Poland, Hungary, Russia and the Czech Republic are endowed with similar competences. In particular, they are required[2] to stir local economic development; to set up and implement land utilisation plans; to outline and pass local budgets; to take care of all aspects of technical infrastructure; and to maintain local roads and communications.

But, as far as the distribution of social policy tasks among different levels of government is concerned, Poland, Hungary, Russia and the Czech Republic differ in four main respects. First, the range of tasks assigned to local governments varies greatly between the four countries. A second difference is that in Poland, the obligation to provide social services lies entirely with municipalities, while in the other three countries it is shared by different levels of government. Third, in Hungary and Russia social tasks are distributed between local governments and the regions, while, until recently, in the Czech Republic social service provision was shared between the localities and the state. Finally, the three systems with shared responsibilities differ in that the Czech Republic and Russia have more flexibility in task assignment among different levels of government, while in Hungary and Poland legal norms are fixed.

With respect to our precise area of investigation, local governments in all the four countries are expected to play a key role in identifying families in crisis, but they differ in terms of the institutions responsible for providing problem families with concrete help. While in Hungary and Poland, local governments are mandated to set up facilities offering advice and temporary shelter, Russian, and until recently, Czech local governments, are free to decide as to whether they want to maintain such costly services. If they decide against setting up the relevant facilities, the respective task is performed either by the regional level, as is the case in Russia, or by the state administration, as in the Czech Republic.[3]

A similar situation exists in the area of child protection. Again, in all four countries, the main tasks of local government consist of identifying children in need of help, protecting them from abuse of alcohol or drugs, prevention of child delinquency, and provision of temporary shelter. But only Polish local governments are obliged to set up and maintain expensive facilities of permanent residence for children. Moreover, in Poland local governments are also responsible for seeking foster families and paying out social payments to young adults who have been brought up in parental care facilities. In the three other countries, local governments play a significantly smaller role in providing childcare services. The Hungarian and Czech systems strictly differentiate between 'basic' services, such as day care centres or temporary shelters guaranteed by local governments, and 'professional' ones or permanent foster care, which is the responsibility of either another level of self-government (Hungary) or the state (Czech Republic until January 2003). Finally, Russian law allows for flexible handling of responsibilities, with local governments free to decide on whether to take over foster facilities or not. Should they decide against it, the region where the locality may be found takes over the performance of the relevant services.[4] To summarise, in the area of social services, Poland has the highest degree of local government autonomy, with the *powiaty* in particular bearing the lion's share of social service provision. In sharp contrast to Poland, the Czech Republic has so far emphasised the principle of efficiency rather than local autonomy. Only recently has the Czech Republic made further steps towards decentralising its social policy. Hungary and Russia may be placed somewhere in between in this respect. In Hungary, it is the larger towns that have to cope with legal obligations similar to those of their Polish counterparts. In Russia, the division of tasks between regional and local levels varies significantly depending on the legislation of the respective regions. In the area of childcare, for example, Staraya Russa performs a remarkably broad range of tasks compared to Balashov. This is because the Saratov oblast has retained authority over childcare services. At the same time, in contrast to Novgorod, the Saratov legislation explicitly provides for women's aid centres. The above differences raise the question of the extent to which the variations in task assignment are responsible for different outcomes at the local level.

Our field research suggests that the answer to this question is clearly negative, a case in point being the variable performance of the two Polish towns. Jelenia Góra complied with all the legal requirements by setting up the relevant social service institutions. The town of Biała Podlaska lags far behind its Polish counterpart in terms of the performance of mandated local tasks. These performance variations suggest that a maximum of local autonomy does not necessarily lead to the availability of social services at a local level. A similar argument may be applied to the quality of social services. Despite the reasonably good quality of childcare services in Jelenia Góra, childcare facilities staff complained in interviews about the recent transfer of competences from the regional to the local *powiat* level.

Hungary, the Czech Republic and Russia illustrate further the issues that exist in the current systems of task assignment between different levels of government. When municipalities are unable or unwilling to perform certain tasks, the regional level hesitates to take them over. Russia is a case in point. At first glance, both Staraya Russa and Balashov appear to be poor performers, as neither of the two operates victims of domestic violence facilities. But there are important differences. In Staraya Russa, there are four institutions – an advisory centre for families, two modern foster homes, and a system of foster parental care – that were set up and operated by the local government, with the region only contributing some funding for special purposes. In contrast, Balashov demonstrates that, should the municipality fail to come up with the finances necessary to maintain the social facilities, the region is unwilling to equip local governments with a dense net of social services. In a personal interview, the Head of the Social Department of the Balashov administration summarised his dissatisfaction with the way the system works. He maintained that the best solution would be for all social facilities to be operated by the federal government.[5]

Similar problems are observed in Hungary. A wider range of services is available here, but neither of our Hungarian towns perform all the legally assigned tasks. Both Sopron and Szolnok lack a facility or a system of foster parents providing children with temporary shelter. The regional level is not only unwilling to fill the gap by setting up the required institutions, but it also fails to sufficiently perform its own mandatory tasks, thus causing further problems for local social policy. In sharp contrast to the above three states, these problems are not an issue in the Czech Republic. In Chapter 2 we demonstrated how our two Czech towns stand out in terms of the variety of local social facilities and services. In the Czech Republic, the state has played an important role in the setting up and maintenance of social facilities. The foster homes in Ústí and Karviná have been for many years operated by the School Office, a decentralised authority of the Ministry of Education. In Ústí, both the Advisory Centre for Interpersonal Relations as well as the House for Mothers with Children were originally set up by the state administration, and then taken over by the local government in the mid-1990s. The Karviná Advisory Centre was operated by the *okres*-authorities before being transferred to the region in January 2003. Although there appears to be a tendency for local governments to take over state responsibilities, a fact which is particularly true for Ústí, many facilities may not have been ultimately set up had it not been for the *okres*-authorities. These authorities set up many important institutions that until recently local governments were not willing to finance themselves. Contrary to the view that the state tends to hamper local government initiative, in the Czech Republic cooperation with state administration was characterised as being 'absolutely problem-free'.[6] The representative of the Silesian deaconry in Karviná maintains, for example: 'The district office has always worked very well and we cooperated very closely and started many common activities.'[7]

The degree of flexibility in task assignment likewise has an impact on performance. The Hungarian town of Szolnok, for example, is mandated to set up a facility of temporary shelter for children, but it has failed to do so for lack of funding. Moreover, since this task is assigned to the local level, the county refuses to assist the town government. A counter-example is the Russian town of Balashov, where the general availability of social services is insufficient, but where the region takes over the responsibilities that the local government is unable to shoulder. Finally, the Polish town of Biała Podlaska demonstrates that even in a system with a fixed distribution of tasks, under conditions of financial shortage, practical requirements outweigh legal considerations. Since Biała Podlaska lacks the funding required to operate the relevant facilities, citizens are allowed to make use of services financed by the region, that is, a level of government that is not required to finance temporary shelters.

To conclude, the availability and the quality of social services at the local level depend on the task assignments among different levels of government. But a high level of local autonomy does not necessarily positively affect social services. The striking performance divergence of our two Polish towns indicates that a simple transfer of the entire burden of social service provision to the local level does not guarantee the availability of social services. In addition, as the Russian and Hungarian cases demonstrate, cooperation between local and regional levels tends to be hampered by the financial problems faced by both levels of government. In Hungary, the rigid and inflexible character of task assignment makes matters even worse with counties not feeling obliged to fill the gaps in local social service provision. In Russia, the more flexible regulations allow the regions to take over responsibilities local governments are unable to fulfil. Balashov illustrates how on the one hand this flexibility saves the local population from being left without any institutions of social care, while on the other, the regional government has few incentives to modernise social service provision.

Although the central state is also not immune from financial shortages restricting its capacity to maintain social facilities, the Czech case shows that the national government – for political or other reasons – is not in a position to ignore its legal obligations in the way some local governments do. In both the Czech towns, not only did we find a complete set of social facilities, but also that citizens have a choice between different providers of the same service. It appears that state involvement works as an insurance of sorts against the financial or political instability from which local governments continue to suffer. This positive assessment of state involvement with local matters runs counter to the widely held assumption that state interference in local matters may negatively affect local governance. The following sections discuss state–local relations and their implications for local performance in greater detail.

Legal review

An important yardstick for assessing the degree of local autonomy and efficiency is the nature of the legal review of local governments. In Poland, legal supervision is the responsibility of the *Wojewoda*, a state appointee and head of state administration at the regional level. The original Law on Municipal Self-Government distinguished between different types of legal review,[8] but recent changes have significantly simplified the review frameworks.[9] The *Wojewoda's* functions are now limited to verifying the compatibility of local government decrees and local activities with national laws. Municipalities have to submit all their decisions within seven days of their passage. In case the *Wojewoda* considers that a decree violates national law, he or she has the right to suspend the decree. The local government can file an objection against the *Wojewoda's* decision to the administrative court, and the court is to decide within 30 days whether the decree can come into force or has to be abolished. Should a local council repeatedly infringe upon the constitution or the law, the Prime Minister can request the *Sejm* to disband it. This in turn leads to the suspension of all political bodies in the respective municipality. In case a repeated violation of the constitution or the law is not caused by the council, but by the executive arm of local government, the *Wojewoda* can call upon the Prime Minister to dissolve the local government without any consequences for the council.

In recent years, Poland has also strengthened the position of local governments vis-à-vis the state. But it has preserved an important feature that at least theoretically renders local governments more vulnerable than their Hungarian or Czech counterparts. In case of a conflict between the state and local government, the final decision does not lie with the constitutional, but with the administrative court. This may lead the state administration to intervene in local politics more often than necessary. But the Polish provision according to which the state can 'fire' a local government without dissolving the local council testifies to the legislators' aspiration to protect local democracy not only from state encroachment but also from incapable local politicians.

The Hungarian system of legal supervision is similar to that of Poland.[10] Here too a state appointee heading the county-based Public Administration Office (PAO) controls municipalities. This official examines the legal compatibility of local governments' activities with national legislation. In contrast to Poland, however, a supervising body's objection does not automatically lead to suspension of the local decision. Instead, the PAO must first initiate legal proceedings at the Constitutional Court, which, at the same time, can be requested to suspend the implementation of the local decision. The government can request the national parliament to disband a local council based on allegations of acting contrary to the Constitution only after it has consulted the Constitutional Court.

Until recently, the Czech Republic had a system of legal review similar to that of its two Central European counterparts, with legal supervision conducted by the 77 district offices (*Okresní úřady*), the lowest level of state administration. But following the abolition of the district offices in January 2003, the task of monitoring local government activities was transferred to the new regional offices with delegated tasks and to the Ministry of the Interior.[11] Thus, in contrast to Poland and Hungary, Czech municipalities are controlled both by the state and by a higher self-governing body. It is important to note here that Czech law continues to distinguish between 'competences proper' and 'delegated tasks', a distinction recently abolished in Poland. Moreover, the Czech legislation differentiates between local decrees and other local decisions. The regional office (*krajský úřád*) scrutinises all municipal activities in the realm of local competences. The regions may also oblige a local government to perform tasks assigned to it by law. Should the regional office question the legality of any local decree or decision, it can request the Ministry to suspend it. If the Ministry agrees to suspend a local decree, it is obliged to obtain the relevant decision from the Constitutional Court. If the Ministry suspends another type of local decision or measure, the local government can submit an explanatory statement to the Ministry. If this explanation is rejected, a normal court decides on the validity of the decision in question.

With respect to delegated tasks, the system is similar, although there are some exceptions. First, all activities of local governments are checked with regard to their compliance not only with national law, but also with legal rules of lower rank, such as government decrees. Second, in case the regional office considers that a local decision or act (but not a decree) is in violation of the law the regional office does not need to contact the Ministry, but may suspend the decision itself. In contrast to Poland, the Czech law limits the possibilities for the state to initiate the dissolution of any body of local government. For example, the law does not mention that a local government may be dissolved if it repeatedly infringes the law. The Ministry of Interior can disband a local council only in case the council lacks a quorum for a period of more than six months or if the council disregards the results of a local referendum.

Until recently, the potential for conflicts between state authorities and local governments was the highest in the Czech lands due to the geographical proximity of the supervising bodies. As of January 2003, however, legal supervision is conducted not by the state administration, but by the regional offices, which reduces the risk of state abuse of legal supervision leading to restricted local autonomy.[12] More importantly, in contrast to the other three countries, the Czech legal system does not allow for the dissolution of local councils if they violate national laws.

While in the above three Central European states legal control over local government activities is subject to detailed regulations, until the recent legal changes passed at the end of 2003, Russia stood out for the striking vagueness of the relevant norms (Kourliandskaia, Nikolayenko and Golovanova 2001: 214). To begin with, the 1995 Law on Local Self-Government lacked precision with regard to institutions that are to inspect local governments and the manner in which such inspection is to take place. According to Article 51, the federal procuracy, a peculiar Russian institution belonging to the executive rather than the judicial branch of the federal government, and its regional offices, are responsible for controlling local government compliance with federal legislation. But the law does not provide a clear-cut answer to the question of which procedure is to be followed in case the procuracy considers that a local government decision violates federal law. Although the 1995 law mentions that such a conflict is to be resolved by 'a court', it is unclear which court should be responsible. What makes the matter even more confusing is that, according to Article 49 of the law, the regional government is also entitled to appeal to 'a court' to scrutinise the legality of a local government decision. If the court finds that a local government has infringed the law, the regional government has the right to dissolve the local council, and remove the local mayor.

The new Law on the Common Principles of Organisation of Local Governments in the Russian Federation, adopted in 2003, likewise endows regional executives with significant power of initiative when it comes to scrutinising local government decision-making, which makes Russia stand out compared to the other three states. Although most of the relevant provisions do contain clauses to the effect that regional authorities may only penalise or disband a local body pursuant to a court decision, it is unclear from the law what type of court should make the decision, and what agency would bring the matter to the attention of the court to begin with. Since the law only has vague references to the 'appropriate courts', it is likely that the governor himself could bring the matter to the court (Lankina 2005).

How do these legal variations affect local government performance? In Poland, Hungary and the Czech Republic, conflicts between the supervising state authorities and local governments are actually an exception rather than the rule. In a personal interview in March 2002, the Deputy Head of the Department for Local Government in the Hungarian Ministry of the Interior estimated that, in 2001, the proportion of local government decisions that caused PAOs' objections did not exceed 1 per cent. In only eight cases did the Constitutional Court have to deal with cases related to the legality of local government decisions. Even in the Czech Republic, where until the recent changes, state control of local government was very tight, legal supervision did not lead to conflicts. Zdeněk Koudelka, a member of the Czech House of Representatives and a leading expert on local self-government, characterised relations between local institutions and state authorities as more or less problem free. In his interview with the authors, he admitted that from time to time, conflicts do occur, the most frequent reason being local regulations that entail specific obligations for residents.[13] Furthermore, the district offices and municipal authorities have repeatedly clashed over the question of whether a certain task falls within the field of 'tasks proper' or 'delegated tasks'.[14] At the same time, Koudelka pointed out that many municipalities benefited from cooperation with the district offices: 'For smaller municipalities in particular the position of state institutions always constitutes important methodological advice as to how to approach a certain problem'. The most controversial issue has been in fact not state supervision, but the government proposal to assign the legal supervision of municipalities to the regional offices.[15]

While in Central Europe legal control over local governments is not an outstanding issue, in Russia the situation is somewhat different. Conflicts between local governments and the regional Prosecutor's Office occur more frequently than is the case in Poland, Hungary and the Czech Republic, the most widespread reason being local finances. The vague definition of tasks of the regional and local levels frequently leads to conflicts over funding for services. At the same time, in order to improve their financial situation, local governments do not hesitate to resort to measures that violate the relevant norms, such as the introduction of local taxes not provided for by federal law.[16] To make matters worse, in Russia the judiciary is not an effective instrument for protecting local governments against state or regional interference. As one study found, 'courts are also equally ready to pronounce judgements against local governments. For instance, the Tver City Duma [council] has had to revoke its decision to cancel entitlements to free public transport for employees of certain federal agencies, a decision originally made due to inadequate funding' (Kourliandskaia, Nikolayenko and Golovanova 2001: 214).

Finally, even the rulings of the Russian Constitutional Court are not always complied with.

The experiences of our eight cases are in line with the above general characteristics of the respective countries. In our Polish, Hungarian and Czech towns, conflicts with state authorities occur rarely. The same applies to our Russian cities. Out of our eight towns, only three experienced conflicts with state authorities. In Poland, in 2000, succumbing to pressure from local traders,[17] the Biała Podlaska council passed a decree prohibiting the establishment of supermarkets on the town's territory. This decision was cancelled by the *Wojewoda* shortly thereafter because it violated Polish law. The local government did not appeal the decision in court. In Szolnok, the local council passed a decree stipulating that farm animals were to be restricted to specific areas of town. After objections by the PAO failed to have an effect, the issue was taken to the Constitutional Court, which then ruled in favour of the local council. Libór Kovács, the then deputy mayor of Szolnok, expressed great trust and satisfaction with Hungary's system of legal review. 'We are not afraid of the control of the county or the state administration … if we don't accept their advice they might take it to the court and that decision is legally binding', he said.[18]

The most interesting case is the Czech town of Ústí nad Labem. Here, in 1999, a town district local council decided to resolve persistent conflicts between residents of Czech and Roma ethnicity by separating the two groups from each other and constructing a high fence made of wooden planks. This decision prompted international criticism, and even threatened to cast doubt on the Czech Republic's 'EU maturity' and Czech respect for human rights. For the purpose of this discussion, it is interesting to note that originally, the district office responsible for legally supervising the town did not see any reason to protest against the fence. However, following international concern and pressure from the EU, the central government ordered the district office to remove the fence.[19] The conflict did not correspond to the local government versus state administration cleavage, since the head of the local district office sided with the local government. Rather, it demonstrated the incompatibility of the Czech government's international interests with a local problem, the perception of which was shared by both the local government and the local branches of state administration. In the end, the local council did not comply with the decision of the district office. The issue was then taken to the Czech national parliament, which voted against the maintenance of the fence. Although, before the vote, the local government had announced that, in case the parliament cast a negative vote, it would appeal to the Constitutional Court,[20] it finally refrained from doing so. Several years later, personal interviews reveal a continued feeling of injustice shared by the members of the local elite and expressed in a view that 'the state should not have interfered in local affairs'.[21]

Although, as we have seen, conflicts between state and local authorities may even acquire international dimensions, in the majority of towns we visited they concerned minor issues. In some cases, controversies were of a financial nature,[22] while very often they occurred because the state administration is the first instance for citizen appeal against local administration, for example, with regard to building permits or social benefits.[23] In general, however, none of our respondents blamed state authorities for hampering local government efforts to improve social services and promote economic development. Our questionnaires administered to the staff of the eight towns' social and economic departments confirm these findings. Table 5.1 shows the differences in the systems of legal review in that the administrative personnel in the two Czech towns is more likely to consider state authorities a hindrance to its work. This may be interpreted as a consequence of the geographical 'proximity' of the district offices. In general, however, the Czech respondents rejected the statement that 'the state interferes too much'.

Table 5.1 Local opinions regarding state intervention (Marks indicate towns' position in terms of degree of approval)

Social Department*	U	K	SP	SZ	JG	BP	SR	B
State authorities interfere too much	4.00	4.93	5.30	4.20	4.91	5.33	5.87	5.11
(average: 5.10)	= 1	= 4	= 6	= 2	= 3	= 7	= 8	= 5
Economic Department								
State authorities interfere too much	4.00	4.20	4.50	5.57	5.30	5.30	4.50	6.00
(Average: 4.92)	= 1	= 2	= 3	= 7	= 5	= 5	= 3	= 8

Note: * Respondents could choose among six degrees of approval, with '1' corresponding to 'I fully agree' and '6' meaning 'I do not agree at all'.

Source: questionnaires administered by authors.

Local finance

A common feature of the four states is that, although local government reform dates back to the early 1990s, the structure of intergovernmental finance remains a subject of considerable debate (Table 5.2). In all our countries, the relevant legislation has undergone several radical changes, but fiscal problems continue to plague local governments. Three main issues are at the centre of debates about the system of local government financing. First, the problem of municipal finances is central to the question of political and administrative decentralisation. If local governments are denied the funding necessary to make real use of their political autonomy, decentralisation is doomed to failure. Much of the relevant literature examines the ratio of 'own' resources, such as taxes, on the one hand, and subsidies or grants, on the other, in local budgets. Although many scholars call for far-reaching fiscal decentralisation, our evidence does not suggest that such arrangements unambiguously lead to political autonomy or improved performance. A second question addressed in much of the literature on fiscal decentralisation is how to provide local governments with sufficient incentives for economic promotion while also guaranteeing a certain degree of economic equality through financial compensation to disadvantaged or undeveloped municipalities. As we shall see, our four countries have found very different solutions to this problem. Finally, a serious issue plaguing all fiscal systems in Central and Eastern Europe is the rising public indebtedness, which also affects local governments. Against this background, national laws related to local finance are expected to prevent local governments from excessively inflating their debts.

Table 5.2 Types of revenues in local budgets (%)

1999	Poland	Hungary	Czech Rep.	Russia
Share, tax revenues*	24.5	33	48	71.1
Share, non-tax-revenues*	24.2	17	36[24]	3.6
Share, targeted grants and subsidies	51.3	50	16	24.3

Note: * Numbers include revenues from own, local taxes and the local share in state-levied taxes.
** Numbers include fees for local services such as waste removal, street cleaning and supply of water and electricity.

Source: *Fiscal Design across Levels of Governments*, OECD, 2000. Available from www.oecd.org; Kourliandskaia et al., 'Local Government in the Russian Federation.'

The four countries are significantly different with respect to the composition of local budgets. While in the Czech Republic and Russia various kinds of tax revenues account for the largest share of local revenues, in Poland and Hungary, financial transfers between different levels of government play an important role in local finance. This is not surprising: as we have shown, task assignment is reflected in local revenue structures. The bigger the role played by local governments in the provision of education and social services, the larger the share of state subsidies and grants in local revenues.

Grants and subsidies

In Poland and Hungary, state grants and subsidies pursue two aims. Both types of payments are intended to support municipalities in performing certain tasks, but also to offset the differences in local budget revenues in order to prevent weaker municipalities from becoming marginalised. While in the Czech Republic, this compensation mechanism is integrated into the system of tax revenue distribution, in Poland and partly in Hungary financial equalisation is achieved through subsidies, and not taxes. The Polish *gminy* receive three types of subsidies. First, the state provides local governments with the so-called basic subsidies, which must amount to at least 1 per cent of the state budget. In general, these funds are distributed among municipalities according to the number of inhabitants. But local governments with less than 85 per cent of the national average of per capita local tax revenues are compensated from these basic subsidies. Second, all tiers of self-government, *gminy*, *powiaty* and *województwos*, receive the so-called education subsidies, which amount to 12.8 per cent of national tax revenues. These revenues are distributed according to the number of school pupils. A third type of subsidy compensates for revenue failures caused by the national government. Finally, all local governments whose revenues from local taxes exceed 150 per cent of the national average are to transfer extra payments to the state, which then redistributes them among all municipalities. The structure of subsidies for the upper tier of local government, the *powiaty*, resembles that of *gminy*. Apart from financial support for education and road maintenance, *powiaty* also receive funds equalising the economic differences between them. Although state subsidies are meant to cover the costs of performance of the numerous assigned tasks, in practice the funding is never sufficient.[25]

In addition to subsidies, grants also play an important role in Polish local government financing. While the state supports *gminy* in their performance of both delegated tasks and certain local tasks proper, such as housing, since 2001, grants, particularly investment grants, have been allocated through the so-called *województwo* contracts introduced in May 2000 by the Law on the Promotion of Regional Development. While these contracts assign state funds to each of the sixteen *województwos*, every contract also includes all local investment projects the respective region plans to support financially in the coming years. In practice, local governments receive financial support for projects identified as 'regionally important' and that have been included in the *województwo*'s regional development strategy.

While the Polish government views *województwo* contracts as regional development instruments,[26] from the perspective of local governments, they entail a significant politicisation of state funding. Municipalities' financial well-being is therefore not only influenced by the regional government's ability to negotiate with the central government, but the fate of the local budget may also heavily depend on the local leaders' bargaining skills and their personal or political contacts with the regional government. This case, as well as examples from Hungary and Russia, illustrates that individual skills of local functionaries, such as those related to 'bringing home the bacon', are an important influence on local outcomes despite the broader institutional rules and constraints within which they operate. The same holds true with regard to EU funding. In order to obtain funds from either the PHARE programme or one of the pre-accession instruments, municipalities have to bargain for, and secure the support of the *województwo*, which proposes concrete PHARE projects to the central government. Funding from the financially more lucrative Instrument for Structural Policy for Pre-accession (ISPA) programme is available only for projects that have been included in the national ISPA Strategy.[27]

The Hungarian system of intergovernmental grants and subsidies is even more complicated. As one study pointed out, '[there] was an attempt to simplify and reduce the number of normatives in 1995–96. However, subsequent modifications further complicated the grant system and the calculation has become less transparent' (Kourliandskaia, Nikolayenko and Golovanova 2001: 41). As in Poland, Hungarian municipalities are eligible for general subsidies, distributed according to the number of residents, the number of beneficiaries of specific public services, the number of beds available in shelters for homeless people, and grants based on the tourist tax. The allocation of these subsidies is decided upon annually, and the criteria for assigning funds are not fully transparent. Moreover, as in Poland, the local government suffers from an increasing range of unfunded mandates, that is, tasks transferred to them by the central government without adequate financing (Pigey and Kálmán 1999).

As the proportion of general subsidies in local budgets has decreased, the role of earmarked transfers has increased in recent years. These transfers are directly allocated to both the relevant institutions, such as health care service providers, and to municipalities. The central government also makes available to municipalities grants for which they have to apply. First, there are the so-called 'deficit grants' designed to compensate local governments for revenue failures beyond their control. Second, municipalities can apply for financial support for large investment projects. In April 2000, the Hungarian government published the Szechenyi Plan, a medium-term state programme 'to mobilise private business, Hungarian and foreign investment as well as the development resources of local administrations'.[28] The plan contains seven programmes whereby both private companies and municipalities are given the opportunity to obtain financial support for development projects in the areas of SME development, investment, tourism, information technology, housing, transport and communications. In general, the Hungarian system of intergovernmental finance is characterised by strong equalising mechanisms, though considerable political discretion is involved, as will be discussed in Chapter 6. Other redistributive mechanisms are the system of normative grants and specific equalisation funds at the county level (Kourliandskaia, Nikolayenko and Golovanova 2001: 42).

While Poland and Hungary have a relatively high share of state transfers in local government budgets, in the Czech Republic and Russia municipal revenues to a significantly lesser degree depend on subsidies and grants. But a closer look at local budgets also reveals enormous differences between the Czech Republic and the Russian Federation. In contrast to the Central European states, Russian municipalities do not have a direct link to central government finances. Instead, external contributions to local budgets almost exclusively come from the regional level in the form of shared taxes or subsidies. Most Russian regions maintain equalisation funds for supporting poor municipalities. However, both the formation and the functioning of these funds differ significantly from region to region. According to one study, '[some] are funded through a share of all taxes collected by the regional budgets, others are linked to a few specific taxes, and in some regions federal transfers are also pooled into such a fund.' The same holds true with regard to the distribution of funding among local governments. While some regions apply standardised formulae for transfers to concrete municipalities, in the majority of regions financial support is a matter of political contacts and bargaining skills. At the same time, the lack of precise rules regulating the distribution of money leaves local governments more or less at the respective regions' mercy (Freinkman, Treisman and Titov 1999: 55).

In sharp contrast to Russia, but also to Poland and Hungary, the Czech system of intergovernmental finance does not provide for any equalisation payments in the form of subsidies. While Polish *gminy* regularly receive general 'survival' or support funding, the Czech *obce* are eligible for state funding only for concrete projects or expenditures. As scholars point out, however, this does not necessarily mean that Czech municipalities are disadvantaged compared to their Polish or Hungarian counterparts. An important difference between the Czech and, for example, the Polish system is that, in the Czech Republic, 'local governments are responsible neither for social benefits (they are in the hands of the central government) nor most health care (it is in the hands of the health insurance system)' (Nam, Parsche, and Reichl 2001: 31). Although they do not receive regular subsidies, Czech municipalities are fully reimbursed by the state for the social benefits that they pay out to their citizens. As we shall see, this might prove to be a larger contribution to local budgets than the subsidies that municipalities in other countries receive. The Czech government also regularly tenders specific state programmes of financial support through investment grants, for which not only municipalities but also individual NGOs are eligible. The money is allocated based on a review of applications and an assessment of the respective projects by commissions generally perceived to be neutral.[29] Procedures for obtaining EU funding resemble those in Poland and Hungary, with the exception of the intermediation role of regional institutions.[30]

To summarise, in Hungary and Poland, a large proportion of local government social expenditure is funded through regular financial transfers from other levels of government. In some cases, these subsidies are directly paid out to social facilities, while in others the money goes through local budgets. According to the Organisation for Economic Cooperation and Development (OECD) estimates, in 1999 state payments amounted to over 94 per cent of Hungarian local health care expenditure and nearly 53 per cent of social policy. In Poland, alcohol license fees that local governments are entitled to issue supplement the resources available for social policy. As far as grants for larger investment projects are concerned, both Polish and Hungarian municipalities depend on good relations with regional authorities, since the regions play an important role in the allocation of state and EU grants. In contrast to

Poland and Hungary, in the Czech Republic and Russia local governments receive far less regular financial support from higher levels of government. But while Russian municipalities are highly dependent on the financial support and political will of the regions, in the Czech Republic both municipalities and social facilities can apply for funding in politically neutral tenders advertised by central ministries.

Tax revenues

There is a common view among scholars of intergovernmental finance in Central and Eastern Europe that 'own' revenues are preferable to financial transfers from state or regional budgets. The following sections therefore examine the local revenue structures in some detail. The four countries display striking variations as to the numbers and types of local taxes. Compared to the three Central European states Russia is marked by a lower number of local taxes, although this is a recent phenomenon. Before 1998, Russian municipalities were entitled to levy up to 23 local taxes. Subsequent amendments to the national tax code shifted jurisdiction over taxes to the regions, leaving local governments with little decision-making power over the levying of local taxes (Kourliandskaia, Nikolayenko and Golovanova 2001: 203; Nam, Parsche and Reichl 2001: 38).[31] In addition to the above taxes, municipalities in all four countries are allowed to keep revenues from local fees paid for different local services, such as administration or licensing. Poland is a particularly interesting case for the purposes of our study. In Poland, the sale of alcohol is strictly licensed, with all three tiers of self-government participating in the licence fees levied from shop owners. Although funds raised in this way may not be used for purposes other than the curbing of alcoholism, the importance of these revenues for social projects should not be underestimated.

In assessing the impact of the variable systems of local taxation on economic performance we differentiate between Hungary and the three other countries. In Poland, Russia and the Czech Republic, local taxation cannot be considered an effective instrument of economic policy, since the localities' influence over local taxes is limited. Not only does the central government in these states determine the kinds of local taxes municipalities have to levy, but also the upper, and in some cases, the lower, limits of local tax rates, thereby restricting municipalities' jurisdiction to the decision on tax reductions or tax breaks (Kourliandskaia, Nikolayenko and Golovanova 2001: 203).[32] The Hungarian municipalities, by contrast, possess a remarkable degree of discretion over local taxes. They have an option of levying five different types of taxes and determining their rates within a centrally prescribed ceiling (Pigey and Kálmán 1999: 22). Similar to their counterparts in the other three countries, Hungarian municipalities may also decide on tax exemptions or breaks. Hungary's localities therefore possess effective means to stimulate local economic development.[33]

With the exception of Hungary, local taxes therefore make up a rather modest share of local budgets. In most cases, the lion's share of revenues from local taxes comes from one or two main taxes, such as the real estate tax in Poland and the Czech Republic or the local business tax in Hungary, while most local taxes are insignificant in the overall structure of local revenues. More important than local taxes are local government shares in state-levied national taxes.

As with local taxes, there are significant cross-country variations in the distribution of national taxes. In Poland and the Czech Republic, local government share in national taxes is fixed in special legislation. By contrast, in Hungary and Russia municipalities are provided with shared taxes based on annually adopted budget laws.[34] Accordingly, while in Poland and the Czech Republic, the proportion of money transferred to local budgets remains stable over time, Hungarian and Russian local budgets are subject to politically or fiscally motivated annual fluctuations. The distribution of income taxes of both physical and legal persons has been at the centre of academic and political debate because these types of taxes are highly relevant for local economic activity and development. Poland has the most liberal and pro-active approach. As early as 1996, Poland amended the relevant legislation to provide *gminy* with strong incentives for local economic development. Instead of distributing the revenues from personal income tax (PIT) and corporate income tax evenly among local governments, the money, subject to a certain coefficient, is returned to the local government where it was collected (Świaniewicz 2001).[35] As far as taxes are concerned, there are no equalising mechanisms of redistribution. In Hungary and the Czech Republic, fiscal reforms followed the opposite trajectory. In both countries, in the course of the 1990s the respective governments changed several times the rules for distribution of tax revenues, with a clear tendency towards equalisation rather than liberalisation.

Between 1990 and 1994, Hungarian municipalities were allowed to retain a certain share of local PIT revenues. In subsequent years, however, local governments' share in PIT revenues was reduced to the point of all but eliminating this type of transfer (Nam, Parsche and Reichl 2001: 41). Moreover, since 1995 local governments have been obliged to pay a certain share of their PIT revenues to the county.

The county in turn distributes these funds in a way that supports economically weaker municipalities.[36] In 1998, the steadily increasing 'solidarity surcharge' amounted to 20 per cent of local PIT revenues, constituting half of the local share in national PIT revenues. Moreover, since 1999 the distribution of PIT revenues has also covered local government potential revenue from local business tax.[37]

The Czech system is even more complicated. Apart from frequent changes in the intergovernmental institutional setting, the Czechoslovak experience of a federation splitting up for economic reasons discouraged the Czech government from creating a simpler fiscal system. As Jiří Blažek notes,

> If the provision of state subsidies is a politically sensitive question almost everywhere, then in our country this is all the more true, because here, until very recently, the question of 'who is paying the bill for whom' was of significant relevance. Providing local governments with subsidies is a very visible thing to do and political parties and movements working towards a greater autonomy for Moravia as a consequence of it being economically disadvantaged could easily abuse any mistake made by the government in this context. (1995, p. 190)

Between 1993 and 2001, the Czech fiscal system combined liberal and equalising principles (Blažek 1995; Marková 2000: 89–92). Since 1994, local governments have been allowed to retain all taxes paid by municipal companies; moreover, every municipality has received the full amount of taxes on income from independent work that it collected from its residents; from 1996, the town where the respective tax-payers lived retained 10 per cent of PIT on dependent work. But the lion's share of revenues from this PIT was always distributed among local governments according to some equalising mechanism, normally based on the number of residents, either within or between the then districts. Although, since 1996 local governments have participated in national revenues from taxes on legal persons, the distribution of these funds has also been based on the number of residents, thus punishing those towns that collect more taxes than the average municipality. The new tax system adopted in 2000 did not incorporate the demands for linking local revenues to local economic activities. Although it significantly expanded the list of taxes shared among the three tiers of government, it endowed local governments with little influence over the amount of money they receive from these shared taxes. Since municipalities receive a portion of local governments' total share exclusively according to their number of residents, there is hardly any incentive for them to engage in active economic promotion.

The same applies to Russia, where there are few incentives for local economic development (Freinkman, Treisman and Titov 1999: 18). The 1991 federal legislation regulating the allocation of shared taxes was never implemented, and the distribution of tax revenues between the federal and regional levels has been annually decided upon in the state budget. It is the regional governments which allocate tax revenues to the localities. The 1995 federal Law on the Financial Foundations of Local Government in the Russian Federation stipulated that regions could choose among several types of taxes in deciding which ones they would share with local governments.[38] Moreover, since 1997, for each type of tax, federal legislation has prescribed a minimum share that regions are obliged to assign to local governments on their territory. This legally determined share applies to all local governments, but the decision on how to distribute the money among municipalities within the region lies completely with regional governments. Despite legal provisions requiring that tax revenues should be assigned according to standardised mechanisms (Kourliandskaia, Nikolayenko and Golovanova 2001: 205), in practice, regional governments have been free to allocate tax revenues more or less arbitrarily (Freinkman, Treisman and Titov 1999: 53).

Accordingly, not only do Russian municipalities lack a stable and reliable basis for financial planning, but the lion's share of their revenues is also subject to lengthy political bargaining processes with regional governments. Moreover, the system tends to discourage economic development because there is no connection between the local tax yield and local share in tax revenues. Economically successful local governments are punished because in return they receive less money from the regional level. In a World Bank Study, Lev Freinkman and his collaborators note that the interconnection between local budgets and regional funds liberates local governments from any budgetary constraints. Since municipal authorities can rely on the financial support of regional equalisation funds, there is no need for them to improve their efficiency. The consequence is widespread expenditure misallocation. Finally, since municipalities have an incentive to conceal their revenues rather than to foster transparency, the existing system of local finance does little to promote democracy and rule of law in Russia. The new 2003 legislation on local government, as well as amendments to tax and budget codes passed in 2004, are meant to do away with these inadequacies of local finance. But because the reforms are still at an implementation stage, it is difficult to assess their impact on local government (Lankina 2005).

Local debt

Since the beginning of the transformation process in the early 1990s, local governments in Central and Eastern Europe have had to cope with a multitude of responsibilities, especially in the fields of social welfare and education. At the same time, a key aim of many towns and villages was to modernise the local technical infrastructure. It became obvious early on, however, that neither tax revenues nor state subsidies would be sufficient to cover the costs related to repairing roads, building water sewage systems and replacing gas pipes. Therefore, in all the countries, other sources of finance have grown in importance. Over the last decade, loans, municipal bonds and other types of securities have increasingly contributed to local budgets. A comparison of the legal frameworks regulating local governments' fundraising activities reveals significant differences. This does not so much apply to municipalities' general right to raise loans or to issue bonds for both investment and current budgeting purposes, but to the legal restrictions and legal control of municipal borrowing.

Poland was the first state to establish rules for municipal debt management, and to place strict limits on local borrowing. As early as in 1993, the Law on Municipal Finances stipulated that local government debt servicing must not exceed 15 per cent of the budget revenues of the same year.[39] In the 1998 Law on Public Finances, the parliament legally restricted local government total indebtedness to a limit of 60 per cent of the annual local budget.[40] Following the Polish example, in 1996, the Hungarian parliament placed legal restrictions on local borrowing, although somewhat more generously than in Poland, the Hungarian legislation has allowed for annual local debt servicing up to a ceiling of 70 per cent of current revenues. In 1997, the Municipal Debt Adjustment Act imposed 'strict financial and moral costs on local governments who default on debt or other payments' (Nam, Parsche and Reichl 2001: 45). In Russia, the 1997 Law on the Financial Foundations of Local Government limited the localities' right to issue obligations to a 15 per cent share of local expenditures in a given year. Moreover, the law also stipulated that proceeds from municipal bonds are to be used for investment purposes only. In order to deprive local governments of access to loans with soft constraints, the law also banned municipal ownership of banks (Freinkman, Treisman and Titov 1999: 43). In 1998, the Budget Code further tightened conditions for local government borrowing with local budget deficits not allowed to exceed 3 per cent of revenues in a given year (Martinez-Vazquez and Boex 2001: 75).

In contrast to Poland, Hungary and Russia, the Czech Republic to date lacks comprehensive legal regulations preventing local governments from plunging into debt. In 2001, the Czech parliament for the first time amended the existing Law on Local Government to restrict local borrowing. According to the relevant provisions, local governments are not allowed to issue guarantees for loans that physical or legal persons raise, with the exception of municipally owned communal businesses. Moreover, the law envisaged that the Czech government is to approve loans raised from foreign creditors. Finally, it stipulated that 'a municipality must not raise a loan in case that its credit service exceeds 15 per cent of the local budget of the previous year' (Vedral 2002). But following criticism from municipalities,[41] a subsequent amendment invalidated all previously introduced restrictions.[42]

The practical implications of the four states' restrictions are difficult to assess, however. To date, local government borrowing does not appear to pose a threat to macroeconomic stability or more generally to the functioning of municipalities in any of the four countries under scrutiny. Nevertheless, significant differences exist with regard to local debt in proportion to total government debt or local budget revenues. Hungarian municipalities have been particularly restrained in raising loans, while local governments in the Czech Republic have made full use of the opportunities that the rather liberal Czech legislation provides.

While local borrowing has not yet acquired dramatic proportions in Central and Eastern Europe, there are also reasons for concern, particularly in the Czech Republic and Russia. In the Czech Republic, throughout the 1990s municipal debts grew rapidly. In 1994, local government debts amounted to 14.3 billion Czech crowns. By 2000, local obligations almost tripled to 41 billion, with recent projections even reckoning with a further increase to 80 billion crowns in 2006. Although these figures reflect the excessive debts of a few large towns, there is widespread acceptance of the need for legal regulation of local borrowing (Eliáš 2003).

The same holds true for Russia, where legal norms and statistical data provide a distorted picture of the actual functioning of local government. Although budget reports suggest that local governments do not suffer from excessive debt, experts consider the overall system of sub-national budgeting a ticking time bomb for several reasons. First, due to the interconnectedness of local and regional budgets, the problem of budget deficits and debts is shifted from the local to the regional level. Since regional governments have to fill the financial gaps in local budgets, many regions tend to accumulate debts noticeably exceeding their annual net revenues. Second, sub-national budget accounting often consciously omits several types of obligations, thus keeping the debt rate down artificially (Freinkman, Treisman and Titov 1999). Finally, in order to bridge financial shortages, local as well as regional leaders reportedly resort to measures that are not financially transparent or that directly infringe upon the law.[43]

The impact of local government financing on performance

Comparing municipal finances in various settings presents formidable challenges. For example, while in Poland housing rental subsidies fall under the 'social' rubric of the budget, in Hungary they come under the 'housing' section. While in Czech local budgets, expenditure for debt service is subtracted from revenues, in Poland it is treated as one item among others on the expenditure side. We therefore begin our analysis of local budgets with a note of caution about possible errors with regard to concrete items. We should also stress that figures that we include in the tables may be imprecise. The goal was not so much to provide the reader with accurate information on the various expenditures, but to sketch a reasonably realistic picture of our eight local governments' financial situation and to demonstrate in what way the system of local government financing may impact on local government performance. A straightforward explanation of performance variations would be the different levels of financial endowment of the respective towns. Table 5.3 demonstrates that there are indeed vast disparities in local budget sizes. For example, in 2002, the Russian town of Balashov spent 117 euros per capita, while the two Hungarian towns spent six times as much.

Table 5.3 Local budgets (euros)

	JG 2002	BP 2001	SZ 2002	U 2002	K 2002	SR 2002	B 2002
Total revenues	46,142,397	30,460,117	63,095,208	34,651,832	25,492,135*	7,634,600	11,430,100
Revenues per capita	496	513	779	361	398	132	117
Total expenditure	51,390,037	32,778,125	65,453,446	34,651,832	25,492,134	8,183,733	11,440,100
Expenditure per capita	553 (92,964)	553 (59,325)	808 (81,000)	361 (96,046)	398 (64,000)	141 (58,000)	117 (98,000)
Saldo	–5,247,640	–2,318,008	–2,358,238	0	0	–549,133	–10,000

Note: * Due to the Czech system of budget accounting, this figure does not reflect the real amount of revenues, which were slightly higher, but only the amount of resources after debt service.

Source: Local budgets, own calculation. Data for Sopron not available.

This difference between the total budgets of the two Russian towns on the one hand, and the other six towns, on the other, becomes even more pronounced if we consider the variations in the purchasing power of the four currencies. This calculation suggests that the financial capacity of Balashov was roughly one tenth of the Szolnok budget. The per capita spending PPP of Jelenia Góra, Biała Podlaska, Szolnok, Ústí, Karviná, Staraya Russa and Balashov in euros in 2002 was 650, 650, 882, 451, 498, 111 and 92, respectively.[44]

The size of local budgets may be an important factor in explaining differences in local government performance, especially if we consider the fact that the financial burdens imposed upon local governments in the four countries vary significantly. As discussed above, Polish, Russian and Hungarian municipalities have to perform a broader range of tasks than their Czech counterparts. An unsurprising but important consequence of these differences in task assignment is that in Poland, Hungary and Russia, local governments' average share in total government expenditure is significantly higher, amounting to 27.6, 23.7 and 27.5 per cent (Kourliandskaia, Nikolayenko and Golovanova 2001: 257), respectively, than in the Czech Republic, where it is 18.4 per cent.[45] In Russia, what makes matters worse is that although they account for the same proportion of total government expenditure as the two Polish municipalities, in terms of financial resources Staraya Russa and Balashov lag far behind the spending capacity of their Central European counterparts. At the same time, the Czech towns of Ústí and Karviná are financially better equipped than we expected with regard to their share in total government expenditure. The Czech Ministry of Finance estimates that in 2002, local governments contributed 23 per cent of all government expenditure while receiving 26 per cent of total revenues.[46] Is the large gap between the per capita spending capacity of the two Russian towns and that of the other six local governments really a consequence of the Russian system of local government financing? The answer to this question is not as straightforward as might appear. The fact that in 2002 Balashov spent only 15 per cent of what the Hungarian town of Szolnok had at its disposal cannot be ascribed to the Russian system of local government financing alone. In 2002, the combined expenditures of local governments of the Saratov *oblast* amounted to 54.4 per cent of the total regional expenditure. At the same time, the proportion of local revenues in consolidated regional revenues was 52.5 per cent.[47] The main reason for the enormous differences in local budgets across countries cannot be found in the different systems of financing, but in the broader national socioeconomic contexts.

Up to this point, we have sought to explain cross-national institutional differences. In the previous chapter, we have demonstrated, however, that there are also significant within-country variations in local outcomes. The question then is whether these *intra*-state variations can be explained by the respective systems of local government financing. With regard to per capita revenues, the intra-state variations in local budgets are rather small, which also holds true for Russia, where one might have expected the most significant variance. It is obvious that in all the four countries, the mechanisms of financial equalisation between local governments work very well irrespective of whether equalisation is maintained through state subsidies, as in Poland, Hungary and Russia, or tax revenue distribution, as in the Czech Republic. The fact that the performance of Biała Podlaska significantly lags behind that of Jelenia Góra is not because the former receives less revenue than the latter. The same can be said about the two Russian towns. The variations in social and economic policy performances of Staraya Russa and Balashov can hardly be explained by the fifteen euros difference in their per capita revenues. Therefore, if the system of local government financing has an impact on local government performance, it does not exert this influence through the general financial endowment of municipalities.

Performance as a consequence of local government spending

The assumption related to spending appears to have greater explanatory power. If two towns with budgets of similar size perform very differently, local government performance may be a function of local spending. A counterargument would be to suggest that local government spending is more a product of political preferences and strategies than of institutional arrangements. The decision to spend money on social facilities rather than on road maintenance might reflect the values of the mayor or successful lobbying by social workers. However, there might be other reasons for supporting facilities at the expense of road maintenance. First, the local government might be legally obliged to spend a certain proportion of money on social issues. Accordingly, shortage of funds for road maintenance may be construed as the product of the system of local financing. Second, the legal, financial and institutional system shaping local government activities might not reward investment into local roads or even discourage it.

One possible explanation for performance differences is that some local governments suffer from severe restrictions on their financial autonomy, preventing them from spending money on either social policy or economic development. Generally, local financial autonomy is considered a function of the availability of 'untargeted' finances. On the revenue side of local budgets, this means that the lower the share of targeted grants in local budgets, the higher the degree of local autonomy.

Similarly, on the expenditure side, local autonomy is heavily influenced by two factors that potentially deprive the localities of their power over financial resources. First, local governments might be to varying degrees obliged to devote a share of their finances to specific policy fields, so that de facto they dispose of significantly less money than their counterparts in other countries. Second, extensive debt and related debt service might reduce the amount of freely available finances.

We begin by looking at local revenues. At first glance, our eight towns can be considered typical examples of their respective fiscal systems. While in Poland and Hungary, subsidies and grants make up a large share of local finance Czech and Russian towns receive a significantly smaller part of their revenues through transfers from other levels of government (Table 5.4).

However, these differences in the composition of local revenues do not necessarily mean that financial restrictions hamper the performance of the eight towns. The fact that, for instance, Szolnok owes half of its total revenues to transfer payments from other levels of government may not imply that the town has less money to dispose of autonomously than Ústí. Rather, in identifying systemic restrictions on local spending we have to look at whether state transfers suffice to cover expenditures for obligatory tasks or whether there are many unfunded mandates. Table 5.5 demonstrates that in general, the eight towns are typical representatives of their national systems of expenditure assignment. In Poland, Hungary and Russia, the lion's share of local finances is allocated to education, while in the two Czech towns education consumes a large share of local expenditure.

Since Polish, Hungarian and Russian municipalities are required to allocate a large proportion of expenditure to education, it appears logical that they spend little on social policy or economic development.

Table 5.4   Proportion of state grants and subsidies in local revenues (%)

	JG 2002	BP 2001	SZ 2002	U 2002	K 2002	SR 2002	B 2002
Total*	55.2	72.2	49.9	15.0**	26.4	28.1	38.3
Of these:							
subsidies	36.4	42.3	23.5	0	0	NA	NA
grants	18.7	29.9	26.4	31.2	26.4	NA	NA

Notes: * Figures include all regular subsidies and individual grants provided by national or regional governments.
** Figure does not comprise grants to municipal districts.

Source: Local budgets, own calculation.

Table 5.5   Key items in local budgets (%)

	JG 2002	BP 2001	SZ 2002	U 2002	K 2002	SR 2002	B 2002
Education	36.2	42.4	48.9	9.7	8.9	41.4	39.1
Social policy	7.8	6.7	5.8	12.6	26.2 incl. health	19.5	9.4
Health care	0.9	2.4	–	–	–	8.3	27.5
Housing	3.5	0.7	1.7*	NA	16.9	11.9 incl. communal services	14.7 incl. communal services
Economic development/ transport/ roads/	10.0	7.2	2.3	34.5	9	4.9	0.05
Tourism** Communal services***	10.9	5.1	22.6	3.9	4.2	NA	NA
Public administration	8.4	7.2	5.5	6.5	14.4	5.5	4.6

Notes: * Figure does not include financial support for young families renting their first flat, since, for reasons of comparability, these payments were included in the list of social payments. ** These figures include expenditures on road maintenance, economic development, tourism and the maintenance of major tourist attractions.
*** Figures include investment in technical infrastructure.

Source: Local budgets, own calculation.

By contrast, the large share of local finances that the town of Ústí dedicates to economic development may appear to be a consequence of the rather small proportion of money spent on education. Nevertheless, of importance is not so much what proportion of expenditure goes to funding mandatory tasks such as education, but rather whether Polish, Hungarian and Russian local governments are fully reimbursed by the state or whether the system of financing education is a reason for steadily growing deficits in local budgets.

Table 5.6 indicates that the four systems of education financing have different consequences for our local budgets. While Polish and Czech municipalities spend similar amounts on education, or roughly 8 per cent of total expenditure, in Hungary the state appears to have transferred fiscal responsibility over education to the local level. Almost a quarter of Szolnok's expenditure goes to bridging the gap between education

Table 5.6   Local expenditure on education

	JG 2002	BP 2001	SZ 2002	U 2002	K 2002	SR 2002	B 2002
Share of total expenditure	36.2%	42.4%	49%	9.7%	8.9%	41.4%	39.1%
Of these: covered by grants and ed. facility revenues	77.9%	82.0%	52.1%	10.1%	12%	NA	NA
Deficit to be covered by LG (euros)	4,111,306	2,503,240	15,386,714	3,021,743	1,996,544	NA	NA
Deficit as share of total LG expend.	8.0%	7.6%	23.5%	8.7%	7.8%	NA	NA

Source: Local budgets, own calculation.

subsidies and the de facto incurred costs related to schools, which is a remarkable restriction on local financial autonomy. In addition to unfunded mandates, a related issue is that of local debt. Admittedly, it does not always stem from the insufficiency of state transfers, but that the Hungarian towns have to cope with a larger proportion of debt service in total expenditure compared to our other cases is not coincidental.

While Sopron's financial problems largely stem from its faulty decision to participate in risky financial operations in the 1990s, Szolnok appears to have been driven into indebtedness by the system of local financing. According to the explanatory statement that the local government issued together with the budget in 2002, in recent years one of the main reasons for raising loans was deficits in financing current expenditure for schools and social facilities.[48] While most of our towns resorted to borrowing for financing larger infrastructure investment projects, Szolnok borrowed in order to perform its mandatory social policy tasks. Although the 4.4 per cent of total local expenditure dedicated to debt servicing cannot be considered a major hindrance in the short run, in the long run, insufficient central state funding and rising indebtedness might increasingly hamper local performance.

To summarise, in the Czech and Polish municipalities the differences in the systems of local government financing do not appear to have tangible consequences for local budgets. Although Polish local governments have to bear the burden of expenditure on education, due to the high proportion of state funding, the de facto financial obligations of

Table 5.7 Debt service as a share of local expenditure (%)

JG 2002	BP 2001	SZ 2002	U 2002	K 2002	SR 2002	B 2002
1.16	3.1	4.4	0.9	1.6	0	0

Source: local budgets, own calculation.

Polish towns are comparable to those of their Czech counterparts. At the same time, as the example of Szolnok demonstrates, in the long run, the Hungarian system of local financing undermines local fiscal autonomy. Finally, the lack of sufficient data on revenues and expenditures in the Russian towns complicates the assessment of the influence of the fiscal system on local performance. Neither town suffers from major indebtedness, but the general feature of the Russian fiscal system is replicated in Staraya Russa and Balashov. If a locality runs out of money to finance the mandated tasks, it shifts the problem to either the potential recipients of payments by simply refraining from paying salaries or bills, or to the regional government, which in turn has to cope with rising debt (Table 5.7).

Impact on social and economic performance

Government spending on social policy

The respective systems of local government financing to various degrees restrict the eight localities' spending autonomy. While the localities in Poland, the Czech Republic and Russia appear to enjoy spending freedom to a similar extent, the Hungarian fiscal system disadvantages municipalities. This would suggest that Hungarian towns significantly differ in their spending patterns from other countries. Data in Table 5.8 do not support this assumption as applied to social policy. In 2002, the eight towns devoted different proportions of their budgets to social policy. At the same time, if we calculate spending on a per capita basis, our Hungarian, Polish and Czech towns display striking similarities rather than differences, with the exception of Karviná, where there are extremely high numbers of recipients of social benefit payments. Surprisingly, the expenditures on social policy of the Russian town Staraya Russa were more similar to the weaker Central European towns than to the other Russian town, Balashov.

The financial restrictions imposed on Hungarian local governments do not lead to significant differences in per capita spending on social policy, which appears to stem from the many legal regulations in this area in contrast to economic promotion. But given the broad similarities in social policy spending, what then accounts for performance variations

Table 5.8 Expenditure on social policy*

	JG 2002	BP 2001	SZ 2002	U 2002	K 2002	SR 2002	B 2002
Prop. of total exp.	7.8%	6.7%	5.8%	12.6%	26.2%	19.5%	9.4%
Total	4,008,699	2,197,889	3,777,025	4,385,170	6,678,367	1,600,033	1,078,500
Per capita	43	37	47	46	104	28	11

Note: * Figures include all expenditure on social benefit payments, social facilities and investment in social facilities.

Source: Local budgets, own calculation.

in the eight towns? In Biała Podlaska, for example, abused women have recourse to one shelter facility, while in Ústí they can choose between several facilities offering accommodation, a fact which can hardly be ascribed to the nine-euro difference in local per capita spending. Since the total *amount* of per capita expenditure cannot account for differences in performance, perhaps the *structure* of local social spending has greater explanatory power. The underlying assumption here is that in some countries, local government financial obligations to provide social benefit payments may be a burden discouraging them from establishing the mandated social facilities. Table 5.9 lays out the structure of social policy expenditure in each of our eight towns.

Table 5.9 shows that in most towns, the lion's share of the total social policy expenditure is devoted to social benefit payments directly paid out to citizens. This does not come as a surprise, since in all four countries local governments are obliged to support financially the poor, the handicapped, elderly people and families. In both Russian towns, these direct payments (mandates) consume almost all of the social expenditure. In Poland, Hungary and the Czech Republic, the structure of social policy expenditure is heavily influenced by the overall socioeconomic situation of the respective towns. This is particularly true for Karviná, which has the highest rate of unemployment compared to our other towns, and where benefit payments make up almost 90 per cent of the total expenditure. A similar situation exists in Biała Podlaska, where social benefits consume nearly 70 per cent of all social spending. At the other end of the scale are Ústí and Szolnok, which spend less then 40 per cent of all social payments on benefits.

These differences in the composition of social expenditure, however, fail to account for the variations in the quality of social services provision in the particular areas of investigation, namely in childcare and women policies. Biała Podlaska and Karviná had at their disposal roughly 800,000 euros for social facilities, while Szolnok and Jelenia Góra had

Table 5.9   Composition of social policy expenditure*

	JG 2002	BP 2001	SZ 2002	U 2002	K 2002	SR 2002	B 2002
Social payments	45.2% 1,813,000	67.3% 1,479,080	36% 1,360,383	23.6% 1,033,333	88.0% 5,878,000	80.6% 1,289,933	100% 1,078,500
Current expenditure, facilities	53.0% 2,124,199	32.2% 708,809	63.7% 2,405,808	65% 2,850,236	12% 800,367	19.4% 310,100	0% 1,078,500
Investment, facilities**	1.8% 71,500	0.5% 10,000	0.3% 10,834	7.4% 322,484			

Notes: * Not all local budgets differentiated between current expenditures for social facilities and investment in their maintenance.
** Including all expenditure for maintenance or restoration of social facilities, regardless of whether they were operated by local government or another organisation.

Source: Local budgets, own calculation.

between 2 and 2.5 million. Nevertheless, there were remarkable variations even among towns that had similar amounts of funding at their disposal. While in Karviná two advisory services offer help to families in crisis and two more institutions provide accommodation to women and children, there were no comparable facilities in Biała Podlaska. Whereas Jelenia Góra operates a variety of facilities for children and one small shelter of 'crisis intervention', there is a paucity of similar childcare institutions in Szolnok. Staraya Russa also serves to refute the assumption that the availability of facilities is a mere function of financial obligations. Although in 2002, Staraya Russa had at its disposal less than half the amount of funding available in other towns, the town has a modern foster care facility that other cities lacked.

One explanation may be the grassroots initiative at the level of social groups or individuals that led to the establishment of these institutions. In this and the previous chapters we have already alluded to the importance of local civic organisations, the skills and values of local personnel, which appear to provide the most adequate explanation for performance variations in otherwise similar structural and socioeconomic conditions. In Karviná, for example, both institutions offering accommodation to women and children owe their existence to either NGOs or individuals who lobbied local government and raised additional funding from external sources. Between 2000 and 2003, facilities for families in crisis and children located in Karviná successfully applied for external funding from the Czech Ministry of Social Affairs amounting to 373,663 euros.[49] This contrasts starkly with Biała Podlaska, where a lack of similar facilities despite the mandate to set them up and perform the relevant services appears to stem from the weakness of the local NGO community and the absence of NGOs specifically addressing social policies. A database on Polish NGOs reveals that between 1994 and 2001, organisations based in Biała Podlaska obtained only 8600 euros for projects dealing with families in crisis.[50]

The women's shelter in Jelenia Góra, the children's home in Staraya Russa, the advisory centre Spirala and the Volunteer Centre in Ústí nad Labem, were likewise institutions that NGOs or even individual activists set up and independently applied for funding. This record suggests that the national systems of local government financing are not an adequate explanation of local government social policy performance, and that local actors account for significant performance variations. The following sections examine the validity of this argument with regard to the second policy area, that of economic promotion.

Local government finance and economic promotion

A comparison of local funding for economic development, technical infrastructure and tourism in the eight towns reveals significant variations.

On the face of it, with less than five per cent of total expenditure, Balashov, Szolnok and Staraya Russa represent the lower end of the scale, while Ústí stands out for its commitment to economic development, with more than one third of total expenditure (Table 5.10).

Table 5.11 shows large differences between the two Russian towns and their Central European counterparts. The amount of money that Szolnok spent on economic development well exceeds the total budget of Balashov, a fact that understandably stems from the lower rates of economic development in Russia as a whole, rather than from the nature of its fiscal system. Another factor influencing the spending patterns of our two Russian local governments is regional economic policies. Although the Russian law provides for municipalities to maintain local roads and stir economic development, in the Saratov *oblast*

Table 5.10 Proportion of economic development expenditure in total local expenditure (%)

	JG 2002	BP 2001	SZ 2002	U 2002	K 2002	SR 2002	B 2002
Economic dev.[51]	10.0	7.2	2.3	34.5	9.0	4.9	0.05
Communal services[52]	10.9	5.1	22.6	3.9	4.2	NA	NA

Source: local budgets, own calculation.

regional authorities almost exclusively regulate larger investment projects. Accordingly, in 2002, Balashov did not spend a single kopek of its budget on economic development, with all relevant funding coming from the regional government.[53] In Staraya Russa, the local spending policies follow the Novgorod regional model of development, hailed as among the most progressive of all Russian regions.

In 2002, the two Polish towns and Szolnok received funding for economic promotion from other levels of government. In the Polish budgets, much of the funding consisted of the so-called 'road subsidy' (*subwencje drogowa*) annually transferred to all Polish *powiaty*. In Szolnok, the national government made a large ad hoc contribution for furthering economic development projects. If we disregard the six million euros that these grants make up, with roughly ten million euros allocated to economic development, Szolnok corresponds to the expenditure patterns of the other larger towns, Ústí and Jelenia Góra.

The above figures suggest that systemic influences fail to explain why some towns experienced more difficulties in implementing their economic strategies than others. With some minor variations, in 2002, our Polish, Hungarian and Czech towns disposed of more or less similar funding for stimulating local economic development. There are, however, remarkable differences in the funding for economic promotion between towns of different *size*, with the larger towns spending roughly twice as much in per capita terms as their smaller counterparts. These differences, however, fail to account for performance variations. While Karviná, the smaller Czech town, may be considered a success story, the larger town of Ústí experienced greater problems in passing and implementing a strategy of local development. Conversely, in Poland, the larger town Jelenia Góra was on the way to implementing its strategy while its smaller counterpart of Biała Podlaska failed to pass the document.

One explanation for these differences may be the system of redistribution of revenues from income and business taxes, which has been

Table 5.11 Local expenditure on economic development and technical infrastructure (euros)

	JG 2002	BP 2002	SZ 2002	U 2002	K 2001	SR 2002	B 2002
Total expenditure	9,874,702	3,431,850	16,303,046	10,784,655	3,147,432	345,033	6,400
Per capita	106	58	201	112	49	6	0

Source: local budgets, own calculation.

Table 5.12   Proportion of grants and subsidies in local expenditure on economic development

JG 2002	BP 2001	SZ 2002	U 2002	K 2002	SR 2002	B 2002
1,985,156 (20.1%)	7,038 (26.4%)	6,351,050 (39%)	0 (0%)	0 (0%)	311,700 (90.3%)	6,400 (100%)

Source: Local budgets, own calculation.

a subject of much debate in the three states due to its implications for development incentives. Poland's system of financing would suggest that the localities would actively pursue economic development because revenues from income taxes are re-allocated to the locality that generated them. By contrast, over the last decade, in the other three countries, the rules for redistribution of tax revenues repeatedly changed in the direction of equalisation. But these differences do not provide a convincing explanation of performance variations. The incentives offered by the Polish system did little to stimulate development in Biała Podlaska, while the 'punitive' system in the Czech Republic did not prevent Karviná from successfully pursuing a strategy of economic development. This is not to suggest that the peculiarities of the tax systems have no impact on local actor incentives. These incentives, however, may have a longer-term effect. For example, in Karviná the high unemployment rate and its negative by-products, such as criminality, provide more incentives to modernise than the longer-term tax yields. Conversely, the strong incentives that the Polish system provides were insufficient to encourage Biała Podlaska to pursue a more active policy of local development.

Conclusion

In this chapter, we have sought to determine the extent to which institutional differences affect local government performance in Poland, Hungary, Russia and the Czech Republic. Our analysis only partly validates the institutional hypothesis. Some institutional settings seem to be more favourable to good local performance than others, but of equal importance appears to be the ability of local actors to explore and seize opportunities for the improvement of social services and economic development. In Russia, the vagueness of legal norms regulating local government activities renders any appraisal of the impact of institutions very difficult. The fact that most Russian regions are economically far less developed on average than the Central European states further complicates the assessment of systemic influences on local government performance.

In general, the quality of Russian local government is strongly influenced by policies pursued by the respective regions. For instance, in the area of childcare, Staraya Russa and Balashov maintain different systems of task assignment. The grotesquely detailed and easily changeable regional tax legislation in Russia fosters financial insecurity and unpredictability, which discourages the localities from opting for large investment projects. Moreover, the loose connection between local economic output and government tax revenues serves to deprive the two towns of incentives for active economic promotion. This fact notwithstanding Staraya Russa has made more efforts to stir economic development than Balashov. If the main feature of the institutional framework of local government activities is a high degree of 'softness', local actors may play a decisive role in local performance. In a system that, both with regard to tasks and finances, allows much room for bargaining between local and regional authorities, the concrete personalities, skills and political connections of local actors become crucial.

The situation is different in Poland, Hungary and the Czech Republic. Here, the institutional frameworks that local governments operate within are more clearly defined and cemented. In the area of local economic promotion, no major differences exist between Poland, Hungary and the Czech Republic. In all three countries, local governments have more or less the same tasks and competences. In social policy, however, the fact that the two Czech towns perform significantly better than our Polish and Hungarian towns, can at least partly be ascribed to the Czech system of task assignment applied until January 2003. In contrast to Poland and Hungary, this system provided for a flexible handling of responsibilities, whereby tasks not taken over by municipalities became state responsibility. This is important considering that it would be more difficult for the national government to shirk its duties. Consequently, the local governments of both Karviná and Ústí owe the former district offices several social facilities for women and children. By contrast, our Polish and Hungarian towns suffer from a system of task assignment that mandates the provision of a broad range of social services while not providing them with support should they fail to do so. Indeed, despite the legal obligations to establish certain social facilities neither the Polish town of Biała Podlaska nor the two Hungarian towns operated all of the required facilities. In Biała Podlaska we had trouble finding *any* of the relevant institutions. Evidently, an inflexible system leads to significant gaps in local social service provision, which can only be closed in the unlikely case that the regional government decides to fulfil the local task of setting up the relevant facility.

To conclude, differences in task assignment to some extent explain variations in performance across nations, but they fail to explain within-country differences, the glaring disparities in performance of Jelenia Góra and Biała Podlaska being cases in point. Similarly, the systems of financing also have limited explanatory power. An interesting finding is that despite remarkable variations in the composition of both local revenues and expenditures, they did not entail direct consequences for the two policy fields. Regardless of whether the respective fiscal system provided for more local fiscal autonomy (Czech Republic) or whether it was more centralised (Poland and Hungary), the six central European towns were similar with regard to the amounts of money allocated to social policy and economic promotion.

This is not to say that there are no differences as to the impact of local government financing on performance. The outcomes of the Czech and Polish systems of local financing are quite similar. In comparison, the Hungarian system appears to be much more disadvantageous than the other two systems. While Czech and Polish municipalities receive a fixed share in taxes every year, Hungarian local revenues largely depend on the annual national budgeting process. In addition, the Hungarian system is a time bomb in the form of unfunded mandates, especially in the educational sector, which leads to local debt. Although, as far as social and economic policy is concerned, Szolnok was able to spend roughly the same amount of money as the other towns, in other policy fields the financial capacities and the performance of Hungarian local governments may be significantly affected by the problems inherent in the system of financing. The lack of funding stability might only reinforce excessive politicisation of economic decision-making in Hungary, whereby lobbying, bargaining and party political criteria, and not long-term fixed standards, are used in annual funding allocations. We discuss this point in detail in the following chapter.

Finally, we have sought to establish whether local government performance is conditioned by different incentives for local actors to engage in local economic promotion. Again, the findings in this respect were inconclusive. Although Poland provides local governments with significantly more incentives to stimulate local economic development than is the case, for instance, in the Czech Republic, Karviná and Biała Podlaska demonstrate that fiscal-institutional incentives cannot alone be held accountable for local actor decisions or strategies. Thus, while institutional variations do have an impact on local performance, this impact is limited and must be highly qualified. To some extent, differences in task assignment and local government financing explain why Czech towns have a tendency to perform quite well, while our Hungarian towns came off rather low on our performance rankings. At the same time, the institutional hypotheses do not explain significant within-country variations.

6
Parties and the Politics of Local Performance

The previous chapters have suggested that socioeconomic or formal institutional intergovernmental arrangements only partly explain performance variations in our eight cases. This chapter investigates political influences on local performance focusing on the role of political parties. The chapter is structured as follows. First, we discuss the importance of political parties in democratic and democratising contexts. Second, we identify the potential influences of various party systems on performance. Third, we examine cross-national institutional variations in local party systems in our four countries. Finally, we zoom into the localities and discuss in greater detail the possible impact of party political factors on performance variations. We also address the question of political culture as it relates to the politics of performance.

Party influences on performance

Political parties have been considered as institutions central to the functioning of a healthy democracy. They articulate and aggregate interests, provide channels for the recruitment of leadership, adjudicate disputes between conflicting interests, and engage in government decision-making. In addition to the above functions, their most important *democratic* normatively desirable role, or raison d'étre is the 'linkage' function that they perform, connecting the ruler and the ruled, the policy maker and the citizen (Lawson 1980: 3). Accordingly, the 'crafters' of new democracies in post-Communist contexts have ascribed special significance to political party development, while also regarding the institutionalisation of party systems as a crucial yardstick for ascertaining the degree of democratic consolidation.

Not just at the national level, but also at the local level party development is seen as an essential aspect of democratisation processes. Parties may play a marginal role in smaller township or village communities where citizens can have regular access to direct forms of democracy, such as township meetings and local plebiscites. But they may have an important democratic role in cities with sizable populations of 50,000 people or more, which may be considered as mini-polities in their own right, given the magnitude and diversity of the local constituencies and their preferences.

Aside from the normative democracy-related aspects of party presence in the localities, parties may also be crucial determinants of performance, the key concern of this book, and, as empirical studies of party politics of national level governments have shown, their role in this respect may not be as straightforward as the normative 'ideal world' linkage paradigm would suggest. At this point it is important to distinguish between parties and party systems. Although this distinction is usually made with regard to national-level party systems, we employ it here for reasons of conceptual clarity, but also because, as the subsequent discussion will show, the parties in our localities have been significantly influenced by or even mirrored national-level party systems. Party systems usually refer to a country's politically significant parties, which impact strongly on national politics, irrespective of their size. Scholars distinguish the various party systems according to the number of key parties, the strength of their links to particular social groups, the ideological distances separating the various parties on issue areas, and the position of the strongest parties on the left–right continuum (Parrott 1997: 18).

The first and most straightforward link between party systems and performance is that various parties may advocate policies that may be widely diverging, and may thus have variable implications for the local community as a whole, as well as for the various segments of the local populations. The second link stems from the degree of conflict that party systems may introduce into community decision-making, irrespective of their political coloration. While healthy from the point of view of democratic theory, conflict may also have negative implications for local policy-making. Parties may check the abuse of power or scrutinise the decision-making of ruling groups, though party polarisation may also significantly hamper agreement on key policy issues, thereby creating gridlock (Tarrow 1977: 228). Third, frequent party turnover may result in the corresponding administrative personnel turnover in local government, which may in turn affect long-term policy consistency (Tarrow 1977: 230). The fourth possible link with performance stems from the fact that politicisation of the local decision-making processes may encourage policy making that is based more on partisanship or clientism or on the 'reciprocation of benefits' (Stone 1980: 989) rather than on long-term policy considerations. This is because in deciding on important policy issues, party members may be motivated more by concerns of vote getting at the next election, or rewarding their narrow client base, rather than by considerations of what is actually good for the community in the longer term. The fifth link with performance is the connection between local party systems and the central state, which remains the largest provider of revenues for the localities in many national contexts. If national reward distribution is coloured by the correspondence of the governing party or coalition with that in the localities, then these national factors may significantly affect local wellbeing. So does the local factor of the skill of the mayor in competing against other cities for such funds (Peterson 1981: 76). The link with national politics may be very important considering that, as we demonstrated in the previous chapter, the localities in our four countries continue to maintain a strong fiscal dependence on the central state or regional authorities even though institutionally they may dispose of wide ranging authorities. The above list is by no means exhaustive; however, it highlights some possible implications of variable party systems for local performance. These links are summarised below.

Party system – party programmes and ideologies – policy choices – performance
Party system – policy agreement/conflict – performance
Party system – party turnover – policy continuity – performance
Party system – short-term electoral considerations – performance
Party system – ability to obtain funding from national government – performance

Although, as the above discussion suggests, political institutional frameworks are important determinants of party systems and the stability of party constellations, they often fail to explain political outcomes if considered in isolation from other factors. Theoretical and empirical studies of other settings have suggested that variable cultural, historical or social contexts may be regarded as important explanatory variables affecting other institutions and actors. For example, in post-communist democratising states scholars have attributed the more successful institutionalisation of party systems in Hungary or Poland compared to Russia to the considerable 'staying power' of the various political cultures of the respective states or to the record of existence of pre-communist parties with strong social roots.[1] Other scholars point to the importance of the existence of civic associations and crosscutting cleavages in affecting the likelihood of cooperativeness of political actors or parties. Moreover, in contexts where party systems remain weakly institutionalised, the personal leadership skills of key political actors also become crucial in affecting local outcomes. We draw on our own research materials and studies conducted by other scholars for obtaining insights into the possible intervening influence of the above factors on party politics in post-communist local settings.

Ranking countries

Before we discuss party-political influences on performance in the eight cities, it is important to identify variations in the national level institutional frameworks creating more or less favourable conditions for institutionalisation of local party systems. If we were to place the four countries on a continuum from more to less local government party institutionalisation, a clear west–east dimension emerges, with the westernmost countries having the most institutionalised party systems in the councils and those in the east, the least. A related tendency, also observed by other scholars, is that the further east the location of a country, the stronger the institutional position of the local executive, and the weaker the control by the legislative bodies (Matsuzato 1999: 191).

The Czech Republic and Hungary rank the highest in terms of the institutionalisation of local party systems. In the Czech Republic, the local electoral system is based on proportional representation. Cities that have between 10,000 and 50,000 inhabitants are entitled to elect 15 to 35 councillors, and those with populations between 50,000 and 150,000 residents, between 25 and 45 councillors (Lacina and Vajdova 2000: 265). Although in addition to party lists, candidates can also run as independents, there has been an overwhelming trend to vote for party-affiliated councillors. In the 1998 local elections, for example, independents obtained only 2.6 per cent of the vote countrywide. This tendency has been particularly pronounced in larger cities. One other indicator of party strength in local government is the council's greater weight in decision-making compared to that of the executive. Moreover, it is the council that elects the mayor as well as other members of the executive board, and also has a right to dismiss the respective officials (Lacina and Vajdova 2000: 266, 268).

In Hungary, cities with a population of over 10,000 have a system which combines the 'short ticket' and 'mixed' forms of election. According to this system, individual constituencies elect a fixed proportion of the councillors, while the remaining deputies are elected by party lists. Although in smaller settlements of up to 10,000 residents independents feature prominently, in towns with populations of over 10,000 the tendency has been to elect councils with party-affiliated majorities. For example, in the 1998 local elections, out of a total of 2743 deputies elected to councils of larger towns, only 191 were listed as independents (Temesi 2000: 355–6). Moreover, a recent survey revealed that while only a negligible percentage of councillors in smaller localities had party affiliation, the figure was quite high for larger cities. In cities with 10,000–49,999 inhabitants, for example, up to 36 per cent of local councillors were affiliated with a council party faction and in those with over 50,000 residents the figure was as high as 91 per cent. The size of party factions is also quite substantial in the larger cities, approximating 18 per cent in cities with 10,000–50,000 residents, and 44 per cent in those with a population of over 50,000 (Soós and Kálmán 2002). In addition to the electoral peculiarities favouring parties in local councils, Hungarian legislation also accords significant weight to the representative branch, which may likewise have an indirect impact on the weight of party factors in local decision-making. However, compared to the Czech Republic, the mayor may be considered to be more independent from and stronger vis-à-vis the council, given that he or she is a popularly elected figure.

Poland, in contrast to the above countries, has been noted for the consistent 'lack of importance of political parties at the local level' through successive elections in 1990, 1994 and 1998. This trend reflects the generally weaker level of party institutionalisation in Poland compared to the Czech Republic and Hungary (Kowalczyk 2000: 228). Mirroring national-level efforts at institutional and electoral engineering to encourage party system development and discourage party fragmentation, the 1998 election law stipulated that municipalities with over 20,000 residents are to have a proportional system of council elections with a 5 per cent electoral threshold. But rather than fostering the development of party systems in the localities, the law encouraged the formation of ad hoc local coalitions of independents or quasi-parties with a low level of survival. In the 1998 local elections, for example, independents and local non-party based coalitions obtained the largest share of the vote, 59.9 per cent. As in the Czech Republic, until recently the council has been institutionally strong vis-à-vis the local chief executive. According to the legislation that existed until 2002, the council elected the mayor and other members of the board, although the mayor did not have to be a local councillor (Kowalczyk 2000: 230).

The direct election of mayors in all towns from 2002 onwards may serve to strengthen the local chief executive vis-à-vis the representative branch of power.

Russia, our easternmost country, has the weakest degree of party institutionalisation in local councils, a fact documented in several studies. Because Russia is a federation, until the adoption of the latest local government law in 2003, its constituent regions were entitled to establish variable institutional arrangements for the election of local councils and their institutional weight in local decision-making.[2] But despite the theoretical possibility of a diversity of institutional choices, two factors have characterised sub-national politics in general in Russia: the weak level of party development and role in local politics; and the marginal position of the local council vis-à-vis the executive. To begin with, the institutional arrangements favoured by a vast majority of Russia's local councils discourage the institutionalisation of parties. Thus, only 0.08 per cent of all local councils in Russia have a proportional system of representation. Moreover, according to the 1998 Russian Central Electoral Commission report, only a negligible 3.03 per cent of candidates for local councils Russia-wide were nominated by electoral blocks. Even in such cities as St Petersburg, Smolensk and Pskov, which tend to have the highest numbers of party or political block affiliated councillors, the figures have been as low as 26.6, 23.2 and 22.4 per cent, respectively. The vast majority of Russia's municipalities, 64.67 per cent, have also opted for institutional arrangements assigning the chief executive key prerogatives in the local government system. An overwhelming majority of mayors, even if they are popularly elected, are also members of the respective councils, have supreme power with the right to chair sessions and possess a decisive vote (Goryunov et al. 1999: 31, 39, 155). The situation contrasts with the Czech Republic and, to a lesser extent, Hungary, where local chief executives are answerable to the council.

Having established the broad cross-country variations in the institutionalisation of party presence in the councils and the weight of the representative versus the executive branches of local power, we now ascertain the *within*-country variations in local party systems. Such an assessment requires both an examination of variation in formal institutional arrangements that the localities choose from a range of institutional options authorised by the national legislation, and the less formal aspects of local decision-making stemming from various party constellations and policy choices aimed at strengthening or weakening the role of party-political actors in decision-making. Accordingly, we here broaden our conceptualisation of local differences and seek to establish city variations by looking at the degree of *politicisation* of local decision-making.

Several yardsticks could be used to assess the degree of politicisation of local decision-making processes. The first is the proportional strength of independent versus party affiliated candidates. The second is the turnover of political parties in councils across time periods. The third is the constellation of political parties within the council and their patterns of interaction and decision-making. The fourth is the formal or informal mechanisms that the council may choose to set up in order to depoliticise decision-making and delegate authority to non-political 'experts'. A final yardstick is the degree to which the administration is purged after each new election.

The impact of parties on local performance

Our findings support the hypothesis that in countries with a greater level of party institutionalisation, party systems exert a strong impact on policy agreement and policy choices in local councils. We found this to be true for both the Hungarian and the Czech towns, where party systems affected such crucial aspects of local economic-development decision-making as the timing of the adoption of the economic strategy, the smoothness of the decision-making process and the likelihood of its implementation in the longer term. The precise impact of party political factors on performance varied, however, depending on the nature of the local party systems and the long-term consistency of the party composition of the local councils. Towns with less ideologically polarised councils and with a lower rate of party turnover, such as the Czech town of Karviná, also had lower levels of administrative personnel turnover, and were more successful in adopting and implementing a comprehensive long-term economic strategy than such towns as Szolnok and Ústí, which had polarised party systems and high rates of electoral turnover. Another important factor shaping local outcomes is the connection between national and local politics. Again, we found this link to be stronger in the above two states with more institutionalised party systems than in Poland and Russia. Tables 6.1–5 contain rough summaries of our findings, as well as data on some of the above dimensions.

In countries where parties are less institutionalised, such as Poland, we found that party systems in the local councils do not have a strong impact on local performance, with other factors providing more convincing explanations of variations in local outcomes. In Russia, where parties are

Table 6.1 Degree of politicisation of local government

Cities	Number of independents in council	Party turnover	Polarisation (left-right)	Engaging 'experts'	Purge of administration after election
Ústí	Low	Medium	High	Low	Medium
Karviná	High	High	Medium	High	Low
Szolnok	Low	High	High	Low	High
Sopron	Low	Low	Medium	Medium	Low
Jelenia Góra	Low	High	Medium	High	Low
Biała Podlaska	Low	High	Medium	Low	Low
Balashov	Low		Medium	Low	Medium
Staraya Russa	High	Low	Low	High	Low

Source: Author assessment.

Table 6.2 Country and within country ranking, degree of politicisation

Czech Republic	Ústí nad Labem Karviná
Hungary	Szolnok Sopron
Poland	Biała Podlaska Jelenia Góra
Russia	Balashov Staraya Russa

Source: Author assessment.

Table 6.3 Number of parties in councils

	Ú	K	SP	SZ	JG	BP	SR	B
1990			6	6				
1994	9	10	8	7	5			
1998	6	8	10	7	4	4		
2002	5	4	8	10	6	7	1	4

Source: Author compilation based on electoral data.

Table 6.4   Turnover of parties[3] and councillors[4] (%)

Parties and Councillors	Ú	K	SP	SZ	JG	BP
Parties in 1998 as compared to 1994	50	66.7	36	0	50	
Parties in 2002 as compared to 1998	37.5	50	20	50	88.9	62.5
Councillors in 2002 as compared to 1994	86.5	68.3			73.91	91.3

Source: Author compilation based on electoral data.

Table 6.5   Councillors without party affiliation (%)

	Ú	K	SP	SZ	JG	BP	SR	B
1990			7	0				
1994			0	3.6	2.27			
1998	10.8	27.3	0	3.6	0	2.5	85.71	68.75
2002	18.9	29.3	0	3.8	0	0		

Source: Author compilation based on electoral data.

underdeveloped even at national and regional levels, it would even be inappropriate to apply the concept of party system to the localities. Significantly, however, one of the towns that we investigated is located in a region where the Communist Party of the Russian Federation, Kommunisticheskaya partiya Rossiyskoy federatsii (KPRF), Russia's most established party, has a sizeable electorate. In this region KPRF's opposition to the regional government has resulted in more competitive electoral politics at the local level compared to the Novgorod region. We found that in Balashov, which is located in Saratov *oblast*, the communist party influenced local policy choices. In general, however, we found that in both Poland and Russia, the party political factors that do influence local outcomes are mostly connected to the regional level. Interestingly, the weaker level of party influence in the two states is also reflected in the generally lower level of administrative personnel turnover in the local administrations.

In all four states, we found that institutional arrangements specifically designed to reduce the politicisation of local decision-making positively affect long-term policy decision-making and implementation. Examples are the setting up of managerial positions in the local administration, or regular consultative mechanisms whereby a variety of non-political actors, such as the local business community, are involved, as was the case in Jelenia Góra and Karviná. The positive role of such arrangements is particularly felt in settings with established party systems. Settings where parties play a negligible role in local decision-making, which is largely managerial and executive driven, such as the Russian town of Staraya Russa, provide further examples of smooth decision-making, as well as greater policy continuity and implementation. In other words, from a pure policy point of view, a lack of parties, but the presence of a will on behalf of the local executive leadership to pursue a given developmental option, may have a positive impact on policy-making and implementation.

Finally, our findings lend support to the contention that the impact of party political dynamics should not be considered in isolation from the locality-specific social, cultural or historical factors shaping both the local political and civil societies. Indeed, there is evidence suggesting that in our towns civil society also to a certain extent shaped or influenced political society. This point of course introduces a new dimension of causality to our argument. But we consider it important to include the evidence that we have on the possible intervening influence of this factor. For example, in the Eastern Hungarian town of Szolnok, and in its Eastern Polish counterpart of Biała Podlaska, the polarised nature of local decision-making, the unstable nature of the local party system and the failure of local political actors to devise inclusive decision-making arrangements could also be products of the weaker traditions of cooperation and citizen involvement in these localities than in some of our other towns.

The above findings apply largely to the area of economic policy. We found that there was only a negligible impact of party systems on social policy outcomes in the precise social policy fields that we investigated. One explanation for this difference is that economic promotion is an area with higher political and economic stakes than social policies concerning smaller segments of the population, such as foster children or 'families in crisis'. Another explanation, suggested in Chapter 5, is that in the four states, social policy continues to be highly regulated at national and regional levels and is not subject to the variety of policy choices that economic promotion entails.

Accordingly, we here focus on decision-making and implementation in the area of economic promotion.

The following sections discuss in greater detail the variable impact of party systems in the eight localities according to the dimensions that we have identified, namely the impact of party systems on policy choices and agreement; personnel and policy continuity; and generating funding from national or regional-level political actors.

Parties and policy agreement

According to our simple ranking in Table 6.2, in the Czech Republic and Hungary parties exert the strongest impact on performance, but with variable effects. The Czech town of Ústí and the Hungarian town of Szolnok have the highest degree of politicisation of local decision-making, while in Karviná and Sopron it is less polarised.

The degree of politicisation of local decision-making and implementation in the four cities stems from the peculiarities of their party systems. In Karviná, left-leaning parties were able to secure majorities in the council in successive elections, and from the mid-1990s onwards there has been a stable and consistent ruling coalition. The smaller parties with a high record of electoral turnover actually helped mitigate political conflict. Compared to Ústí, Karviná also had significantly higher percentages of party-unaffiliated candidates in successive councils. The rate of re-election of councillors was also relatively high, with roughly one third of all councillors remaining in office in the period between 1994 and 2002. The relative consistency of the council composition across electoral periods made it less likely that the initially adopted economic plan would be identified with the opposition or would be discarded altogether.

In Ústí, by contrast, the local council's ability to agree on long-term policy goals was significantly hampered by a party ideological split between the Civic Democratic Party (ODS) and the Communist Party of Bohemia and Moravia (KSCM), which also reflected national-level party polarisation. The strength of the ODS in Ústí corresponds to the centre–periphery and industry–agriculture cleavage observed by scholars of the Czech Republic and the higher probability of success of the ODS in larger cities compared to smaller or more rural localities (Kostelecký 2002: 95). The ODS, a successor to the Civic Forum which was the driving force behind the Czech Velvet Revolution, espouses a Thatcherite free market ideology, with its national leader Vaclav Klaus frequently citing the former British Prime Minister as a role model. The party advocates minimal state intervention in the market, low taxation and a reduction of state bureaucracy.[5] The KSCM is a successor to the Communist Party of Czechoslovakia (KSC), which ruled the country from 1948 until 1989. The party contrasts with its counterparts in Poland and Hungary in that in the post-communist period the reformist elements within it failed to devise a political programme with a greater social-democratic orientation (Kostelecký 2002). It has been regarded as 'one of the few largely unreconstructed Communist parties' in all of the post-communist states of Central and Eastern Europe, retaining the communist label and overtly taking pride in its communist past.[6] In contrast to the ODS, the KSC advocates strong state control over the economy and state ownership of its key sectors.

The above party ideological differences substantially affected policy preferences at the local level, as well as policy agreement and implementation success. The ODS, that has dominated the local scene since 1990, has tended to follow the economic model imposed by the national-level ODS party of Klaus with its preference for fiscal austerity over public investment and the avoidance of debt accumulation. In contrast to the parties of the left, it also advocated the selling off of municipal assets, rather than maintaining municipal ownership over them. The ODS ideology, with its stigmatisation of the left as responsible for the evils of communism, also precluded effective cooperation between parties. Left-leaning parties, particularly the KCSM, have been consistently marginalised in the Ústí council, a fact fostered both by the dogmatism of the ODS and the unreformed nature of the KCSM. This dogmatism is well illustrated by a statement from Ústí's mayor. 'I cannot accept that people responsible for the overall devastation of the country and crimes against humanity should be included in the political decision-making process. I reject the opinion that on the local level these things do not matter. This question should not be restricted to the national level only', he maintained. In contrast to Karviná, where the opposition, including the ODS, was invited to participate in important committees, in Ústí the opposition communists were excluded from key council decision-making bodies.

In Hungary, the greater degree of political polarisation of the Szolnok council had similarly negative effects on policy agreement and implementation. In the 1990 local elections, in an apparent backlash against communism, the electorate voted overwhelmingly for centre to right wing parties, such as FIDESZ (Federation of Young Democrats), SZDSZ (Alliance of Free Democrats) and MDF (Hungarian Democratic Forum). In the successive elections of 1994 and 1998, however the MSZP (Hungarian Socialist Party), which obtained only three out of 33 seats in the 1990s council, was the party which secured the largest number of seats (11, 12 and 15 out of 28) in the 1994, 1998 and 2002 councils, respectively. At the same time, despite the dispersion of the right vote among several parties, such as the SZDSZ (Alliance of Free Democrats), FIDESZ (Alliance of Young Democrats), MDF (Hungarian Democratic Forum), KDNP (Christian Democratic People's Party) and FKGP (Independent Smallholders' Party), their combined number of seats in 1994 and 1998 resulted in councils split almost fifty-fifty between left- and right-leaning parties. The right constellation centred on FIDESZ, whose candidates, as well as those nominated jointly by FIDESZ and smaller right-wing parties, obtained the largest number of seats after the socialists, eight and ten seats in the 1994 and 1998 councils, respectively.[7]

The polarisation of the council was exacerbated after the 1998 Hungarian parliamentary elections. In 1998 the majority of the seats in the national parliament were won by FIDESZ-MPP and its ally the MDF, while the MSZP (Hungarian Socialist Party) followed closely in terms of the number of seats it was able to obtain. The Hungarian Socialist Party, which was the ruling party between 1994 and 1998, had already established a reputation for itself as a pragmatic reform party enjoying broad social support. It prioritised pro-market economic reforms, proclaimed its Western orientation, and also declared its wish to improve relations with neighbouring states with large Hungarian minorities. Scholars have identified this party as an example of a 'successful social democratic communist successor party', whose former *nomenklatura* elites were instrumental in fostering alliances not only with the new business groups and former trade unions, but also such 'losers' of the transition as pensioners and farmers (Orenstein 1998: 485). The MSZP thus represented a classical catch-all party of the centre. It was at this time that the then opposition FIDESZ party radically shifted its orientation from a liberal party to a more right-wing and nationalist orientation with government and opposition diverging not on pragmatic policy issues but on concepts of nation and state (Kostelecký 2002). The fact and presence of the centre party thus only served to encourage polarisation and 'centrifugal' rather than 'centripetal' party faction dynamics within the parliament (Sartori 1976: 135).

These polarised party dynamics were reproduced at the local level reflecting national-level politics with parties of right-wing orientation finding it necessary to pursue politics of issue outbidding that would make them more distinguishable from the more moderate parties. In Szolnok, further exacerbating the situation was the fact that while the socialists were the party with the largest number of seats in the successful councils, the popularly elected mayors in 1994 and 1998 were affiliated with FIDESZ. The result was that many important decisions considering town redevelopment, tourism and industry promotion were blocked at the council decision-making stage because of political conflicts. One example is the city's failure to push through a plan to restore the historical part of town. Once the opposition socialists found out that FIDESZ, the party faction that was pushing the plan, owned property on the street, its implementation was stalled. Another example was the failure of the council to advance the development of the industrial park. 'As far as I know the reason why it has not been realised so far is because of this political cat-and-mouse game: in the previous council term what FIDESZ proposed MSZP voted against. What MSZP proposed FIDESZ voted against', complained one entrepreneur, whose company has been eager to participate in the inhabitation of the park.[8] As one businessman maintained with regard to the 1998–2002 council, 'I think that some kind of local political interests may have clashed with the idea of development. The percentage of socialists and FIDESZ representatives in the council was almost the same. And maybe this was the problem. FIDESZ may have proposed things which were not approved by the socialists, following the rationale "just because they shouldn't succeed."'

The other Hungarian town of Sopron is located in a traditionally more conservative area, but as in Szolnok, the Socialists have maintained a strong presence in successive councils. In 1994 and 1998 they were the party with the largest number of seats (seven and nine out of 25, respectively). As in Szolnok, the right-wing vote had been dispersed among several parties, such as FIDESZ, the KDNP, MDF, SZDSZ, FKGP, and MIEP (Party of Hungarian Truth and Life), which combined possessed enough seats to result in council polarisation.

In Sopron, however, the significant distinguishing characteristic of local politics has been the presence and strength of a purely local party, the Szövetség Sopronért (Alliance for Sopron). In the 1994 and 1998 councils, with five seats, it was the largest party faction after the MSZP and those of the right-wing parties, such as the MDF/ KDNP faction in the 1994 council, and the FIDESZ/ MDF/ MDNP (Hungarian Democratic People's Party)/ MKDSZ (Hungarian Christian Democratic Federation) faction in the 1998 representative body.[9] Moreover, the mayor who was elected in 1994 and re-elected in 1998 was also from this party, although his two appointed deputy mayors represented FIDESZ. Although the party is considered to be right-leaning, its local nature and rhetoric of politics for the 'common good' prevented council polarisation to the extent observed in Szolnok.

Compared to Hungary and the Czech Republic, Poland has a weaker level of party institutionalisation, and this situation is mirrored at the local level. In both the Polish cities parties and party politics play a weaker role in local administration than they do in our Hungarian and Czech towns. The absence of party-unaffiliated candidates in the councils in the two cities compared to those in the Czech Republic and Hungary would suggest a stronger level of party institutionalisation. This superficial impression is misleading, however. The introduction of the 1998 legislative provision whereby cities with populations of over 20,000 are to elect councils based on PR with a five-per cent electoral threshold resulted in councils whose deputies are 100-per cent formally affiliated with a party. But close scrutiny reveals that many of these parties are actually ad hoc constellations of local groups with a very low survival rate. For example, in Jelenia Góra between 1994 and 2002 five local parties were elected, only one of which (Razem) survived from one electoral period to the other. In Biała Podlaska, of the three local parties elected between 1994 and 2002, only one (Akcja Samorządowa) survived the subsequent elections.

This is not to suggest that national level parties have a small presence in or lack influence over Polish local politics. In Jelenia Góra council decision-making benefited from the overwhelming majority of the seats (33 out of 40) that the left-wing SLD (Democratic Left Alliance) and the centre Unia Wolności (Freedom Union) parties were together able to capture in the 1998 elections and form a coalition. It also benefited from the fact that the council-elected mayor represented the majority party, the SLD. In Biała Podlaska, the council elected in 1998 has been more polarised between the SLD-UP and the anti-communist WAS (Solidarity Election Action), which obtained 14 and 12 seats, respectively. But it is also important to note that there has been reportedly very little discipline in party faction voting within the council, and decision-making in general has been characterised as personalised.

In Russia, party political factors play a much weaker role in the localities compared to the above three states. Political factors that do influence local developments are linked to the regional level. Indeed, one study found that the greater the representation of parties in regional-level power bodies, the greater their role in the political process at a municipal level (Luchterhandt-Mikhaleva 1999: 137).[10] The Novgorod region is typical of the Russian regional scene in its 'consensual'-style politics. The region's long-serving governor Mikhail Prusak has been successful at crowding out and undermining his political opponents, with opposition parties enjoying limited electoral success. In the course of the 1990s, the head of the local branch of KPRF, which has a sizable electorate in the region, was only once able to obtain a seat in the regional Duma (legislature), while the ultranationalist LDPR (Liberal Democratic Party) of Vladimir Zhirinovsky, which likewise enjoys a degree of popular support, failed to elect a single candidate at either regional or local level (Petro 2004). Generally, in the regional level legislature the presence of party-affiliated candidates has been negligible (Golosov 1999: 1337). Not only at the regional level, but also in the localities, Prusak has sought to depoliticise the local administration considering the importance of local governments as support structures for the regional regime. Virtually all mayors have been loyalists of the regional governor. The Novgorod legislation has allowed the heads of the local administrations to sit simultaneously as deputies in the regional legislature, and 30–40 per cent of the regional Duma deputies have been local heads of administration.[11] Accordingly, both regional rhetoric and practice with its stress on 'conflict-free' and 'consensual' decision-making have also been replicated at the local level.

Saratov *oblast* is similar to Novgorod in that the regional governor has sought to centralise power and undermine political opposition to his regime including by such means as subordinating local governing institutions to the regional bodies (Gel'man et al. 2002: 173; Malyakin and Sveshnikov 1999). There are, however, important political differences between the two regions. Saratov, a largely agrarian region, has traditionally been a stronghold for KPRF, to a much greater degree than the Novgorod region. For example, in the 1996 Presidential elections, the leader of KPRF, Gennadiy Zyuganov, was the clear favourite in the region obtaining 41.59/49.94 per cent in the first and second rounds of the elections, compared to Yel'tsin's 28.38/44.8 per cent. By way of comparison, in Novgorod, Zyuganov obtained 23.76/33.99 per cent of the vote, while Yel'tsin obtained 35.76/59.14 per cent (Orttung, Lussier and Paretskaya 2000: 496, 382). As is well known, in Russia KPRF remains the only party which is able to mount substantive opposition to non-KPRF actors at both federal and regional levels. Because KPRF has not been a strong force in the Novgorod region, Prusak did not find it difficult to weed out contenders against his rule from this and other parties, such as LDPR. By contrast, in Saratov KPRF presented challenges to the rule of its then governor Ayatskov. It is the smaller rural towns like Balashov that KPRF has regarded as its strongholds.

In contrast to Novgorod, the local councils in Saratov *oblast* were seen by KPRF as institutions that would facilitate the preservation of the party's power in the localities and would also strengthen its hand in the struggle with the *oblast* governor. In the mid-1990s, it was KPRF that insisted on holding elections to the local councils. By contrast, the governor was opposed to elections, fearing that KPRF would capture many local council seats. Although as a result of massive electoral manipulations, the Ayatskov administration was able to prevent the communists from electing a single head of administration and from obtaining a majority of seats in any local council, in a number of cities, KPRF has been able to maintain a relatively strong presence (Luchterhandt-Mikhaleva 1999: 141).

Balashov's economic decision-making has been significantly coloured by KPRF presence in the council and administration, although the council also has deputies from LDPR, as well as the more centre-right Union of Right Forces (SPS) and United Russia (YR) parties. The town's policies with regard to the sale of land are illustrative of this influence. The *oblast* has been singled out as 'the leader in land reform' and as 'the only' region in Russia where legal conditions for the development of a land market had been created at the time of research for this book.[12] These legal frameworks allow for the lease of land by investors for 49 years, including by foreigners, or for purchase. But although the *oblast* has been a pioneer in land privatisation, the Balashov local government functionaries that we interviewed maintained that they were staunchly opposed to the sale of land. The city only sells small plots of land for garages, mini-markets and private houses. No sale of agricultural land is permitted for fear that it would be used for purposes other than agriculture.

In Staraya Russa, the parties in the council exert a negligible impact on local decision-making, which is executive driven. Staraya Russa's council, which consists of seven deputies, has only one party-affiliated councillor, a member of KPRF. As in most other Russian towns the local chief executive dominates local decision-making. Potential threats from opposition party contenders are also undermined with the help of the notorious 'administrative resource', although Staraya Russa comes nowhere close to some of the more crass practices of other regions. One example of the undermining of political opponents by the mayor was his Decree on the Improvement of the Order of Trade in Periodicals and Press, whereby newspapers were only allowed to be sold in official state kiosks and other state mandated places, but not by street vendors. According to the candid admission of the mayor, the decision was prompted by the desire to undermine competition presented to the official city newspaper *Staraya Russa* by a paper sponsored by the opposition, *Zhivoy most*.[13] In a personal interview with the authors, the town's Head of Administration indicated that the paper was funded by a candidate fielded by economic interests from Moscow, who was interested in establishing control over the city's wood processing assets.[14] This example illustrates how political opposition actors are marginalised and prevented from obtaining office.

Parties, administrative turnover and policy continuity

Our findings also support our second expectation with regard to the impact of party systems on administrative turnover and policy continuity. In Karviná, the Czech Republic's less politicised town, there was a higher record of re-election of councillors and greater continuity of senior executive staff. Between 1990 and 2002, Karviná had one mayor, Lubomir Kuznik (born in 1956), who headed coalitions of social democrats allied with either left- or right-leaning parties, and was himself member of the Social Democratic Party. The mayor elected in 2002, Antonin Petras (born in 1941), though a member of the communist party, professes an 'impartial' approach to local administration and is critical of 'politics' in local governance. There was also a low record of turnover of key personnel within the economic department, which had been headed by one individual over the period of ten years.

By contrast, the turnover of councillors in Ústí has been relatively high. For example, only 14 per cent of local councillors elected in 1998 also had a council seat in the body elected in 1994. The composition of executive bodies has also been more fluid. Since the Velvet Revolution, Ústí has been governed by five different mayors. Miroslav Pátek (born in 1944), who was in office from 1999 until the end of 2002, subsequently obtained a seat in the Czech national parliament. His successor, Petr Gandalovič (born in 1964) was a leading figure of the Ústí dissident movement in 1989. He also boasts extensive Western exposure – between 1997 and 2002 he was Consul in New York; he is fluent in English and can converse in German. Early on during his mayoral spell, he demonstrated great enthusiasm for rejuvenating the city and attracting foreign investment. He too, however, left his post having barely served for a few months, and was appointed to the post of Minister for Local Development in the national shadow cabinet of the ODS.[15] Now, in 2006, at the time of the writing of this book, he is widely rumoured to become the Minister for European Affairs in the new Czech Government. These facts illustrate the connection between national and local politics in Ústí. On average relatively young and well educated, ODS local politicians have tended to consider the local seat as a stepping-stone to higher national office. The size of the city – Ústí is one of the Czech Republic's largest towns – likewise accounts for its nationwide party-political significance. The above record contrasts with the more elderly and working class membership of the KSCM, and the greater rootedness of communist politicians in the smaller localities. This explains the greater stability of the Karviná council with its strong KCSM presence. Moreover, in Karviná, the fact that the current mayor is a former national senator suggests that the post of key local executive may be even considered a retirement position.

In Hungary, towns with high party political polarisation also had higher turnover of executive personnel. Although Hungary-wide statistics suggest that the turnover of mayors (as opposed to councillors) has been quite low, with approximately two thirds of all mayors re-elected,[16] the tendency is reversed in Szolnok. Within a period of eight years, between 1994 and 2002 Szolnok elected three different mayors. In Hungary, the record of mayoral turnover may have a significant bearing on policy implementation, as it concerns not just the political office of the mayor, but also the ostensibly purely administrative core of civil servants subordinate to him or her in the local administration. At this point it is important to discuss the position of the mayor in the Hungarian public administration system. The mayor is a political figure whose legitimacy derives from his elected mandate, but he does have authority over civil servants. Civil servants are de jure employed by the Chief Administrative Officer (CAO), also called the notary. Although the CAO is a civil servant nominated by the council for an indefinite period, the mayor exercises a strong influence on the process of appointments. Hungarian public administration scholars write that the country's 'strong mayoral system' ensures that the mayor's position in the choice of local civil servants is dominant. The fact that the CAO is in turn dependent on the council, a political body, likewise reinforces the influence of politics on the local civil service. According to Hungarian scholars, 'although their [the civil servants'] position is regulated and guaranteed by the Civil Service Act, it cannot be interpreted as a politically neutral status since they are too dependent on politicians' wishes' (Horváth and Kiss 2001: 33).

It is therefore not surprising that in Szolnok, the high turnover of mayors, as well as the polarised nature of successive councils, has been accompanied by a strikingly high record of post-election turnover within the local administration, as well as of inter-organisational change. For example, after the local elections in 2002, which brought victory to a socialist mayor, 18 out of the 31 key local administration civil servants were reshuffled from one department to another, and eight new civil servants were hired. The change concerned such key departments as the city development bureau, and departments and sub-departments in charge of the economy, investment and town property.

The new head of the economic department, a member of the ruling Socialist Party, maintained that only 'professional changes, nothing of a personal kind' occurred in the composition of administrative personnel following the 2002 elections. He also defended the organisational change on the grounds that 'it is good to … refresh the civil servant staff of the local government a bit'. 'These times of change are always good to filter out those whose capabilities don't fit the job', he maintained.[17] The optimism of this functionary, however, was not shared by other civil servants responsible for policy implementation. According to the candid admission of one local official, 'here a public administration officer has the feeling after each election that everything starts from scratch again'.[18]

Our respondents in the business community likewise criticised the politically motivated turnover, which arguably significantly hampers long-term economic development and policy consistency. Thus, the director of one of the town's largest enterprises maintained: 'You can't change people in the administration every four years depending on whether the council is left or right. … I think the greatest responsibility of this local administration should be to depoliticise this town, so that economic decisions would not be based on political decisions, but on careful consideration of business plans.' The director of another large enterprise complained: 'It takes at least one and a half years for them to learn how to do things. It is actually pretty sad that the work of these civil servants is so politicised. Here in Szolnok this is the case. I would expect those who were good at their jobs to stay in their positions regardless of the political membership of the new mayor. Qualified people should be allowed to stay.'[19]

In Sopron, the lesser degree of politicisation of local decision-making is reflected in the noticeably lower record of post-electoral reshuffle of the local administration compared to Szolnok. The mayor elected in 2002 appointed new deputy mayors, which is not uncommon considering that deputy mayors are political appointees. But in stark contrast to Szolnok, here no organisational changes took place within the local administration itself. Only three new civil servants were hired, the remaining 32 key individuals retaining their posts in the departments that they had previously worked for. Significantly, civil servants in charge of such key departments as those concerned with economic development and business promotion also retained their positions. 'We didn't do any political cleansing', maintained the deputy mayor.[20] This continuity has also been observed with previous administrations.[21] In Sopron, the survey of staff in the administration in charge of economic policy revealed a lower level of approval than in Szolnok that political conflicts hamper their work.

Another important factor which impacts on local electoral and administrative personnel turnover stems from the peculiarity of Hungary's central–local relations, whereby local political preferences are significantly coloured by national-level politics. Despite the relatively high level of party institutionalisation in Hungary compared to other post-communist countries, scholars have noted the high volatility of Hungarians' voting preferences in national elections. One standard way of measuring volatility is by examining the rate of parties that enter subsequent elections and the likelihood of the same parties obtaining similar results in successive elections. By applying this method, scholars have estimated that for votes cast for regional party lists in the 1990 and 1994 parliamentary elections, the volatility index is more than three times higher than the average in Western Europe observed between 1885 and 1985, although it is relatively low compared to other post-communist countries such as Poland. The volatility rates in Hungary remained significantly high throughout the 1990s, while voter party loyalties were low, with surveys revealing high levels of preference for a swing from government to opposition (Tóka 1999a: 155, 177).[22]

Hungary-wide electoral statistics indicate that there is a strong correlation between the ruling government at the national level, and electoral preferences in the localities.[23] This tendency goes back to 1990 when the localities sought to punish the national government for performance weaknesses by electing opposition parties. The result of the discrepancy between the national government ruling coalition and party constellations in local councils was the over-politicisation of central–local relations. The response of the voter has since been to either elect non-party affiliated mayors and councillors (almost 70 per cent), as in 1994, or to elect local governments roughly corresponding to the central government ruling coalitions, as in 1998 and 2002. For example, in the October 2002 elections, of the cities with county rank, 16 elected mayors belonging to the ruling coalition parties, four – to the opposition, and only two – not affiliated with any party. In the smaller municipalities as many as two thirds of all elected mayors were independents, but even here the socialists, who were victorious in the national elections, achieved the highest results ever in local elections (Thelen 2002). This strategic voting has done little to depoliticise centre–periphery relations or to introduce greater continuity of council and executive actors.[24]

Another consequence of the politicisation of local decision-making in the Czech Republic and Hungary is that local functionaries are more under pressure to pursue policies that make them more visible, particularly at election time. It also encourages the distribution of rewards according to political criteria, which in turn negatively affects the perceived legitimacy of policy-makers. The town of Ústí's deputy mayor in charge of economic development[25] provides one example of policy agreement and implementation failure in the area of economic promotion as a result of short-term electoral considerations of the local actors. He maintained:

> There were two main reasons why the economic strategy was never implemented. First, there was a lack of political will ... If all councillors had adopted the strategy as 'their' strategy, things would have developed in another way. The second reason was that the executive board did not want to burden the budget with the projects suggested by the Barents Group ... Nobody wanted to 'reduce' the budget by investing in these projects, because they would not have had any immediate effects, it would have taken some time, until the first results would have become visible. And this made many politicians think: OK, but by then, I will not be in office any more.[26]

The short-term electoral mentality may explain the local council's approval of a decision to build a very costly and extravagant, but 'visible', bridge across the river Labe. The bridge may have appeared to generate greater political dividends compared to the pursuit of the long-term development strategy, whose implementation time frame exceeded the electoral term of the council.[27]

The more politicised nature of local government is also reflected in perceptions regarding the transparency of local decision-making of outside actors, as revealed by our surveys. For example, in Ústí, interviewees were more likely to indicate that they believed public tenders not to be sufficiently transparent. These attitudes reflect the legitimacy of local decision-making by actors within the local business community. A recent survey of local companies conducted by the highly respectable *Prague Business Journal* confirms this tendency. The study revealed that among the country's ten largest towns, Ústí ranked the highest in terms of the perceived level of corruption.[28] Similarly, in Szolnok, another town with highly polarised council politics there was a high level of agreement among the largest entrepreneurs that we surveyed that 'interest groups' – a term which in Hungary is also understood as a euphemism for corruption – hamper the economic policy of the local administration.

A recent comparative study of local government performance in other settings helps further explain the links between parties and performance. The study, based on data from Mexico and Bolivia, found that local councils exceeding a set margin of numbers of parties and with greater fragmentation of local electoral politics were more likely to have graft, 'financial impropriety' and 'economically inefficient policies' than those with less fragmentation. Moreover, political fragmentation was also found to significantly affect municipal hiring practices. Municipalities with over four effective parties were found to have a 5 per cent increase in government employment, and also had greater municipal debt. In other words, in such municipalities, resources were invested in maintaining clientelistic networks, rather than improved and more efficient government services. The study's suggested margin of parties actually supports the observations in our cases. Negative tendencies associated with party fragmentation appear when there are more than 4.7 parties contesting elections (Singer 2004). In our study, in countries with more institution-alised party systems, the strongest economic performer, Karviná, in 2002 also had the lowest number of council parties, while the weakest performer, Szolnok, had ten parties. As we move eastwards, we see that in Poland and Russia, there is a greater continuity of local executive person-nel, which reflects the weaker influence of local- and national-level parties on local decision-making. In Poland, in both the towns while council electoral turnover has been high, there has been a low level of executive personnel change corresponding to electoral cycles. In Russia, where local elections are often non-competitive, and where the local administration staff does not depend on the council, electoral politics likewise exert a weak impact on administrative personnel composition. What does affect personnel stability is often the preferences of the regional-level governor, and the nature of relationships between regional and local actors.

In the Novgorod region, most of the mayors are loyalists of the regional governor. The mayor according to Novgorod legislation supervises both executive and legislative branches of local power, and is a chairman of the city and *rayon* Duma, a fact that gives him a high degree of autonomy (Petro 2004). In Staraya Russa the mayor, Yevgeniy Ryabov (born in 1951), during the communist times a *rayon* party functionary, has occupied the post for several successive terms. He was elected as head of Staraya Russa town and *rayon* in May 1992 according to the procedure that existed at the time, namely by the local council. Then in 1993–5 he was the deputy head of administration in charge of agriculture. In 1996 he was popularly elected as head of administration. At the time of preparation of this manuscript for publication – 2006 – Ryabov is still the Mayor of Staraya Russa.

In Balashov, the mayoral candidacy strongly depends on the preferences of the regional governor, with the two mayors elected in the 1990s known to have been regional loyalists. Institutionally, the council does, however, play a stronger role in Balashov than in Staraya Russa, as it is the council that elects the chief local executive from its ranks. It is for this reason that the regional 'party of power' has sought to exert control over elections to the local councils. In so doing, however, in some localities it met with limited success considering the strength of the opposition KPRF and its efforts to prevent and report on electoral manipulations. The current mayor, in 2006, is different from the individual that occupied the post when we conducted field research in 2002 and 2003, which confirms the trend of more frequent executive turnover in this locality.

These findings have strong implications for debates on elite turnover or continuity in post-communist settings (Machonin and Tucek 2000; Tokes 2000). There is little agreement as to whether greater or lesser elite continuity has negative or positive effects on performance. Some scholars have argued that during early stages of transition, greater elite continuity might be good for performance. At the same time, they warned against the risks of negative implications for democracy of low elite turnover. This is because lengthy terms in office negatively affect the responsiveness of local decision-makers (Stoner-Weiss 1997). Greater levels of consensus and 'quasi-solidarity' arguably also breed clientism (Frane and Matevž 2002: 439). Our findings should qualify the assumption that greater turnover at regular intervals reduces clientism and improves performance; in fact, the opposite seems to be the case, though more evidence is needed over a longer period of time about the impact of the *rate* of turnover on performance and the ideal-type balance between low versus high turnover. We should also note that much of the literature on post-communist elites has focused on the national level, where turnover would not have such immediate effects on local performance as would be the case in the small settings that we are investigating.[29]

Aside from the question of elite turnover, the very background of elites is also deemed to be 'one of the questions of post-communist transformation'. This is because the old communist elite 'reproduction' versus 'circulation' and influx of new forces untainted by the old regime, might crucially impact on developmental outcomes in the respective states or localities. Scholars have, for example, pointed to the contrast between the high performing Czech Republic, where thorough systemic changes occurred and the communist elite was 'practically thrown out of power', and the extreme case of backward and stagnating Belarus where both the elite makeup and the 'modes of government' have remained communist (Frane and Matevž 2002: 436, 437). At the same time, even if the old party *nomenklatura* may have lost office, the 'new' forces elected on the wave of change may have actually come from the old managerial elite and now use the resources of public office for private gain and whose 'commitment to ... democratic and market values is highly suspect'.[30] In such a scenario, bureaucratic allocation, and not markets, will continue to be the defining feature of the local economies (Walder 2003).

With regard to the backgrounds of local elites, our own findings are mixed. Mayors in some of our higher performance towns, such as Staraya Russa, actually came from the old Soviet *nomenklatura*, while senior local functionaries in some economically low performing towns, as in the Czech Republic's Ústí, were resolutely opposed to any involvement of the old elites in local decision-making. Our focus on institutional arrangements for party representation in local councils, the balance between the executive and representative branches of local power, and arrangements to depoliticise local decision-making, is therefore more appropriate in our view than a simple look at the background of the local elite. We therefore concur with other scholars of post-communist change who found that it is not the persistence of the old elite per se, or the respective merits of the old versus new forces, but the establishment of a 'dynamic balance between two or more pillars of the political elite' that is important for positive developmental outcomes (Frane and Matevž 2002: 449). Again, our evidence suggests that political institutions and their effects on partisanship in local decision-making are central to striking or, alternatively, undermining such a balance.

The link with national parties

In the preceding discussion we have suggested that in countries where party systems are more institutionalised, such as the Czech Republic and Hungary, national party political factors affect local electoral dynamics. But if we look at the other dimension of the possible influence of national politics on local performance, namely national government financial and economic support for localities, the empirical record is mixed.

Our findings only partly support the hypothesis that the correspondence between national and local party systems affects performance variations. What does seem to make a difference for success or failure in generating economic support for a given locality is the skill of the mayor in exploiting political connections with the national party of power. Sydney Tarrow's classic study of centre–periphery relations in France and Italy suggests the conditions under which the central–local political links may be exploited differently in various institutional or political settings. Tarrow distinguished between systems with *a*-political civil services and clientelistic ones where the bureaucracy is politicised and rewards are distributed 'to the benefit of friends of the government' (1977). 'Clientelism', writes Tarrow 'is an irrational and unpredictable way of distributing resources, since it mixes political preferment with more objective factors in awarding contracts, locating public works, or giving jobs out to the constituents'. In such systems, the role of the mayor becomes crucial in securing central funding for the community (Tarrow 1977: 197–8, 138).

Of our countries with more institutionalised party systems, Hungary most closely approximates Tarrow's clientelistic system with its implications for central–local relations. There are numerous anecdotal accounts, as well as concrete evidence of the central government allocating grants to localities with mayors of the same political colour as the national government. Such practices only concern addressed or targeted grants, including those involving EU PHARE and similar funds, disbursed by the central ministries. These grants admittedly represent a small portion of central funding for municipalities,[31] but considering that they concern matching capital investment and regional development grants they can nonetheless make a big difference for a particular locality.[32] According to such schemes, local governments come up with a share of their own funding required for a particular project, while the rest, which could be as high as 70 per cent, comes from sectoral ministries. The local governments must prepare special applications for such funding, which are then reviewed on an ostensibly non-political and impartial basis. The government ministries play a key role in the application selection process. The ministries are also increasingly influential players in the regional development councils, which exist at regional, county and sub-county levels, and which handle the allocation of most of the EU and PHARE funding to the localities.

Despite the ostensible impartiality of the ministerial actors in grant-related decision-making, it is frequently discretionary and politicised with localities whose mayors are party affiliates of the ruling national government enjoying preferential treatment in the process. The FIDESZ government of Viktor Orbán elected in 1998 became notorious for such clientelistic practices.[33] According to the estimates of a respectable Hungarian academic journal, over 70 per cent of all targeted grants in 2001 went to localities with loyal mayors, with 17.59 per cent going to those with independents and only 12.3 per cent to those run by the opposition.[34]

In line with the above tendencies, in Szolnok, most of the respondents indicated that the 'connections' of the mayor Ferenc Szalai to national politicians played a key role in their decision to cast the vote for him in 1998. Not only was Szalai affiliated with the then ruling FIDESZ party, but the family of the wife of FIDESZ Prime Minister Viktor Orbán came from Szolnok. At the time of the electoral campaign, Szalai promised to exploit these connections, while national politicians pledged the city concrete benefits, such as the building of a highway and the modernisation of the dilapidated airplane landing facility. But none of these promises came to fruition, a fact that, as local observers like to point out, contrasts with the ability of FIDESZ mayors in other depressed towns of Jász-Nagykun-Szolnok County, such as Debrecen, to 'bring home the bacon' (Tarrow 1977: 211). There is evidence supporting the contention that the county as a whole benefited quite well from targeted grants under the previous FIDESZ government, ranking tenth in terms of the amount of targeted funding that it received in 2001. The only significant grant that Szolnok received was 545,000 forints for rebuilding the town's waste disposal facility.[35]

The disappointment with Szalai's failure to profit from his political connections and to exploit the patron–client grant-making system is illustrated by a quote from the town's new head of the Economic Department. He argued:

> We could have started some kind of development during the last four years, especially because we had a FIDESZ local government in Szolnok, just like the central government in Budapest. There were expectations with regard to this FIDESZ government. After 1994 there were more and more opportunities to obtain EU funds for example … In general half of economic planning is about politics. If economic lobbying works, political lobbying also works. When there are forty-three applications of similar quality and you can only provide for ten, how do you rank them? There are several aspects in this ranking and one aspect is definitely political.[36]

Partly dovetailing with the above argument that the mayor's relations with national politicians are seen as crucial for the local economy, in Szolnok there was the highest agreement among the largest entrepreneurs surveyed that conflicts between the mayor and the central authorities hamper local economic development. The results of the 2002 elections, which brought to power a socialist mayor, illustrate this disappointment with the previous mayor, but also faith in his or her party political role in centre–local relations. In Sopron, the mayor was more successful in exploiting his links with the national FIDESZ government. Despite the fact that Sopron is smaller and more economically developed than Szolnok, in 2001 it was able to attract a larger amount of targeted funding from the central government.[37]

In Russia and Poland, the impact of national-level politics on the localities is weaker. In both these states, however, there is a stronger impact of regional-level political and electoral dynamics on the respective towns considering that the regions in Russia, a federal state, and the *powiat* level in Poland, are also institutionally stronger than the *meso* level in the Czech Republic or Hungary. Significantly, the regional level is also endowed with important fiscal decision-making powers vis-à-vis the local level, a fact which strengthens the political link between the two administrative tiers. In Poland, in both Jelenia Góra and Biała Podlaska, the *powiat* authorities were blamed for exercising political favouritism in disbursing funds to the localities. A respondent in Jelenia Góra, for example, maintained: 'It is important whether the *wojewoda* and the mayor come from the same party or not.' In Russia, fiscal decision-making is concentrated in the regions, and there is considerable political discretion as to how funds are allocated to various localities. For example, Balashov, which is considered to be within the Saratov *oblast* an economically successful town, obtained the status of a 'subsidised' locality, a fact attributed to friendly relations between the governor and the town's mayor.

Institutional arrangements to depoliticise decision-making

Our findings suggest that the introduction of 'impartial' or 'technocratic' managerial positions in the local administration could offset the politicisation of local decision-making and policy implementation. The setting up of ad hoc or more formal consultative mechanisms, with the respective individuals free to pursue long-term developmental objectives irrespective of political pressures, could likewise have a positive impact on local performance.

In the Czech Republic, Karviná delegated functions related to the implementation of key economic development objectives to expert or 'non-political' bodies. In 1998, the government economic department made an agreement with a private company to help implement the economic strategy. The Karviná city government also solicited several surveys of the local economy, which the local government used in policy planning and which served as the basis for its new development strategy.[38] A special centre was also set up at the university specifically aimed at developing small and medium-sized businesses in town. Other consultative bodies, involving external actors, such as the Commission for Economic Development, likewise ensured that political figures would not be the sole decision-makers in the area of economic development.

By contrast, in Ústí, no impartial implementation or consultative mechanisms were set up. This corresponds to the ODS dictum whereby parties are seen as the most important and legitimate pillars of the political system, hence the distrust of 'so-called experts', 'intellectuals', and 'civil society'. This mentality is reflected in the fact that rather than entrusting a professional agency with the task of economic planning, the mayor, a political figure, was responsible for much of the relevant planning and implementation work in the town.[39] The weight of politicians in various policy bodies was also not matched by the presence of non-political actors. The Strategic Development Committee, for example, largely consisted of political figures, while such professionals as architects or urban planners were underrepresented or marginalised. In contrast to Karviná, the town also failed to establish effective consultative arrangements with the local academic community, most notably Ústí University (UJEP).[40]

Likewise, in Szolnok no professional advisory bodies existed in the local government until 2003. A special town development bureau staffed with 'impartial administrators' and specifically trained in the skills of applying for external funding was established only in 2003 following the victory of the MSZP (Hungarian Socialist Party). The development advisory bodies that had been previously set up were along party lines. For example, the owner of a local hotel maintained that a local government committee on tourism established in 2002 of which he is a member is composed of politicians nominated by parties. 'It isn't my fault', maintained the entrepreneur, who is also a member of the FIDESZ party. 'I would have preferred to sit on a body with more businessmen than politicians.' 'I would have been happier if there were more professionals', he maintained.[41]

In addition to the lack of full-time 'expert' agencies in local government specifically charged with long-term economic development policy implementation, there is also a striking lack of less formal consultative mechanisms involving concerned agencies. When asked about the extent of involvement in local economic decision-making, the owner of one of the best hotels in Szolnok complained: 'They never involved businesses, neither during the first eight years, nor during the last four years. Although businesses would need this and would be happy to help.'[42] The executive of another large enterprise maintained: 'We are among the five largest taxpayers in Szolnok but our director did not know the previous mayor. We don't know the new one either. She hasn't tried to contact us yet. We have never turned to the local government with a request either ... The local government hasn't involved us in any kind of decision-making or economic planning.'[43]

In Sopron, unlike in Szolnok, 'professional' business associations, including the Chamber of Commerce, the Industrial Association and the Manager Club, are engaged in much tighter interaction with the local government attending council deliberations and committee meetings. Sopron has a Council for Interest Reconciliation, which meets every month and involves local government representatives, small and large businesses, employer associations and employees. The main purpose of the forum is to discuss the major decisions considered by the local government.

The two Polish towns likewise differed in the choice of policy implementation and consultative mechanisms. In Jelenia Góra there are regular monthly meetings between local councillors and the Directors' Council, which is a business association aimed at 'exchange of views'. By contrast, in Biała Podlaska, the planning commission was almost exclusively staffed with local politicians and did not include members of the local business, cultural or intellectual community. Accordingly, it took over three and a half years of debate for the council to pass the development strategy in 2000. Many business respondents in Biała Podlaska maintained that contacts with the local government were more accidental than regular in character.

Significantly, the Russian town of Staraya Russa maintained some of the most intensive consultative mechanisms for policy formulation and implementation. The practice originated with the Novgorod regional government, which is a pioneer in Russia in social and business partnerships. In 1998 it adopted a law on social partnerships aimed at encouraging cooperation between state and local government bodies and private and non-profit organisations.[44] There is also a so-called Social Chamber established as a public forum for 'all social forces interested in non-crisis development, in search of mutually acceptable decisions and in their timely correction' and which scrutinises all legislation before it is passed by the regional Duma (Petro 2004).

Social Chamber-type consultative forums now exist also at district level, including in Staraya Russa. Similar to the above regional frameworks, Staraya Russa's administration maintains strong informal partnership links with both business and non-profit organisations. The deputy head of the Staraya Russa medical and recreational facility, one of the largest contributors to the local budget, for example, also sits on the city's urban planning committee. In general, most businesses that we interviewed admitted to being consulted on major economic decisions made by the local government. Representatives of the largest enterprises, for example, participated in the development of the economic strategy. Although the strategy was solicited from and drafted by an independent research institute in Moscow, prior to its adoption the city administration solicited inputs from local businesses.

No such consultative mechanisms exist in Balashov. Balashov, a town located in eastern Russia, is actually very similar in this respect to Szolnok, located in our westernmost country. When asked if the town has engaged 'external experts' in developing a local economic strategy, the head of the economic department of the administration maintained: 'We are all highly qualified people here, and we don't need external experts to help us.'[45] Significantly, there were no formal or informal consultative mechanisms or forums that would engage the business community in local decision-making on a more or less regular basis. The Balashov textile plant, which is now a private shareholding enterprise, illustrates this point. Although the city to a large extent depends on revenues generated by the plant, according to its director there is limited contact with the local administration, and this is also the case with other enterprises in town.

The impact of civil society on local politics

The within-country contrasts in the degree of inclusiveness of the local decision-making process and cooperation of local actors actually correspond to broader regional variations observed by other scholars of post-communist politics and attributed to historical, cultural or other social-contextual factors. In Hungary, Szolnok's record of high volatility of voter preferences, for example, corresponds to broader patterns observed by the country's political geographers in the economically depressed eastern areas. While western Hungary and Budapest have been classified as 'stable and politically mature', and as having high citizen turnout rates at elections and ideologically consistent party preferences, eastern Hungary has been described as an 'unstable, politically less motivated and mature region, with generally low turnout rates and considerable swings in party preference' (Kovács 2001: 270). A recent survey also found that the more developed cities closer to Hungary's western border generally scored higher on key democracy and civil society indicators, such as the likelihood of holding public forums and discussions. Another study suggested that in Hungary the density of civil associations positively correlated with the affluence of the locality and the size of its budget, with the western areas scoring higher on key civil society indicators (Soós and Kálmán 2002: 45–7).

Our qualitative evidence also suggests strong contrasts between the generally apathetic nature of local actors, and weaker levels of cooperation between them in the eastern town of Szolnok, on the one hand, and greater community participation in local affairs in the western town of Sopron, on the other. In Szolnok, the businessmen that we interviewed admitted to being weakly or not at all involved in business or other associations. The businesses showed a striking lack of awareness of local economic policies, or a lack of familiarity with local government functionaries. For example when asked to name the issues that have elicited the biggest debate in town in recent years, a senior executive of one of the town's largest companies maintained: 'We don't know. Don't watch local TV or read local newspapers. We don't know the local gossip.'[46] Another entrepreneur, when asked about his opinion with regard to the economic policies of the newly elected mayor, declared: 'I haven't heard of anything.'[47]

Sopron contrasts starkly with Szolnok in terms of the involvement of local actors in local government decision-making. One example is the decision by businessmen of various political orientations to come up with a common pool of money that would help reduce the city's debt that came as a result of the speculative 'Globex affair'. 'Now everyone can show what a local patriot town this is', maintained one local businessman in this context.[48] Another example that the local respondents gave is that Sopron is unique among cities that are not regional capitals in that it has its own Chamber of Commerce in addition to the one located in the county capital Győr.[49]

We also found strong contrasts in the levels of local citizen participation in the improvement of social welfare. We devised a simple test for establishing if variations exist in this respect. Local government actors involved in social policies were asked if they solicit charity donations from businessmen, and businessmen were in turn asked if such solicitations were made by the local government, and if so, with what result. This test revealed significant variations between the two towns. In Szolnok, the officials scoffed at the question and reported that no special solicitations were made. The businessmen in turn reported that the local government does not generally approach them with such requests. The donations that they reported were ad hoc in nature. By contrast, in Sopron, the local government, businesses and NGOs responded positively to the question of whether they regularly engaged in charity activities. Most of the senior executives of the town's largest enterprises that we interviewed also maintained that they organise or participate in joint charity events involving the local churches, the NGO community and municipal officials.[50] These events range from the annual 'charity ball', attended by the local notables, to the more frequent meetings organised by the owner of the John Bull Pub, a well known local community activist.

In the Czech Republic, there are reportedly no significant regional variations to the extent observed in Poland or Hungary. But one possible influence on local societal activism is the record of post-Second World War displacement of ethnic Germans, which affected some areas of Czechoslovakia particularly strongly. Northern Bohemia, of which Ústí nad Labem forms a part, was particularly hard-hit by this displacement. After the Germans were deported en masse to Germany, in a desperate effort to bring labour force to the region, the Czech government encouraged the settlement in Ústí of Czechs, but also Slovaks, Roma and other ethnic groups, with no roots in the locality. This record might explain the relatively weaker levels of social cooperation and engagement in local politics in Ústí compared to Karviná, where no such popular dislocations took place.

In Poland, scholars have observed significant regional variations in levels of civil society development. A recent study by Paweł Świaniewicz, for example, found that local government performance varies depending on whether a given municipality is located in the eastern or western part of the country. Those in the east (with the exception of some regions in the southeast) scored significantly lower on many indicators of performance, such as the propensity of local government to take bribes, its budget promptness and the quality of administrative services. Significantly, the eastern areas also ranked lower on the indicators of political stability, such as the turnover of mayors. Our own case studies of Biała Podlaska and Jelenia Góra, the eastern and the western town, respectively, would support this contention further. In Biała Podlaska, decision-making is more politicised, while the involvement of NGO, business or other community actors in municipal affairs is very low. In Jelenia Góra, by contrast, the town's policy agreement and implementation success could be largely explained by the inclusive nature of local government decision-making, and the presence of various formal and informal mechanisms of cooperation involving various public and private actors.

As in Hungary, the developmental disparities of the two Polish towns complicate the drawing of causal inferences. Like Szolnok, Biała Podlaska is a less economically advanced town located in the east, and further from borders with developed EU states than is the more prosperous western town of Jelenia Góra. Świaniewicz's study, however, found that levels of economic development and modernisation of the respective regions do not provide an adequate explanation for this discrepancy. Instead, he argues that the differences in the maturity of civil society, which are in turn arguably influenced by the variable historical trajectories of Polish regions, prove to be a much stronger explanatory factor for performance variations. Świaniewicz suggests that the formerly Russian ruled areas in eastern Poland continue to be influenced by the more centralist and authoritarian tradition of the absolutist Russian tsarist state which discouraged the development of civil society. This contrasts with western Poland, where the record of a much earlier development of the bourgeoisie and territorial self-government in Prussia and Austro-Hungary-ruled areas fostered a greater degree of civic consciousness and engagement (Świaniewicz 2001).

Within Russia itself, some scholars have argued that the variable historical record of Russia's constituent regions has likewise had an impact on civil society. The Novgorod region, where Staraya Russa is located, has a particularly strong claim to a 'civic tradition' arguably influencing its present-day political development. From the early twelfth century until 1471, Novgorod practiced a republican form of government involving the election of princes and magistrates, neighbourhood and district assemblies that sent their delegates to the city-wide popular assembly, the *veche*, and a confederation or even subsidiary-type form of territorial administration in an area that became the largest state in Europe since the Holy Roman Empire. More than any other area in Russia, Novgorod was also subject to extensive Western influences, which manifested themselves in the proliferation of trading guilds similar to those that existed in medieval European cities, and the existence of educational establishments and grammar schools. Despite the republic's subjugation by Muscovy in the late fifteenth century, elements of the city's democratic traditions, such as the practice of popular election of district self-governments, continued to resurface in the following centuries when the liberalisation of the Tsarist regime allowed this (Petro 2004).

Although Novgorod Velikiy's glorious past dates back to the twelfth–fiteenth centuries, as one scholar of post-communist trans-formations wrote, 'national memories or even myths of a democratic past

may facilitate popular acceptance of democratic political structures'
(Parrott 1997: 11). In Novgorod, the regional elite has made a conscious
effort to exploit these historical memories of the 'cradle of Russian
democracy' in an effort to gain popular support for economic reforms
and to lure in Western investors. Scholars of Russian regional politics
have debated the extent to which the region is actually more democratic
or 'civic' than Russia's other regions. The above discussion of the political
processes within the region supports the contention that, as in many
other Russian regions, there is little tolerance for political opposition in
Novgorod.

But there also appears to be a genuine interest on behalf of the
regional administration in the development of the NGO community
and the inclusion of NGOs and businesses in the regional decision-
making process.[51] This conscious policy is in turn replicated at the local
level, and cooperation between various local actors extends beyond the
official 'social chambers'. Local businessmen, for example, reported
regular donations for local charity causes, in a practice that contrasts
with Balashov, where cooperation between businesses, NGOs and the
local government is very weak. In Staraya Russa, the social department
of the local administration also makes regular solicitations from
businessmen in an effort to build 'community spirit'.

A cynical observer might suggest that such 'solicitations' are no more
than an official racket, of the kind practiced by the Moscow Mayor Yuriy
Luzhkov and reminiscent of the Soviet-style *dobrovol'no-prinuditel'nye*, or
'voluntary-coerced' acts. But the Saratov *oblast*'s town of Balashov pursues
no such policies. Another example of genuine grassroots rather than
'top-driven' involvement in local community affairs is the childcare
facility run by Leonid Kirillov. Kirillov was originally seen as a nuisance
by the Staraya Russa local government considering his staunch criticism
of the archaic municipal Soviet-style foster care policies. In cooperation
with other local activists, his lobbying at both regional and local levels
subsequently resulted in the reform of regional and local childcare
systems. Kirillov, who has been awarded a special Soros Foundation Open
Society Institute prize of *Podvizhnik*, an old Russian word for a citizen
concerned with the well being of the community, is now well known
Russia-wide, as well as in child welfare communities in Europe.[52]

Conclusion

The foregoing discussion has shown that party systems have had a strong
impact on local performance. While their impact has been weaker the
more eastwards the location of a given country, with parties playing a

negligible role in Russian local governments, their impact is stronger in states with more developed local party systems. The aspects of party systems most relevant for explaining performance are the degree of party institutionalisation; the constellations of parties in local councils and their ideological makeup; and the connections between local and national-level politics. The explanatory power of these factors as weighed against the other sets of independent variables, namely socioeconomic and structural institutional ones, is discussed in the following, concluding chapter.

7
Conclusions

Local government matters. Uncontroversial as it sounds, there remains a considerable amount of debate as to the question 'in what way?' Answering this question has been particularly pertinent in post-communist states. Initially, in the fledgling democracies of Central and Eastern Europe, as indeed in many established ones in the West, there has been an almost unquestioning assumption of the normative desirability of decentralisation, which coloured both the processes of institution building and the academic and policy debates on the matter. Some of the initial institutional design choices influenced by these assumptions proved to be false early on in the process, such as the hyper-fragmentation of Hungary's local units leading to a multitude of self-governing, but powerless municipalities. But many other aspects of local governance, such as institutional design, relations with state authorities, finance, and so forth, and their impact on local perform-ance, have continued to be under-researched.

This study may be called a second-generation exploration of local governance in post-communist settings. While in the early to mid-1990s scholars were only in a position to discuss the initial political debates on, the first elections to, and processes of institution-building of local government, the timing of this study has allowed us to make the initial steps in the exploration of the actual longer term impact of local institutions. Thus, while critical of the assumptions or findings of the earlier studies, the authors of this monograph are very much aware of the objective limitations and constraints facing researchers of the earlier institution-building phase. Likewise, we are conscious of the possible weaknesses of the present study considering the short period of time that has passed since the institutions were set up, and the relevant methodological challenges. Our findings should nevertheless contribute to the debates on local performance and the reassessment of earlier arguments with regard to decentralisation in post-communist settings.

In contrast to much of the earlier scholarship on local government in the newly democratising states of Central and Eastern Europe, this study has examined not just cross-country, but also within-nation variations. Such a research design appears to be logical if we take as a starting point the premise that local government does make a difference. Nevertheless, many other works on the subject have explored the various aspects of local government as an institution without making a distinction between developments within separate localities. For example, scholars have conducted survey research on the 'responsiveness' of local government as a whole, or the degree of general citizen involvement in local governance in a given state. While providing rich insights into the decentralisation processes in the new democracies, such a methodology does not allow us to assess the extent to which an individual locality might make a difference for the local population within the broadly set national legal and institutional frameworks. If local government developmental efforts can make a substantial impact on a locality's developmental trajectory, perhaps it would be less appropriate to conduct state-level comparative analysis of local performance, and more logical to compare performance at the level of municipalities across various national settings.

With only eight cases, it is difficult of course to make generalisations about the other towns in the four countries. Nevertheless, as we discussed in Chapter 1, our cities are fairly representative of the small and medium town municipalities and the issues that they have had to grapple with in the post-communist decade and a half. More research is needed, but our case selection and methodology should allow us to make inferences about municipal performance in general, and to hope that our findings would stand up in other localities as well.

Surprisingly, we found that the performance record of the Russian town of Staraya Russa was more comparable to its Central European counterparts than to Balashov, the other Russian town that we researched. At the same time, the Szolnok municipality in Hungary, one of the most developed post-communist states and one with arguably the most progressive local government, lags behind or is comparable to many of the other less advanced cities we examined, including in Russia. Such a methodology has allowed us to draw broader conclusions about the impact of social-economic and infrastructural, institutional or political factors on local performance, and about how their constellation constrains or enables the localities as they adapt to new post-communist realities.

We found that the socioeconomic conditions, the structural 'givens' of a given town only partly account for performance outcomes, and our findings in this regard are mixed. A western location is a definite advantage that facilitates the localities' developmental efforts. How a western location translates into better outcomes is illustrated by the examples we gave of EU cross-border cooperation and other developmental projects in pre-accession countries. Even in non-candidate countries, such as Russia, the more western localities experience greater diffusion of Western influences, as is evident from Staraya Russa's developmental ethic and, in social policy, the exposure of its social professionals to Western training and ideas about child and family welfare. Even the influence of the western location factor has to be qualified however. For example, Hungary's border town of Sopron was a very modest economic performer: while it may rank high on 'outcomes' considering the general prosperity of the broader area in which it is located, and the constellation of its industries, it was relatively low on 'outputs', that is, the performance of the local government. Likewise, such factors as the broader regional environments, transportation links and the socialist economic inheritance do not adequately explain local variations, and assertions about their impact should be highly qualified. In our case sample, some of the more remote towns with less developed transport infrastructure performed better than others with more favourable structural conditions. At the same time, towns that at the time of transition found themselves with similar inheritances, such as communist-era large enterprises, ended up having quite different developmental trajectories. For example, in the towns of Staraya Russa, Karviná, Szolnok and Ústí nad Labem the local economies were overly dependent on large enterprises. The towns that made a consistent effort to diversify the local economies in particular by stimulating small and medium-sized enterprise development, such as Staraya Russa or Karviná, by the end of the 1990s could compare more favourably in terms of policy outcomes than their counterparts with similar starting conditions, but where the local administrations failed to agree on long-term developmental objectives. These examples also suggest that the structure of local economies, dispersed versus concentrated, agrarian versus industrial, also do not hold up as the main explanation for performance differences.

The national frameworks shaping local institutions and regulating local government of course do matter. Our findings, however, do not always correspond to the normative prescriptions regarding decentralisation. More centralist arrangements in fact appear to be desirable in certain policy fields, such as social service provision. But excessive regulation and rigidity in task assignment between various levels of government may also have significant negative consequences. Enveloping local governments in a web of regulations and mandates does not guarantee compliance with the law or the performance of all state-required services. Poland, for example, has a high degree of local autonomy in the sense of the magnitude of tasks the municipalities have to perform, but this autonomy hardly translates into high quality service delivery. The Czech Republic, where social service provision is more centralised, but where task assignment is more flexible, by contrast maintains some of the best social service practices. Another finding is that more centralist arrangements in the form of stronger state legal review or lesser ones where the courts play a stronger role appear to have a negligible, if any, impact on local performance.

The systems of intergovernmental finance likewise do not always account for divergent outcomes in social policy fields or economic promotion. Cities located within the same state have very similar budget sizes, suggesting that equalisation mechanisms work very well in all four countries. There are of course some well-known differences in intergovernmental finance. The sources of funding, the method of allocation (annual or fixed), and the amount of expenditure going to various fields vary between the four countries. These broader variations between the four states are nevertheless not sufficient to explain within-country differences, that is, the variable performance of towns operating within one common framework of national intergovernmental finance. For example, the Czech method of financing social services, whereby much stress is laid on impartial tenders administered by the central state, helps explain why the Czech Republic in general compares very favourably to the other states. But it does not explain why one Czech town was successful in setting up a very modern system of social service provision, and another one did not. Likewise, it does not explain why the more punishing Czech and Hungarian systems of national tax distribution did not prevent some cities from developing better than others, or why some towns did not take advantage of the less equalising Polish system.

The most plausible explanation for observed differences relates to political factors shaping local policy choices and implementation. In particular, we found that political parties or party systems might influence local performance in the following ways. On the one hand, a higher degree of party institutionalisation appears to positively affect performance as it reduces the likelihood of frequent and unpredictable swings in voter preferences and hence frequent party turnover in local councils. On the other hand, a higher institutionalisation of party systems might strengthen the link between national and local politics. This factor may also negatively affect the stability of local party systems. This is because local voter preferences may be guided less by considerations of the performance of the local council than by party political constellations at the national level.

Another link with national-level politics is that in countries with a higher degree of party institutionalisation, parties also provide more stable and established channels of political recruitment. For the politically ambitious, it may mean that a local political office is but one step on the career ladder leading to national level politics. This fact may negatively affect the stability of local administrative personnel, while also encouraging local office holders to politicise local decision-making as it increases the visibility of the respective actors. A factor that may offset this tendency is the presence of strong and established local parties. Overall, the constellations of parties in the local councils, even if we consider them in isolation from national-level politics, do impact on performance. These findings are straightforward and confirm the theoretical postulates about party systems in other settings. The absence of parties with stable majorities in the council leads to policy gridlocks and conflict. The presence of strong centre parties encourages ideological polarisation and issue outbidding. Ideological polarisation in turn encourages a purge of administrative personnel following the victory of the party previously in opposition. It also encourages newly elected local governments to discard policies associated with the previous government.

The above arguments do not uniformly apply to all issue areas of local performance, however. Social policies, unlike economic promotion, might not be affected as strongly by political factors at the council decision-making phase. This finding challenges the 'partisan' model of local decision-making advanced by scholars of local government in other, particularly Western European and American settings, which suggests that left–right political ideological variations in the council or executive preferences may significantly affect social spending and service priorities (Clark 1985; Aiken and Martinotti 1985). It also supports the findings of some other studies of post-communist states, suggesting that the 'old timer' mentality continues to be a strong feature among leaders. This finding has important implications for our understanding of performance in post-communist states. It suggests that a strong egalitarian and socially-oriented tradition continues to influence national institutional frameworks for social services, as well as the local social policy choices that the localities make within the framework of nationally set standards.

The above findings are also related to debates on the post-communist turnover of the local elite. Greater continuity of the local elite, even that with an old Soviet party or managerial background, might be better for local performance than rapid turnover, as is demonstrated in towns like Staraya Russa, which still has a mayor from the Soviet party *nomenklatura*. An alternative example is the Czech town of Ústí, where ideologically inspired intolerance of politicians from the communist era ironically did not perform a particularly good service to the city in terms of developmental outcomes on its transition to capitalism. Again, it is not the background as such – communist or non-communist – that matters, but the institutional mechanisms that would ensure a rate of turnover of administrative personnel that is not so frequent as to disrupt long-term policy planning. These mechanisms should also affect the degree of politicisation of local appointments and encourage or discourage the mayor to purge local professional staff because of their party affiliations.

Our findings on parties challenge the spirit of the democratisation related institutional reforms in post-communist contexts, whereby party development at both national and local levels was seen to be intrinsic to democratic consolidation. Our study does not belittle the importance of party systems for the *representation* aspects of democracy. But we suggest that while desirable at the national level, and while important from the point of view of *representation*, party presence in local governments may not necessarily have a positive impact on *performance*, the key concern of this book. As a cautionary note, one may suggest that this argument holds true for the early phase of transitions in these countries, where party systems continue to be weakly institutionalised.

In both economic promotion and social policy, institutional and political factors are not always adequate explanations of particular performance outcomes, however. For example, the institutional factors tell us little about why party system development took such a different course in our towns. Biała Podlaska and Jelenia Góra may appear to have similar party systems and may be similarly influenced by the respective national political contexts. As our case studies have shown, a more nuanced look at local politics reveals significant differences. Voters in such towns as Szolnok and Biała Podlaska appear to be more prone to change of electoral preferences; local parties and electoral blocks less stable and durable; and political dynamics within the council conflictual and polarised, as in the case of Szolnok, and personalised as in the case of Biała Podlaska. By contrast, decision-making in Sopron and Jelenia Góra is less politicised; local parties more durable; and turnover of administrative personnel less frequent.

Our findings suggest that there may be a possible link between the above variations and the various cultural or historical trajectories of the towns and broader regions in which they are located. A systematic evaluation of political culture, civil society, social capital (Putnam 1993) or the historical traditions of different settings affecting local party development would require more research into local citizen or leadership values, patterns of civil cooperation, density of civic associations, and so forth, which is beyond the scope of this study. Still, what limited evidence we have suggests that longer term historically-conditioned political cultural factors, that is, those related to patterns of historical development of the respective areas, their imperial incorporation, or, in the case of Russia, exposure to West European civilisation, do affect various aspects of performance (Fish 1999). These influences are felt in the institutional choices that are made, party political dynamics, the willingness of local governments to cooperate with civil society, the activeness of civil society itself, and the civic consciousness of businesses and other local leaders. For example, in the western town of Sopron, the politicisation of local decision-making appears to have been mitigated by a strong tradition of trust and civic cooperation: businessmen are involved in regular networks of interaction, hold annual 'charity balls', and are willing to pool their resources to bail the local government out of the 'Globex affair' fiscal mess. This contrasts starkly with the eastern town of Szolnok, where an atmosphere of mistrust and conflict prevails among local businessmen and decision-makers, and where the local government suffers from high administrative turnover after an election. And in Staraya Russa, in Kirillov and other local social activists we likewise see the confirmation of the political culture thesis when we contrast it with Saratov, which lacks a historical tradition of civic engagement, as indeed exposure to the West dating back to the Middle Ages of the kind that the Novgorod region can boast (Petro 2004).

One overall conclusion that could be drawn from the above discussion is that performance could be a function of the ability of actors of political and civil society to influence local processes. To put it differently, performance could be affected by the degree to which the existing intergovernmental and finance systems, national and local party systems, as well as local institutional arrangements, which may vary from town to town, enable or constrain local actors. In terms of the impact of national factors, in countries such as Hungary, where intergovernmental finance is characterised by a high degree of softness, that is, where allocations are made annually, political bargaining becomes crucial. In the Czech Republic, the process of impartial tenders for social funding in which

NGOs compete against each other serves to develop the third sector and enables the influence of NGOs on local policies. In contexts of weak levels of institutionalisation of local government and of institutional frameworks regulating social and economic policies, which continues to be characteristic of many post-communist contexts, such as Russia, political or civic actors and their leadership skills may play a particularly strong role. Consider the role of the director of the children's home Nadezhda in Staraya Russa, who initiated the reform of not just local and regional, but also the archaic Soviet-era federal legislation on childcare. The fact that there was greater flexibility in the legal frameworks for child protection, with the regional government encouraging experimentation, as well as the presence of activist civic leaders, in our view accounts for the striking performance success of Staraya Russa in the area of social services.

Our findings should be encouraging for local government practitioners who seek to make a difference for their locality irrespective of the multitude of objective challenges. Neither the disadvantageous infrastructural inheritance, nor remote geographic location, predetermines a municipality to failure, although a western location does facilitate local government developmental efforts. Likewise, a distorted economic structure, shared by many of the post-communist localities, should not be seen as an obstacle to long-term economic development. Finally, even within the same nationally set institutional and legal frameworks, individual localities can make a difference for the well-being of their populations, providing that local political pressures are channelled such that they encourage rather than constrain local social and economic development efforts.

Notes

1 Methodology and case selection

1. These theories suggest that the larger dominant economic units wield considerable influence over the well-being of the locality as a whole, as they provide the employment and other benefits on which a given city depends.
2. Institutional analyses have been a particular growth industry for scholarship of post-communist states, considering the variable implications of different institutional choices for their prospects of democratic consolidation (Offe 1996). The literature on post-communist institutional choices, however, has largely dealt with national-level institutions. Local government has received much less extensive treatment aside from the many descriptive or policy prescriptive studies.
3. He drew the concept from the work of James Coleman (1990).
4. Study by Rossi et al. (1974) (cf. Clark et al. 1981).
5. One possibility is the approach that Robert Dahl used in his classic study of New Haven. Dahl chose to study policies arguably most salient for the local citizenry, namely urban redevelopment and public education, as well as political nominations. A classic study of Birmingham by Kenneth Newton focused on three issue areas: housing, education and race relations (1976). These issue areas are important, concern large numbers of people and involve substantial sums (Judge 1995: 22). Dahl's focus on these fields has been criticised on the grounds that other important issue areas were left out of the research because they were turned into 'non-issues' by certain business or other interests in the city (Judge 1995: 17). Numerous other methodological complexities of evaluating local performance exist (Clark et al. 1981; Clark and Ferguson 1981).
6. For an overview of the impact of decentralization on social policy in Hungary, see also Kremer et al. (2002).
7. Other studies provide further evidence of this practice (Kopányi et al. 1999: 9, 21).
8. As of 1989, 16.9 per cent people lived in cities of up to 50,000 people (considered to be small); 11.8 per cent in cities of 50–99,000 people (medium); and 71.3 per cent in cities of over 100,000 people (large cities).
9. http://www.Szfki.hu/meco27/venue.htm (accessed 15 December 2001).
10. http://www.sopron.hu/maneu-piknik/elozm_uk.htm (accessed 15 December 2001).
11. HCSO.Regionaldata.1999.http://www.ksh.hu/pls/ksh/docs/eng/free/e6/fe62513.html (accessed 15 December 2001).
12. http://www.gyaloglo.hu/megye/jasnsz_e.htm;http://gyaloglo.hu/megye/gorms_e.htm(accessed 15 December 2001).
13. Czech Statistical Office, http://www.czso.cz (accessed 15 December 2001).
14. Czech Statistical Office, Ostrava branch, http://www.czso.cz/kraje/ov/publika/8102/2001/q4/8102q4b1.pdf (accessed 15 December 2001).

15. http://www.rusline.com/oblast/novgorod/novgorod.html (accessed 15 December 2001).
16. Approximate figures.
17. http://www.rusline.com/oblast/saratov/gover.html (accessed 15 December 2001).
18. http://www.balashov.san.ru/balashov/index.html (accessed 15 December 2001).
19. *Saratovskaya guberniya*, 2, no. 11 (2000), 11.
20. *Saratovskaya guberniya*, 2, no. 11 (2000), 5.

2 Local government performance in social policy

1. According to the head of the department of social work, 'before 1989, the Czechoslovak social system rather resembled a health care system. The system was focused on stationary centres for elderly people, most social workers were nurses, and these homes for elderly people looked like hospitals where residents were expected to die soon.' Personal interview with Helena Herbstova, May 2002.
2. *1. Komunitní plan péče ve městě a okrese Ústí nad Labem na rok 2001–2003* (Ústí nad Labem: Město Ústí nad Labem, June 2001).
3. Personal interviews, January 2003.
4. This despite the fact that Ústí is similar to the other towns surveyed in terms of personnel shortages. With a total number of 77 employees, the Ústí social administration appears to be very lean compared to other Czech towns of similar size. For example, the number of social administration staff in the town of Liberec is 92; in Olomouc, the town social administration has 109 staff.
5. Personal interview, January 2003.
6. For example, between 2000 and 2002, Spirála successfully applied for funding in the amount of 2,262,400 Czech crowns, or over 75,000 euros, from the national government. Information provided by the Ministry of Social Affairs.
7. According to the plan of communal care, in 2000 the local government advertised a grant to initiate the founding of the Centre. Moreover, the head of the Centre told us that the local government supported the Centre in its search for an appropriate building. Personal interview, January 2003. For details see http://www.volny.cz/spirala.cki/dotace.htm (accessed 30 January 2003).
8. In 2000, the facility's budget amounted to over two million Czech crowns (roughly 70,000 euros).
9. These projects relate to various segments of local society, such as elderly people, hospitals or the unemployed, http://dcul.cz (accessed 30 January 2003).
10. For more details, see the DC's annual reports at http://dcul.cz (accessed 30 January 2003).
11. http://soros.novgorod.ru/grants/IEA718/law/govern/gov009.htm (accessed 18 September 2002).
12. Personal interview with Yevgeny Ryabov, Head of Administration of the City of Staraya Russa and Starorusskiy District, Staraya Russa, 22 January 2002.

13. Laws available from: http://iatp.tsu.ru/grant/mt-34/loaw96.html (1 August 2002); http://www.fw.ru:8101/Law/Texts/govern10.htm (accessed 1 August 2002); http://www.fw.ru:8101/Law/Texts/govern9.htm (accessed 1 August 2002); http://www. fw.ru:8101/Law/Texts/govern26.htm (accessed 1 August 2002).
14. Government provision on 'Social Standards and Norms', adopted in July 1996 and amended in July 2001 is available at http://npa-gov.garweb.ru:8080/public/default.asp (accessed 7 August 2002). For a comprehensive list of laws pertaining to children, see http://vse-vmeste.ru/specialist/legislation.htm (accessed 1 August 2002).
15. Articles about him have appeared in the national press. See, for example, Liliya Mukhamedyarova, 'Staraya Russa. Samyy dobryy gorod na svete', 30 January 2003, http://2003.novayagazeta.ru/nomer/2003/07n/n07n-s21.shtml (accessed 21 May 2003).
16. Personal interview, 22 January 2002. Another of Kirillov's innovations is to create a unified system of childcare that would replace the current system, which divides responsibilities over childcare between education, health and police institutions.
17. Personal interview, Staraya Russa, 22 January 2002.
18. See *Press Centre of Novgorod Administration*, 10 December 2002, http://niac.natm.ru/presscentr.nsf (accessed 6 August 2003).
19. Novgorod *oblast* legislation on children without parents is available from http://www.ngosnews.ru/aro_pgs/law.htm (accessed 24 September 2002).
20. Information available at www.czso.cz.
21. In 1995, Karviná registered 1911 people who, due to insufficient income, were eligible for social benefits. By the end of 2001, the number had risen to 4673. *Sociální problematika–rozsah poskytované podpory z prostředků státu a města, služby sociální péče pro občany města* (Karviná: Město Karviná, odbor sociálních věcí a zdravotnictví, March 2000); *Sociální problematika–rozsah poskytované podpory z prostředků státu a města, služby sociální péče pro občany města* (Karviná: Město Karviná, odbor sociálních věcí a zdravotnictví, February 2002). We would like to thank Blanka Dadoková for making these materials available to us.
22. Information provided by Blanka Dadoková, Head of the Social Department. Personal interview, January 2003.
23. With 27 per cent, the neighbouring town of Havířov, another coal-mining town, ranked second. Information provided by Milan Lipner, Moravian-Silesian Institute for Social Analysis, personal interview, January 2003.
24. Personal interview, January 2003.
25. Personal interview, April 2002.
26. They may live there for up to two years.
27. In 2001, the local government spent 2,627,000 Czech crowns (over 87,500 euros) for the operation of the DMD. In recent years, this sum has slightly increased. *Sociální problematika–rozsah poskytované podpory* (Karviná: Město Karviná, odbor sociálních věcí a zdravotnictví, February 2002), 10. The DMD also applies for financial support from the Ministry of Social Affairs. For instance, in 1998 the DMD received over 155,000 Czech crowns (roughly 5200 euros). In 2000, it obtained 25,000 crowns (800 euros). *Sociální problematika–rozsah poskytované podpory z prostředků státu a města, služby sociální péče pro občany města* (Karviná: Město Karviná, odbor sociálních věcí a zdravotnictví, 1999, 2001).

28. In the last two years, the Ministry has provided SARA with over 2.5 million crowns, or roughly one third of its budget. (Information provided by the Ministry of Social Affairs, Prague.) Regional and local authorities also support the facility financially. For the first time, in 2001 the local government contributed 50,000 crowns (over 1600 euros) to the budget of over 3.1 million (roughly 105,000 euros). Ibid., 11.
29. Personal interview, April 2002.
30. For more detailed information see the Centre's website at www.sweb.cz/pppkarvina/ (accessed 30 January 2003).
31. *Sociální problematika–rozsah poskytované podpory z prostředků státu a města, služby sociální péče pro občany města* (1999).
32. *Sociální problematika–rozsah poskytované podpory z prostředků státu a města, služby sociální péče pro občany města* (1999, 2000).
33. *Sytuacja rodzin jeleniogórskich* (Jelenia Góra: Specjalistyczny Ośrodek Pracy Socjalnej w Jeleniej Górze: Biuletyn SOPS Nr. 8/1999), 39. We would like to thank Barbara Wielichowska for making this study available to us.
34. Ibid., 31. This assessment was given in the district unemployment office report (*Powiatowy Urząd Pracy*), which was included in the study mentioned above, 62.
35. Ibid., 96
36. The local MOPS has 59 employees which is lower than in Ústí, where there are 77 social staff members, although the two towns have similar population sizes.
37. Personal interview, December 2002.
38. Personal interview, December 2002.
39. According to the law, the sale of alcohol is strictly licensed, with all three tiers of self-government participating in the licence fees levied from shop owners and food stores. *Ustawa z dnia 26 października 1982 r., o wychowaniu w trzeźwości i przeciwdziałaniu alkoholizmowi* (Law on the Prevention of Alcoholism, first adopted in 1982).
40. *Budżet miasta na prawach powiatu na 2002 rok* (Jelenia Góra: Urząd Miasta, 2002), 52.
41. *Uchwała Nr 276/ XXIII/ 2000 Rady Miejskiej Jeleniej Góry z dnia 23 maja 2000* (Jelenia Góra: Urząd Miasta, 2000).
42. Apart from the two institutions, there are four stationary facilities for children operated by the *powiat grodzki*: two foster homes and two institutions for married couples.
43. Personal interview with Elżbieta Hamer, December 2002.
44. Personal interview with Elżbieta Hamer, December 2002.
45. For example, the Catholic Church runs at least three youth centres for children. *Budżet miasta na prawach powiatu na 2002 rok* (Jelenia Góra: Urząd Miasta, 2002), 51–3.
46. This is a result of a comparative study conducted in 2000 by the Association of Polish towns. *Pomoc społeczna w Białej Podlaskiej na tle innych miast członkowskich Związku Miast Polskich*. We would like to thank Maria Parafiniuk for making this study available to us. See also *Raport z monitorowania problemów alkoholowych w gminie miejskiej Biała Podlaska 2001* (Biała Podlaska: Urząd Miasta Biała Podlaska, Pełnomocnik ds. Zdrowia i Patologii

Społecznych, 2002); http://www.stat.gov.pl/urzedy/lublin/miesieczne.htm (accessed 30 January 2003).

47. Personal interview, December 2002.
48. In 2001, the local court received 264 requests to commit people to some kind of withdrawal treatment. *Raport z monitorowania problemów alkoholowych w gminie miejskiej Biała Podlaska 2001* (Biała Podlaska: Urząd Miasta Biała Podlaska, Pełnomocnik ds. Zdrowia i Patologii Społecznych, 2002).
49. *Działalność organizacji pozarządowych na rzecz ofiar przemocy w rodzinie* (Biała Podlaska: Urząd Miasta Biała Podlaska, Pełnomocnik ds. Zdrowia i Patologii Społecznych, 2002).
50. Ibid. The de facto figure may be even higher considering that there are social taboos on reporting family abuse.
51. Ibid.
52. Ibid.
53. *Pomoc społeczna w Białej Podlaskiej na tle innych miast członkowskich Związku Miast Polskich* (Warsaw: PARPA).
54. While 22,000 złoty came from the regular powiat budget, 12,000 złoty were added from the local Alcohol Prevention Programme.
55. *Działalność organizacji pozarządowych na rzecz ofiar przemocy w rodzinie* (Biała Podlaska: Urząd Miasta Biała Podlaska, Pełnomocnik ds. Zdrowia i Patologii Społecznych, 2002). In 2001, the local government supported the facility with 17,520 złoty (roughly 4,400 euros).
56. *Sprawozdanie z Realizacji Programu Profilaktyki Rozwiązywania Problemów Alkoholowych Gminy Miejskiej Biała Podlaska w 2001 roku* (Biała Podlaska: Biuro Pełnomocnika ds Zdrowia i Patologii Społecznych, Komisja Rozwiązywania Problemów Alkoholowych, March 2002), 16.
57. Personal interview with the Director of Dziupla, December 2002.
58. This figure was given in a questionnaire distributed among all local governments by the Państwowa Agencja Rozwiązywania Problemów Alkoholowych (State Agency For Alcohol-Related Problems), PARPA. *Roczne Sprawozdanie z działalności samorządów gminnych w zakresie profilaktyki i rozwiązywania problemów alkoholowych w 2001 roku* (Biała Podlaska: Urząd Miasta Biała Podlaska, March 2002), 8; *Sprawozdanie z Realizącji Programu Profilaktyki Rozwiązywania Problemów Alkoholowych Gminy Miejskiej Biała Podlaska w 2001 roku* (Biała Podlaska: Biuro Pełnomocnika ds Zdrowia i Patologii Społecznych, Komisja Rozwiązywania Problemów Alkoholowych, March 2002), 15.
59. The Saratov *oblast* Law on Social Protection of the Population is available from http://www.srd.ru/documents/social/t35-1389.html (accessed 11 September 2002).
60. Personal interview with Teréz Sütő, Head of Social Department, Sopron, 11 February 2003.
61. Personal interview with Antal Tengerdi, head of CWS, Sopron, 13 February 2003.
62. Personal interview with József Eszes, Director of the Child Protection Centre, Sopron, 14 February 2003.
63. According to the Head of the Social Department, after 2006 it will be mandatory for county ranking towns to maintain special/professional child welfare services.

64. Says the Director of the family shelter: 'This [legislation] made us very sad because we would like to help these people. And this decree is a problem because there are many people in Sopron who come from the surrounding small settlements or from the Great Plain and they have been living here for years. They work, or they are in the process of looking for a job but they don't have a permanent address because the authorities don't let them have it. And when they get into a difficult situation, we cannot help them. The local government is trying to protect the institute by saying that this is only for people from Sopron.' Personal interview with Rita Palotai, Director of Temporary Family Shelter, Sopron, 13 February 2003.

65. An example given by the shelter staff member illustrates this point: 'We cannot take these families in because of the decree. We had one case where a young mother was brought up in a foster-home in Sopron and then moved to Kaposvár. When she got into crisis, she called her teachers here in Sopron and came here for help. We could take her in for only three days because she didn't have a permanent address in town. I almost had to evict her from here. But then here is an example of how well cooperation can work sometimes: the foster home got in contact with us and they gave her a permanent address there, so she could stay here with us. She stayed here for three or four months and then moved back to Kaposvár.' Ibid.

66. Personal interview with Teréz Sütő, Head of the Social Department, Sopron, 11 February 2003.

67. Personal interview with Mrs Ferenc Berki, Head of the Social Department, Szolnok, 6 February 2003.

68. The centre, whose work is regulated both by the 1993 family legislation and the 1997 law on child welfare, coordinates its work with CWS and the Court of Guardians.

69. Personal interview with Ilona Bozsó, Head of the Child and Youth Protection Institute, Szolnok, 6 February 2003.

3   Local government performance in economic promotion

1. The following information is based on personal interviews and the following documents: *Průmyslová zóna Karviná-Nové Pole. Informativní zpráva k 31.12. 2001* (Karviná: Město Karviná, odbor majetkoprávní a rozvoje, January 2002); *Strategický plan ekonomického rozvoje města Karviné–vyhodnocení k, 31.3. 2002* (Karviná: Město Karviná, April 2002).

2. In June 1998, the Czech government adopted a special support programme to promote the establishment of local industrial parks. For a detailed overview, see Czechinvest Newsletter 3, 2002, 6, http://www.czechinvest.cz. By the end of 2001, Karviná had received a sum of roughly 2,828,331 euros from the government to build and equip its industrial park. *Průmyslová zóna Karviná-Nové Pole. Informativní zpráva k 31.12. 2001*, 21.

3. Shimano (Japan), Mölnlycke (Sweden) and Belfort (Belgium).

4. *Czechinvest News*, 13 November 2003.

5. *Karviná: Strategický plán ekonomického rozvoje* (Karviná: Agentura pro Regionální Rozvoj Severní Moravy a Slezska, August 1996), 7.

6. In 1992, the Czech Ministry of Industry and Trade set up a network of Regional Advisory and Information Centres (RPICs). These centres provide SMEs with advisory services concerning economic and legal questions, national and international support programmes and access to foreign markets. Although in many cases these RPICs are private, for-profit companies, ministerial subsidies allow SMEs to make use of the relevant services for relatively small fees. For detailed information about the RPIC system, see *Agentura pro rozvoj podnikání*, www.arp.cz (accessed 30 January 2003).

7. Interview with Martina Zbožínková, January 2003.

8. A project called Infobusiness aims at setting up an information network of Czech and Polish SMEs on both sides of the border. In another project, businesses located in Karviná are offered the opportunity to have their own website integrated into the local business information system. *Strategický plan–vyhodnocení k 31.3.2002*, 22; personal interview with Martina Zbožínková, January 2003.

9. Since 1997, the Silesian University has annually published a report called *Sborník výzkumných prácí Ústavu malého a středního podníkání*. Moreover, in recent years, the University has conducted several polls concerning the local quality of life.

10. In 2002, the town was awarded a national prize for its tourism promotion materials; personal interview with Ingrid Szczypková, January 2003.

11. Personal interview, January 2003.

12. *Strategický plan–vyhodnocení k 31.3.2002*, 31–38.

13. Ibid., 31.

14. Lidmila Janečková et al., *Kvalita života ve městě Karviné, příloha 1* (Karviná: Městský úřád, 2000), 11.

15. All information provided in this paragraph is based on: *Strategia Rozwoju Jeleniej Góry* (Jelenia Góra: Urząd Miejski w Jeleniej Górze, 1998).

16. *Uchwała Nr 405/XXX/2000 Rady Miejskiej Jeleniej Góry z dnia 5 grudnia 2000 r.* (Jelenia Góra: Urząd Miejski w Jeleniej Górze, 2000). In March 2002, the council adopted a regulation waiving registration fees for businesses set up by unemployed residents. A few weeks later, it passed a decree establishing tax breaks for companies creating new jobs. In October 2002, the local council agreed on a decree allowing local companies to restructure their liabilities towards the local government. In May 2003 the local government reduced the rents for municipal premises used by local enterprises. *Uchwała Nr 405/XXX/2000 Rady Miejskiej Jeleniej Góry z dnia 5 grudnia 2000 r.; Uchwała Nr 646/XLVII/2002 Rady Miejskiej Jeleniej Góry z dnia 5 marca 2002 r.; Uchwała Nr 700/ L/ 2002 Rady Miejskiej Jeleniej Góry z dnia 14 maja 2002 r.; Uchwała Nr 756/LV/2002 Rady Miejskiej Jeleniej Góry z dnia 10 października 2002 r.; Uchwała Nr 71/iX/2003 Rady Miejskiej Jeleniej Góry z dnia 27 maja 2003 r.* (Jelenia Góra: Urząd Miejski w Jeleniej Górze, 2000, 2002, 2003).

17. *Strategia Rozwoju Jeleniej Góry*, 14, 15.

18. Figure contained in the monitoring report of April 2002, 8. It should be noted, however, that this sum also includes financial contributions from the state, as well as loans. *Realizacja Strategii Rozwoju Jeleniej Góry* (Jelenia Góra: Urząd Miasta, 2002).

19. We would like to thank Barbara Chrebor for making the list of public investment activities available to us.

20. Personal interview with Barbara Chrebor, Head of the Department of Economic Development, December 2002. PHARE stands for Poland and Hungary: Assistance for Restructuring their Economies. It was subsequently expanded to include other pre-accession countries.
21. For more details see the local government website, www.jeleniagora.pl (accessed 10 July 2003).
22. For more details, see www.parp.gov.pl (accessed 11 July 2003).
23. For more details, see www.karr.pl (accessed 11 July 2003).
24. Personal interview with Elżbieta Kopecka-Malara, December 2002.
25. *Uchwała Nr 507/XXXIX/2001 Rady Miejskiej Jeleniej Góry z dnia 17 lipca 2001 r.* (Jelenia Góra: Urząd Miejski w Jeleniej Górze, 2001).
26. Personal interview, December 2002.
27. *Realizacja Strategii*, 8.
28. *Realizacja Strategii*, 9.
29. *Strategia Rozwoju Jeleniej Góry*, 54, 55.
30. *Realizacja Strategii*, 36.
31. Ibid., 51.
32. Personal interview, January 2003.
33. Personal interview with Václav Fridrich, Head of Economic Department, Ústí nad Labem, May 2002.
34. Altogether, the financial support from the Czech government and the EU amounted to 1.27 million euros. Information provided by the local government's official spokesman, *Právo*, 19 November 2002.
35. 'Ústecký kraj láká stále více investorů' (Czechinvest Newsletter 1, 2002), http://www.czechinvest.cz.
36. Information contained in the strategy follow-up document of 1998 suggests that SMEs were listed as priority areas in the Barents group strategy. *Strategie ekonomického rozvoje města a okresu*, available at http://web.usti-nl.cz/msp/index_dokumenty.htm (accessed 30 January 2003).
37. The Chamber is institutionally and financially independent of the local government. It is funded by company membership fees.
38. Concretely, these aims and measures were to facilitate access to capital by supporting restructuring, providing subsidies and establishing a guarantee fund; to support and provide advisory and training services; to foster co-operation between SMEs and larger companies; to assist the introduction of modern technology and management; and to stir technological innovation. *Komplexní projekt rozvoje malých a středních podniků* (Ústí nad Labem: Okresní hospodářská komora, November 1999).
39. The first round of selection of the RPICs was conducted in 1992. It is unclear why, at that time, the then management of the OHK did not apply for the status of RPIC. In 2000, the Ministry of Industry and Trade advertised a further opportunity for private as well as public institutions to obtain the status of RPIC. Interview with Jiří Kalach, Managing Director of the OHK, January 2003. In 2002, 94 local SMEs were provided with 800 hours of advisory services. Moreover, the OHK organised two seminars with information on programmes of financial support. *Zpráva o činnosti 2002* (Ústí nad Labem: Okresní hospodářská komora, 2002), 8.
40. Ibid., 9.

41. In January 2003, during personal interviews with local economic and political actors, several interviewees indicated that they suspected that the local government did not handle public tenders in a transparent way.

42. *Zpráva o činnosti 2002*, (Ústí nad Labem: Okresní hospodářská komora, 2002), 10.

43. Personal interview, January 2003.

44. *Severočeské Deníky Bohemia*, 24 May 2002, http://www.ecmost.cz.

45. Between 1998 and 2001, the local council discussed the possibility of purchasing a small castle, located above the river that, after 1989, had been sold by the state to a private owner, who had neglected it. Although in April 2001 the local council decided to buy the castle for roughly 67,000 euros and to take over at least part of the cost of restoring it, during the election campaign of 2002, photos of the rundown castle tower were used by the opposition parties to challenge the ruling government's political legitimacy. In the summer of 2002, a similar situation occurred with regard to a baroque monastery located in the town centre, when the local government did not respond to pleas from local politicians to purchase the building in order to prevent it from 'becoming another disco or gambling house'. *Mladá Fronta Dnes*, 30 August 2001; *Právo*, 5 April 2002; *Právo*, 8 July 2002. In an opinion poll conducted in January 2001 by the Gallup Organization Česká republika, out of 194 respondents, 135 said the outward appearance of the town was a reason for dissatisfaction with the local government, and 59 respondents praised the town hall for having brought about an improvement in this respect. *Některé výsledky projektu 'Region a Politika', Část Ústí nad Labem pro tiskovou konferenci na FSE UJEP Ústí nad Labem, 5 April 2001* (Ústí nad Labem: Gallup Organization Česká republika, April 2001). In January 2002, high-ranking representatives of the opposition Social Democrats started a debate on whether Ústí is an 'ugly town' or not. *Právo*, 12 January 2002, 25 January 2002.

46. *Roční zpráva 2001* (Ústí nad Labem: Okresní hospodářská komora, příloha 2, 2001).

47. On average, guests stayed for 2.9 nights, while the regional average was 3.5. Figures are taken from *Statistická ročenka Ústeckého kraje 2002* (Ústí nad Labem: Český statistický úřad, Krajská reprezentace Ústí nad Labem, 2003), 182.

48. *Uchwała Nr VII/64/2000 Rady Miejskiej w Białej Podlaskiej z dnia 20. września 2000 r.* (Biała Podlaska: Urząd Miasta, 2000).

49. www.bialapodlaska.pl (accessed 30 January 2003).

50. Since 2002, this department has been directly accountable to the mayor.

51. *Uchwała.*

52. *Sprawozdanie z Działalności Zarządu Miasta Biała Podlaska w latach 1999–2002*, (Biała Podlaska: Urząd Miasta, 2003), 11.

53. Personal interview, December 2002.

54. *Strategia Rozwoju* (Biała Podlaska: Urząd Miasta, 2001), aneks Nr. 2, 3.

55. Personal interview, December 2002.

56. Personal interview, December 2002.

57. *Strategia Rozwoju*, 16, 17.

58. *Sprawodanie z Działalności Zarządu Miasta Biała Podlaska w latach 1999–2002*, 43.

59. Personal interview, December 2002.

60. Personal interview with Nikolay Zanin, Deputy Head of Administration, Staraya Russa, 22 January 2002.
61. http://www.WOMNET.ru/db/Russian/organiz/topics/org1488.html (accessed 6 August 2003).
62. *Novgorod Oblast Press Centre*, 20 August 1998, http://niac.natm.ru/ presscentr. nsf (accessed 6 August 2003).
63. Personal interview with Zanin.
64. http://www.gm.hu/Ippark/English/xmagyar/ndt/sopron_txt.html   (accessed 25 July 2003).
65. http://gm.hu/kulfold/english/economy/counties/gyor.htm (accessed 25 July 2003).
66. http://gm.hu/kulfold/english/economyipariparkang_021003.htm   (accessed 25 July 2003).
67. Ibid.
68. Personal interview with József Hruby, Deputy Mayor in charge of economic development, Sopron, 12 February 2003.
69. Lucy Mallows, 'Springtime in Sopron', *The Budapest Sun*, 2 May 2002.
70. Personal interview with Gyula Varga, member of the Social Committee and President of the Town Development Committee, Sopron, 12 February 2003.
71. Personal interview with Tivadar Csonka, member of the local government Property Committee and owner of enterprise Csonka and Sons Glass Technology, Ltd., Sopron, 14 February 2003.
72. *Saratovskaya guberniya* 2, no. 11 (2000), 11.
73. Personal interview with Attila Agócs, Financial Director, GITR, Szolnok, 6 February 2003.
74. Personal interview with József Kéri, Head of Economic Department; Tamás Treffler, Head of the Budget Committee; and Zoltán Radócz, Deputy Mayor, Szolnok, 6 February 2003.
75. Personal interview with János Lipóczki, Director of Tisza Hotel Ltd., Szolnok, 6 February 2003.
76. Ibid.

4   Socioeconomic contexts

1. Data for 1994.
2. http://www.efe.hu/english_page/doc3.html (accessed 19 February 2002).
3. These disparities are to a large extent the product of the federation's hyper-decentralisation in the 1990s, whereby the regions were able to retain authority over the taxation of the immobile, but high-yielding resources, such as oil or gas. Public finance theorists suggest that these resources should be the preserve of central government in order to enable redistribution of the relevant yields to poorer areas not endowed with resources (Hanson 2004).
4. http://www.bisnis.doc.gov/bisnis/country/9710novg.htm (accessed 7 December 2001).
5. www.rusline.com/oblast/saratov/saratov.html (accessed 2 January 2002).
6. Alaksandra Malinina, 'Dorogie zemlyaki!' (campaign article for Alexander Vetrov, Baltex Director, http://www.vetrov.info/?action=list& id= 1070524953&type=news (accessed 5 January 2004).

7. For more information, see the World Energy Council report, *Restructuring the Coal Industries. Central and Eastern Europe and the CIS*. Part II: Country Profiles: Czech Republic, www.worldenergy.org (accessed 16 December 2003).
8. Figure taken from *Prague Business Journal*, City Invest Czech 2001, Prague 2001, 188.
9. *Roční zpráva 1999* (Ústí nad Labem: Úřad práce v Ústí nad Labem, 2000), 4.
10. Cited from CzechInvest news, 27 November 2003.
11. CzechInvest news, 2 October 2003.
12. CzechInvest Newsletter 3, 2002, 4.
13. Figures obtained from *Finanční zdroje EU poskytnuté České republice před vstupem do Evropské unie v letech 1990–2003* (Prague: Informační Centrum Evropské unie při Delegaci Evropské unie v České republice, June 2003), 3. The report is available from the EU delegation's website, www.evropska-unie.cz (accessed 18 December 2003).
14. Personal interview with Tomáš Krejčí, general director of the *Komunitní nádace Ústí nad Labem*, January 2003.
15. *Strategie regionálního rozvoje České republiky* (Prague, July 2000), available from the website of the Czech Ministry of Local Development, www.mmr.cz.
16. Based on the EU regional policy template, the Czech Republic is divided into eight units corresponding to the NUTS-2 level. In this framework, the Ústí region, together with the Karlsbad region, forms the NUTS-2 Northwest unit, whereas the region of Moravia-Silesia is a separate NUTS-2 unit.
17. Program regionální podpory malého a středního podníkání; Program Region 2; Regiozáruka 2.
18. Figures for 1996 are based on Příloha č. 1 ke Strategii regionálního rozvoje České republiky, usnesení vlády č. 682/ 2000, July 2000. Figures for 2002 are available from the Czech Statistical Office, www.czso.cz.
19. As of 30 September 1999. Polish Statistical Office, http://www.stat.gov. pl/english/serwis/polska/praca.htm (accessed 30 January 2003).

5 Intergovernmental setting and local performance

1. Apart from political disagreements on the concrete shape of the regions, the main factor hampering reform was the former Prime Minister Klaus's reluctance to share political power with regional governments before the political and economic transition was completed (Vodička 1997).
2. This section is based on Ustawa z dnia 8 marca 1990 r. o samorządzie gminnym, amended several times (Poland); Act. No. LXV 1990 on Local Government, amended (Hungary); federal Law on General Principles of Local Self-Government in the Russian Federation (28 August 1995); Zákon č. 128/ 2000 Sb. o obcích, amended several times (Czech Republic).
3. Ustawa z dnia 29 listopadu 1990 r. o pomocy społecznej, amended several times; Zákon č. 114/ 1988 Sb. o působnosti orgánů České republiky v sociálním zabezpečení, amended several times; Novgorod *oblast* Law on the Regulation of Certain Questions of Family Relations in Novgorod Oblast, adopted 31 July 1996, and amended several times; Saratov *oblast* Law on Social Protection of the Population, adopted 10 January 2001.

4. Ustawa z dnia 29 listopadu 1990 r. o pomocy społecznej; Zákon č. 114/ 1988 Sb. o působnosti orgánů České republiky v sociálním zabezpečení, amended several times; Zákon č. 359/ 1999 Sb. o sociálně-právní ochraně dětí; Decree of the Novgorod Oblast Administration on the Oblast Targeted Programme Children of Novgorod Region for 2001–2003, adopted 29 January 2001; Saratov *oblast* Law on Social Protection of the Population, adopted 10 January 2001.
5. Personal interview, January 2003.
6. Personal interview with Ivana Šťastná, Head of the Social Department in Ústí nad Labem, May 2002.
7. Personal interview with Renata Trombíková, January 2003.
8. According to earlier versions of the law, the *wojewoda*'s competences depended on whether the local decree in question referred to the realm of municipal competences proper or to state-delegated tasks (Wollmann and Lankina 2003: 114).
9. Ustawa z dnia 11 kwietnia 2001 r.o zmianie ustaw: o samorządzie gminnym, o samorządzie powiatowym, o samorządzie województwa, o administracji rządowej w województwie oraz o zmianie niektórych innych ustaw.
10. Act LXV on Local Government, amended.
11. Zákon č. 128/ 2000 Sb. O obcích, jak vyplývá ze změn a doplnění provedených zákonů č. 273/ 2001 Sb., č. 320/ 2001 Sb., č. 450/ 2001 Sb., č. 311/ 2002 Sb. a č. 313/ 2002 Sb.
12. During the process of drafting and passing the new legislation, the national Association of Towns and Municipalities (*Svaz Měst a Obcí*) lobbied *against* transferring the responsibility for legal review from the state to the regions, arguing that this would establish a hierarchy between the two tiers of self-government. Personal interview with Jaromir Jech, Deputy President of SMOČR, 16 May 2002.
13. Conducted on 12 February 2002.
14. As an example Koudelka mentions local fees (2001, p. 75).
15. This provoked criticism both from the Czech Association of Towns and Municipalities and from impartial academic observers. Personal interview with Zdenka Vajdová, expert on local government at the Czech Academy of Sciences, 16 May 2002. For the position of the Association of Towns and Municipalities of the Czech Republic see the 'Prípomínky SMOČR k návrhu zákona, kterým se mění zákon č. 128/ 2000' available at http://www.smocr.cz/prip01prosinec.htm (accessed 30 January 2003).
16. Corruption and nepotism are also widespread with investigations revealing that organisations and enterprises in a number of municipalities had been exempt from payment of taxes and fees to local budgets for no lawful reason (Kourliandskaia, Nikolayenko and Golovanova 2001: 214).
17. Personal interview with Mirosław Radecki, local councillor, December 2002.
18. Personal interview, March 2002.
19. *Mladá Fronta Dnes*, 27 May 1999.
20. *Mladá Fronta Dnes*, 14 October 1999.
21. Personal interviews conducted in May 2002 and January 2003.
22. For the Czech case, Ondřej Brdičko, Deputy Mayor of Karviná, reported on the distribution of money within the former districts. Personal interview, January 2003.
23. Helena Bogoczová, Head of the Economic Department, Karviná; and Blanka Dadoková, Head of the Social Department. Personal interviews, January 2003.

24. It should be noted that, in 1999, the share of non-tax revenues in local budgets was extraordinarily high with many municipalities selling their shares in gas and electricity companies (Nadvorníková 2002).
25. *Rzeczpospolita*, 31 May 2001.
26. See, for example, *Projekt Polska–Zintegrowany Program Operacyjny Rozwoju Regionalnego 2004–2006*; and *Wersja Robocza 4*, 1, Warsaw, September 2002, available from the website of the Polish Ministry of the Economy www.mg.gov.pl (accessed 15 October 2002).
27. http://fundusze.ukie.gov.pl (accessed 15 October 2002).
28. Hungarian Ministry of the Economy, Budapest 2001, p. 31. The Programme is designed for a period of six years. In 2001 and 2002, the programme amounted to roughly 2.6 billion euros.
29. Our doubts as to the impartiality of this commission were resolved during a personal interview with Helena Herbstová, head of the Ústí department of social work. She maintained she was not aware of the names of people who sat on the commission, and so she would not know who to turn to in order to lobby for projects from Ústí. Personal interview, January 2003.
30. For more details, see the website of the Czech Ministry of Local Development, www.mmr.cz.
31. Ustawa z dnia 10 grudnia 1993 r. o finansowaniu gmin, Art. 4. See also the website of the Hungarian government, www.kormanyportal.hu; OECD Country Report, *Czech Republic: Fiscal Design across Levels of Government*, 25. In contrast to Poland, the Czech Republic does not have a special law on municipal finances. In 1999 and 2000, a draft law outlined by the Czech government was repeatedly rejected by the Czech parliament.
32. For the Czech Republic, see OECD, p. 26; Poland: OECD, p. 31; Hungary: OECD, p. 42.
33. Data based on OECD report, p. 42.
34. In Hungary, the distribution of revenues from the tax on motor vehicles and on property is regulated by special laws. The most important type of shared taxes, that is, personal income tax, is determined in the annual state budget.
35. See also OECD report.
36. Local governments whose per capita personal income tax revenues fall short of 90 per cent of the national average are entitled to compensation payments, while local governments with tax revenues above the national average are not equalised down.
37. OECD, pp.18–19.
38. This list included VAT, PIT, enterprise profit tax, tax shares regions received from federal taxes, enterprise profit tax, forest tax, education tax and sales tax.
39. Ustawa z dnia 10 grudnia 1993 r. o finansowaniu gmin, Art. 24.
40. OECD, p. 47.
41. This criticism concerned several aspects of the law. While, according to the Association of Czech Towns and Municipalities (SMOČR), some paragraphs of the law remained so unclear as to make it impossible to apply it in practice, local governments objected to the idea of the central government interfering with their financial tasks (Vedral 2002).
42. The only innovation that survived the renegotiation of the law is the provision whereby local governments are not allowed to issue guarantees for loans other than those raised by municipality-owned businesses.

43. Examples are bank loans which are often gained only through disadvantageous side-payments. Many governments reportedly provide 'friendly' banks with additional benefits such as tax exemptions, preferential access to municipal real estate, and so on. The *vekseli* are an infringement upon existing laws. These are promissory notes that, though legally banned in 1996, in the late 1990s continued to be issued by regional as well as local governments (Freinkman, Treisman and Titov 1999: 41–2).
44. Data for Sopron not available. Data for BP are for 2001. Own calculation based on German Statistical Office information. These figures do not reflect purchasing power as of 2002, but as of August 2003. Moreover, all data concerning PPP refer to the *capital* cities, which generally have price levels significantly exceeding the national average.
45. Own calculation based on figures provided in OECD (2001), pp. 17, 23, 30.
46. www.mfcr.cz (accessed 14 November 2003).
47. Saratov field research material.
48. *2002.évi Költségvetése*, Szolnok: Szolnok Megyei Jogú Város önkormányzata 2002, p. 13.
49. Information provided by the Czech Ministry of Social Affairs.
50. http://bazy.ngo.pl (accessed 14 November 2003).
51. Figures include expenditure for economic promotion, road maintenance, transport, tourism and the restoration of tourist attractions.
52. Figures include investment in technical infrastructure.
53. Saratov material.

6   Parties and the politics of local performance

1. While Hungary has an estimated party survival rate of 90 per cent, and Poland close to 72 per cent, in Russia it is as low as 53 per cent (Golosov 1998: 511–12).
2. The new law mandates the setting up of uniform local structures throughout the federation.
3. Number of parties which either lost representation or, for the first time, won mandates in the council as a percentage of all parties that were represented in either of the councils.
4. Share of councilors not in the council in 1994.
5. 'ODS: Civic Democratic Party', *Radio Praha*, http://www.radio.cz/en/html/ods.html (accessed 8 October 2003).
6. KSČM: The Communist Party of Bohemia and Moravia, http://www.radio.cz/en/html/kscm.html (accessed 8 October 2003).
7. http://www.vokscentrum.hu/mvkgy/o18.htm (accessed 15 October 2003).
8. Personal interview with Attila Agócs, Financial Director, GITR, Szolnok, 6 February 2003.
9. http://www.vokscentrum.hu/mvkgy/014.htm (accessed 15 October 2003).
10. For other aspects of Russian party development at the regional level, see also (Golosov 1999; Brown 1998).
11. The region was recently made to change this provision under pressure from federal government because of its ostensible violation of federal legislation (Petro 2004).
12. IEG, 1999.

13. Mihail Mel'nikov, 'Regional'naya pressa vzyata v okruzheniye vlastyami vsekh urovney', *Sovershenno sekretno* 8, 2003, http://www. sovsekretno.ru/2003/08/5.html (accessed 2 September 2003).
14. Personal interview with Evgeniy Ryabov, Head of Administration, Staraya Russa, 22 January 2002.
15. *Právo*, 3 March 2003.
16. Personal interview with Gábor Péteri, Open Society Institute, Budapest, 14 March 2002.
17. Personal interview with József Kéri, Head of the Economic Department, Szolnok, 6 February 2003.
18. Personal interview with Mrs Ferenc Berki, Head of the Social Department, Szolnok, 6 February 2003.
19. Personal interview with Attila Agócs, Financial Director, GITR, Szolnok, 6 February 2003.
20. Personal interview with József Hruby, Deputy Mayor responsible for economic development, Sopron, 12 February 2003.
21. Personal interview with Gyula Varga, member of the Social Committee and President of the Town Development Committee, Sopron, 12 February 2003.
22. Evans and Whitefield found that the salience of economic ideology was low in voter preferences, while ethnic issues and the fate of the Hungarian diaspora were high. This might partly explain high volatility, since there is no clear social basis for party divisions (1995).
23. In general scholars have noted the high volatility of Hungarian citizens' voting preferences, which likewise points to the instrumental, rather than ideological, nature of their vote (Tókab 1999: 155, 169).
24. As a Hungarian public administration expert put it, here 'political difference is not between the local and the central, political difference is between the parties and the big groups in the society'. Personal interview with László Vass, Institute of Communications, Budapest, 18 March 2002.
25. Personal interview, January 2003.
26. Personal interview, January 2003.
27. Between January and November 2002, the local government faced attacks from opposition parties accusing the ODS of neglecting the renovation of historical buildings. *Právo*, 12 January 2002; 25 January 2002; 2 October 2002.
28. *Prague Business Journal*. City-Invest Czech 2001, 18.
29. For the importance of the sub-national level in exploring post-communist elites, see the article by James Hughes (1997).
30. As was the case in Russian regions (Hughes 1997).
31. Personal interview with László Vass, Institute of Communications, Budapest, 18 March 2002.
32. Personal interview with Tamás Horváth, Institute of Public Administration, Budapest, 14 March 2002; and with Gábor Péteri, Open Society Institute, Budapest, 14 March 2002.
33. For a discussion of FIDESZ, see Kiss.
34. *Ön-Önkormányzat* 11, no. 12 (2001), 15.
35. *Ön-Önkormányzat* 11, no. 12 (2001), 16.
36. Personal interview with József Kéri, Head of the Economic Department, Szolnok, 6 February 2003.
37. Szolnok received 545,000 forints for its waste disposal facility, while Sopron received 587,000 forints for a water project. *Ön-Önkormányzat* 11, no. 12 (2001).

38. Personal interview by Anneke Hudalla with Martina Zbožínková, Head of the Sub-Department for Economic Development, Karviná, January 2003.
39. As a result of administrative delays, Ústí was unable to participate in external funding programmes set up in 1998. According to Tomáš Krejčí, Managing Director of the *Komunitní nadace* in Ústí, the most important incentive for the *Aktivní politika* was the realisation by the local government that it had not made use of 80 million euros provided by the CBC PHARE programme. Personal interview with Anneke Hudalla, January 2003.
40. Assessment by Miloslav Šašek, Head of the Institute for Regional and Local Development at Ústí University. Personal interview with Anneke Hudalla, January 2003.
41. Personal interview with János Lipóczki, Director of Tisza Hotel Ltd, Szolnok, 6 February 2003.
42. Ibid.
43. Personal interview with Attila Agócs, Financial Director, GITR, Szolnok, 6 February 2003.
44. For the text of the law, see http://soros.novgorod.ru/grants/IEA718/law/govern/gov009.htm (accessed 18 September 2002).
45. Personal interview with the Head of the Economic Department, Balashov, January 2003.
46. Personal interview with Éva Dernyei, Ramexa Company, Szolnok, 6 February 2003.
47. The apparent lack of a vibrant civil society in Szolnok is likely to foster conflictual rather than accommodative and consensual decision-making. As scholars of party politics in other settings maintain, cleavages that 'entail multiple and neutralising loyalties' may reduce the likelihood of party political polarisation (Sani and Sartori 1983: 331).
48. Personal interview, Sopron, 14 February 2003.
49. Personal interview with László Gyarmati, Economic Director, Water Utilities Company, Sopron, 12 February 2003.
50. As one local entrepreneur declared: 'I think those who are present at these events truly believe in these things. [Charity events] for nurseries, hospitals, institutions, foundations for children with cancer, Rotary Club balls. ... I can go on and on. These are annual events and we all believe that we are doing a good thing and the money gets to the right place. For good causes local entrepreneurs get together and they truly do something.' Personal interview with Tibor Josan, Director, GYSEV railway company 11 February 2003.
51. Civic education classes are taught in schools, and historical records of Novgorod's political institutions, such as those related to district self-government, are studied in an effort to look for models for the present. Nicolai Petro, the authority on the region, argues that these efforts have borne fruit. Novgorod now boasts one of the most active NGO communities compared to other Russian regions, while surveys have revealed that regional residents also score higher on such democratic values as trust and interest in public affairs compared to the national average (Petro 2004).
52. Articles about him have appeared in the national press. See for example, Liliya Mukhamedyarova, 'Staraya Russa. Samyy dobryy gorod na svete', 30 January 2003, http://2003.novayagazeta.ru/nomer/2003/07n/n07n-s21.shtml (accessed 21 May 2003).

Bibliography

Aiken, Michael, and Guido Martinotti (1985) 'The Impact of Political and Urban Systems on Municipal Expenditure.' In *Urban Innovations as Response to Urban Fiscal Strain*, edited by Terry Clark, Gerd Michael Hellstern and Guido Martinotti, 33–57. Berlin: Europäische Perspektiven.

Almond, Gabriel A., and Sidney Verba (1963) *The Civic Culture: Political Attitudes and Democracy in Five Nations*. Newbury Park: Sage Publications.

Bachrach, Peter, and Morton S. Baratz (1962) 'Two Faces of Power'. *The American Political Science Review* 56, no. 4: 947–52.

Baldersheim, Harald, Michal Illner, Audun Offerdal, Lawrence Rose and Pawel Świaniewicz (eds) (1996) *Local Democracy and the Processes of Transformation in East-Central Europe*. Boulder: Westview Press.

Baldersheim, Harald, and Michal Illner (1996) 'Local Democracy: The Challenges of Institution-Building.' In *Local Democracy and the Processes of Transformation in East-Central Europe*, edited by Harald Baldersheim, Michael Illner, Audun Offerdal, Lawrence Rose and Pawel Swianiewicz, 1–22. Boulder: Westview Press.

Baldersheim, Harald, Michal Illner and Hellmut Wollmann (eds) (2003) *Local Democracy in Post-Communist Europe*. Opladen: Leske und Budrich.

Banfield, Edward C. (1961) *Political Influence*. New York: The Free Press.

——— (1985) 'The Political Implications of Metropolitan Growth.' In *Here the People Rule: Selected Essays*, xviii, 348. New York: Plenum Press.

Banfield, Edward C., and James Q. Wilson (1963) *City Politics*. New York: Vintage Books.

Bartik, Timothy (2002) 'Evaluating the Impacts of Local Economic Development Policies on Local Economic Outcomes: What Has Been Done and What Is Doable?,' paper presented on 20 November 2002 at Conference on 'Evaluating Local Economic and Employment Development', organised by the Local Economic and Employment Development (LEED) Programme of the OECD.

Bennett, Robert J. (1990) 'Decentralization and Local Economic Development.' In *Decentralization, Local Governments, and Markets: Towards a Post-Welfare Agenda*, edited by Robert J. Bennett, 221–44. Oxford University Press.

——— (1990b) *Decentralization, Local Governments, and Markets: Towards a Post-Welfare Agenda*. Oxford University Press.

——— (1993) 'European Local Government Systems.' In *Local Government in the New Europe*, edited by Robert J. Bennett, 28–50. London: Belhaven Press.

——— (1994) 'An Overview of Developments in Decentralization.' In *Local Government and Market Decentralization: Experiences in Industrialized, Developing, and Former Eastern Bloc Countries*, edited by Robert J. Bennett, 11–37. Tokyo: United Nations University Press.

Bish, Robert L., and Vincent Ostrom (1973) *Understanding Urban Government: Metropolitan Reform Reconsidered*. Washington: American Enterprise Institute for Public Policy Research.

Blažek, Jiří (1995) 'Nový systém financování místní správy v České republice a jeho regionální dopady,' in *Území v procesu změn*, edited by Gilles Lepesant, 181–99. Prague: Francouzký ústav pro výzkum ve společenských vědách.

Brown, Archie (2005) 'Conclusions.' In *Political Culture and Post-Communism*, edited by S. Whitefield, 180–202. New York: Palgrave Macmillan.

Brown, Ruth (1998) 'Party Development in the Regions: When Did Parties Start to Play a Part in Politics?' *The Journal of Communist Studies and Transition Politics* 14, no. 1 & 2, March/June: 9–30.

Bunce, Valerie (2003) 'Rethinking Recent Democratization: Lessons from the Postcommunist Experience,' *World Politics* 55, no. 2: 167–92.

Chagin, Kirill (2005) 'The Problems of the Implementation of the Competitive Procurement of Social Services in Russia: The Practical Experience of the Project "Improvement of Social Service Delivery System in the Russian Federation"' http://www.nispa.sk/ news/papers/wg2/Chagin.rtf (accessed 18 January 2005).

Clark, Terry N. (1973) *Community Power and Policy Outputs: A Review of Urban Research*. Beverly Hills [Calif.]: Sage Publications.

————— (1985) 'Local Government Growth and Retrenchment: Lessons from American Cities.' In *Urban Innovations as Response to Urban Fiscal Strain*, edited by Terry Clark, Gerd Michael Hellstern and Guido Martinotti, 1–12. Berlin: Europäische Perspektiven.

Clark, Terry N., and Lorna Crowley Ferguson (1981) 'Political Leadership and Urban Fiscal Policy.' In *Urban Policy Analysis: Directions for Future Research*, edited by Terry N. Clark, 81–101. Beverly Hills, Calif.: Sage Publications.

Clark, Terry N., Ronald S. Burt, Lorna Crowley Ferguson, John D. Kasarda, David Knoke, Robert L. Lineberry, and Elinor Ostrom (1981) 'Urban Policy Analysis: A New Research Agenda.' In *Urban Policy Analysis: Directions for Future Research*, edited by Terry N. Clark, 13–22. Beverly Hills, Calif.: Sage Publications.

Clark, Terry N., Gerd-Michael Hellstern, Guido Martinotti, and European Research Group on Fiscal Austerity and Urban Innovation (1985) *Urban Innovations as Response to Urban Fiscal Strain*. 1. Aufl. ed. Berlin: Europäische Perspektiven.

Coleman, James (1990) *Foundations of Social Theory*. Cambridge, Mass.: Harvard University Press.

Csóka, István (2000) 'The Relationship between the Governmental and Civil Sectors – Hungary'. *International Journal of Not-for-Profit Law*, no. 1, www.icnl.org/ journal/vol3iss1.

Dahl, Robert (1966) *Who Governs? Democracy and Power in an American City*. New Haven: Yale University Press.

Dahl, Robert (1967) 'The City in the Future of Democracy.' *The American Political Science Review* 61, no. 4: 953–70.

Domhoff, G. William (1998) *Who Rules America? Power and Politics in the Year 2000*. Mountain View, CA: Mayfield Publishing Company.

Dövenyi, Zoltán (2001) 'Development and Spatial Disparities of Unemployment in Hungary.' In *Transformations in Hungary: Essays in Economy and Society*, edited by Peter Meusburger and Heike Jöns, 208–24. Heidelberg: Physica.

Eckstein, Harry (1988) 'A Culturalist Theory of Political Change,' *The American Political Science Review* 82, no. 3: 789–804.

Eckstein, Harry, Frederic J. Fleron, Jr., Erik P. Hoffmann and William M. Reisinger (1998) *Can Democracy Take Root in Post-Soviet Russia? Explorations in State-Society*

Relations, Dilemmas of Democratization in Post-Communist Countries. Vol. 1. Lanham, Md.: Rowman & Littlefield.

Eisinger, Peter K. (1973) 'The Conditions of Protest Behavior in American Cities.' *American Political Science Review* 67, no. 1: 11–28.

Eliáš, Antonin (2003) 'Rozpočty územních samospráv,' *Obec & finance* 8, no. 1, http://denik.obce.cz (accessed 8 October 2003).

Evans, Geoffrey, and Stephen Whitefield (1995) 'Social and Ideological Cleavage Formation in Post-Communist Hungary,' *Europe-Asia Studies* 47, no. 7: 1177–204.

Evans, Peter B., Dietrich Rueschemeyer, and Theda Skocpol (1985) *Bringing the State Back In.* Cambridge University Press.

Fish, M. Steven (1999) 'Post-Communist Subversion: Social Science and Democratization in East Europe and Eurasia,' *Slavic Review* 58, no. 4.

Frane, Adam, and Tomšič Matevž (2002) 'Elite (Re)configuration and Politico-Eocnomic Performance in Post-Socialist Countries,' *Europe-Asia Studies* 54, no. 3: 435–54.

Freinkman, Lev, Daniel Treisman, and Stepan Titov (1999) 'Subnational Budgeting in Russia.'

—— (1999) 'Subnational Budgeting in Russia: Preempting a Potential Crisis.' Washington, DC: World Bank.

Friedgut, Theodore H., and Jeffrey W. Hahn (eds) (1994) *Local Power and Post-Soviet Politics.* London: ME Sharpe.

Friedland, Roger, and William T. Bielby (1981) 'The Power of Business in the City.' In *Urban Policy Analysis: Directions for Future Research,* edited by Terry N. Clark, 133–51. Beverly Hills, Calif.: Sage Publications.

Gel'man, Vladimir, Sergey Ryzhenkov, Yelena Belokurova and Nadezhda Borisova (2002) *Avtonomiya Ili Kontrol'? Reforma Mestnoy Vlasti V Gorodakh Rossii, 1991–2001.* Moscow: Letniy Sad/European University in St. Petersburg.

Gel'man, Vladimir, Sergey Ryzhenkov, and Michael Brie (eds) (2000) *Rossiya Regionov: Transformatsiya Politicheskikh Rezhimov.* Moscow: Ves' Mir.

Goldsmith, Michael G., and Kenneth Newton (1988) 'Introduction.' *European Journal of Political Research, Special Issue: Centralisation and Decentralisation: Changing Patterns of Intergovernmental Relations in Advanced Western Societies* 16, no. 4: 359–63.

—— (1998) 'Who Survives? Party Origins, Organizational Development, and Electoral Performance in Post-Communist Russia.' *Political Studies* 67: 511–43.

Golosov, Grigorii V. (1999) 'From Adygeya to Yaroslavl: Factors of Party Development in the Regions of Russia, 1995–1998.' *Europe-Asia Studies* 51, no. 8: 1333–65.

Goryunov, P.A., N.A. Kulyasova, V.A. Malyshev, S.Yu. Nesterov, V.G. Sitnik, E.V. Shloma and S.N. Shusharin (1999) *Formirovanie Organov Mestnogo Samoupravleniya V Rossiyskoy Federatsii: Elektoral'naya Statistika.* Moscow: Ves' Mir.

Gottdiener, Mark (1987) *The Decline of Urban Politics: Political Theory and the Crisis of the Local State.* Beverly Hills, Calif.: Sage Publications.

Grabher, Gernot, and David Stark (1997) 'Organising Diversity: Evolutionary Theory, Network Analysis, and Post-Socialism.' In *Restructuring Networks in Post-Socialism: Legacies, Linkages, and Localities,* edited by Gernon Grabher and David Stark, 1–32. Oxford University Press.

Hahn, Jeffrey W. (2005) 'Yaroslavl' Revisited: Assessing Continuity and Change in

Russian Political Culture Since 1990.' In *Political Culture and Post-Communism*, edited by S. Whitefield, 148–79. New York: Palgrave Macmillan.

Hanson, Philip (2004) 'Federalism with a Russian Face: Regional Inequality and Regional Budgets in Russia.' In *The Dynamics of Russian Politics: Putin's Reform of Federal-Regional Relations*, edited by Peter Reddaway and Robert Orttung. Lanham, Md.: Rowman and Littlefield.

Hatry, Harry (1994) 'Accountability for Service Quality, Performance Measurement, and Closeness to Customers.' In *Local Government and Market Decentralization: Experiences in Industrialized, Developing, and Former Eastern Bloc Countries*, edited by Robert J. Bennett, 163–81. Tokyo: United Nations University Press.

Hawkins, Brett W. (n. d.) 'A Comparison of Local and External Influences on City Strategies for Coping with Fiscal Strain.' *Research in Urban Policy* 3: 73–90.

Helgason, Sigurdur (1997) 'International Benchmarking: Experiences from OECD Countries.' Paper presented at the conference on International Benchmarking, Copenhagen, 20–21 February.

Horváth, Tamás M. (2000a) 'Directions and Differences of Local Change.' In *Decentralization: Experiments and Reforms*, edited by Tamás Horváth, 19–60. Budapest: Local Government and Public Service Reform Initiative.

——— (ed) (2000b) *Decentralization: Experiments and Reforms*. Vol. 1. Budapest: Local Government and Public Service Reform Initiative.

Horváth, Tamás M., and József Kiss (2001) '*Politico-Administrative Relations in Local Governments: The Hungarian Case*'. *Ten Years of Transition: Prospects and Challenges for the Future of Public Administration Edited by Jal Jabes*. Bratislava.

Huérou, Anne Le (1999) 'Elites in Omsk.' *Post-Soviet Affairs* 15, no. 4: 362–86.

Hughes, James (1997) 'Sub-national Elites and Post-communist Transformation in Russia: A Reply to Kryshtanovskaya and White,' *Europe-Asia Studies* 49, no. 6: 1017–36.

Hunter, Floyd (1968) *Community Power Structure: A Study of Decision Makers*. Chapel Hill: University of North Carolina Press.

——— (1980) *Community Power Succession: Atlanta's Policy-Makers Revisited*. Chapel Hill: University of North Carolina Press.

Illner, Michal (1997) 'The Territorial Dimension of Public Administration Reforms in East Central Europe.' Working Paper. Prague: Institute of Sociology, Academy of Sciences of the Czech Republic.

——— (2003a) 'The Czech Republic 1990–2001: Successful Reform at the Municipal Level and a Difficult Birth of the Intermediary Government.' In *Local Democracy in Post-Communist Europe*, edited by Harald Baldersheim, Michal Illner and Hellmut Wollmann, 61–90. Opladen: Leske und Budrich.

——— (2003b) 'Devolution of Governments in the Ex-Communist Countries: Some Explanatory Frameworks.' In *Local Democracy in Post-Communist Europe*, edited by Harald Baldersheim, Michal Illner and Hellmut Wollmann. Opladen: Leske und Budrich.

Institute, Metropolitan Research (2002). 'Performance Measurement.' Budapest: Energy Regulators Regional Association and Local Government and Public Service Reform Initiative.

Jones, Bryan D. (1995) 'Bureaucrats and Urban Politics: Who Controls? Who Benefits?' In *Theories of Urban Politics*, edited by David Judge, Gerry Stoker and Harold Wolman, 72–95. London: Sage Publications.

Judge, David (1995) 'Pluralism.' In *Theories of Urban Politics*, edited by David Judge, Gerry Stoker and Harold Wolman, 13–34. London: Sage Publications.

Judge, David, Gerry Stoker and Harold Wolman (1995) 'Urban Politics and Theory: An Introduction.' In *Theories of Urban Politics*, edited by David Judge, Gerry Stoker and Harold Wolman, 1–12. London: Sage Publications.

Keating, Michael (1991) *Comparative Urban Politics: Power and the City in the United States, Canada, Britain, and France*. Aldershot: Edward Elgar.

——— (1995) 'Size, Efficiency and Democracy: Consolidation, Fragmentation and Public Choice.' In *Theories of Urban Politics*, edited by David Judge, Gerry Stoker and Harold Wolman, 117–34. London: Sage Publications.

Kopányi, Mihály, Samir El-Daher, Deborah Wetzel, Michel Noel and Anita Papp (1999) 'Hungary: Modernizing the Subnational Government System.' In *Hungary: Subnational Modernization Challenges*, edited by Mihály Kopányi, Samir El-Daher and Deborah Wetzel, 1–47. Washington: World Bank.

Kopstein, Jeffrey S., and David A. Reilly (2000) 'Geographic Diffusion and the Transformation of the Postcommunist World,' *World Politics* 53: 1–37.

Kostelecký, Tomáš (2002) *Political Parties after Communism: Developments in East-Central Europe*. Washington, DC: The Johns Hopkins University Press.

Koudelka, Zdeněk (2001). *Obce a kraje. Podle reformy veřejné správy v roce 2001*. Prague: Linde.

Kourliandskaia, Galina, Yelena Nikolayenko and Natalia Golovanova (2001) 'Local Government in the Russian Federation.' In *Developing New Rules in the Old Environment: Local Governments in Eastern Europe, the Caucasus and Central Asia*, edited by Igor Munteanu and Victor Popa, 161–264. Budapest: Open Society Institute.

Kovács, Zoltán (2001). 'The Geography of Post-Communist Parliamentary Elections.' In *Transformations in Hungary: Essays in Economy and Society*, edited by Peter Meusburger and Heike Jöns, 249–71. Heidelberg: Physica.

Kowalczyk, Andrzej (2000) 'Local Government in Poland.' In *Decentralization: Experiments and Reforms*, edited by Tamás Horváth, 217–53. Budapest: Local Government and Public Service Reform Initiative.

Kremer, Balázs, István Sziklai, and Katalin Tausz (2002). 'The Impact of Decentralization on Social Policy in Hungary.' In *The Impact of Decentralization on Social Policy*, edited by Katalin Tausz. Budapest: Open Society Institute Local Government and Public Service Reform Initiative.

Kubik, Ian (2005) 'How to Study Civil Society: The State of the Art and What to Do Next,' *East European Politics and Societies* 19: 105–20.

Kulesza, Michal (2001) 'Public Administration Reform and Decentralization as a Factor of the Development of Poland.' In *Ten Years of Transition: Prospects and Challenges for the Future of Public Administration*, edited by Jak Jabes, 331–48. Bratislava.

Lacina, Karel, and Zdenka Vajdova (2000) 'Local Government in the Czech Republic.' In *Decentralization: Experiments and Reforms*, edited by Tamás Horváth, 258–95. Budapest: Local Government and Public Service Reform Initiative.

Lallemand, Jean-Charles(1998) 'Gouvernance Introuvable à Briansk et Smolensk.' *La Revue Tocqueville/The Tocqueville Review* 19, no. 1: 75–102.

Lamentowicz, Wojtek (1990) 'Political Culture and Institution-Building: Democratic Evolution at Work.' In *Eastern Europe and Democracy: The Case of Poland*, edited by Wojtek Lamentowicz, 1–14. New York: Institute for East-West Security Studies.

Lankina, Tomila, and Lullit Getachew (2001) 'A Geographic Incrementalist Theory of Democratization: Territory, Aid, and Democracy in Post-Communist Regions.' *World Politics* 58, no. 4 (July 2006): 536–82.

Lankina, Tomila (2001) 'Local Government and Ethnic and Social Activism in Russia.' In *Contemporary Russian Politics: A Reader*, edited by Archie Brown, 398–411. Oxford University Press.

—— (2002) 'Local Administration and Ethno-Social Consensus in Russia.' *Europe-Asia Studies* 54, no. 7: 1037–53.

—— (2004a) *Governing the Locals: Local Self-Government and Ethnic Mobilization in Russia*. Lanham: Rowman and Littlefield.

—— (2004b) 'President Putin's Local Government Reforms.' In *The Dynamics of Russian Politics: Putin's Reform of Federal-Regional Relations*, edited by Peter Reddaway and Robert Orttung. Lanham, Md.: Rowman and Littlefield.

—— (2005) 'Explaining European Union Aid to Russia,' *Post-Soviet Affairs* 21, no. 4: 309–34.

Lappo, G.M. (ed) (1998) *Goroda Rossii: Entsiklopediya*. Moscow: Terra Knizhnyy Klub: Nauchnoe izdatel'stvo 'Bol'shaya rossiyskaya entsiklopediya'.

Lawson, Kay (1980) 'Political Parties and Linkage.' In *Political Parties and Linkage: A Comparative Perspective*, edited by Kay Lawson, 3–24. New Haven: Yale University Press.

Leif, Irving P., and Terry Nichols Clark (1972) *Community Power and Decision-Making: A Trend Report and Bibliography*. Vol. 2, *Current Sociology*. The Hague, Paris: Mouton and Co.

Lineberry, Robert L., and Edmund P. Fowler (1967) 'Reformism and Public Policies in American Cities.' *The American Political Science Review* 61, no. 3: 701–16.

Lobatch, Andrei I. 'EU Membership and Growing Regional Disparities: Poland's Strategy Options to Optimise Structural Transfers from the Union.' NISPACEE.

Lowndes, Vivien, Lawrence Pratchett, and Gerry Stoker (2002) 'Trends in Public Participation: Part 2 – Citizens' Perspectives,' *Public Administration* 79, no. 2: 445–55.

Luchterhandt-Mikhaleva, Galina (1999) 'Partii V Regionakh I Na Munitsipal'nom Urovne.' In *Reforma Mestnogo Samoupravleniya v Regional'nom Izmerenii*, edited by N. Vinnik, 134–48. Moscow: Moskovskiy obshchestvennyy nauchnyy fond.

Mabileau, Albert (1989) *Local Politics and Participation in Britain and France*. Cambridge University Press.

Machonin, Pavel, and Milan Tucek (2000) 'Czech Republic: New Elites and Social Change.' In *Elites after State Socialism: Theories and Analysis*, edited by John Higley and György Lengyel, 25–45. Lanham: Rowman and Littlefield Publishers.

Malyakin, I., and A. Sveshnikov (1999) 'Saratovskaya Oblast': Munitsipal'naya Klientela Gubernatora.' In *Reforma Mestnogo Samoupravleniya V Regional'nom Izmerenii*, edited by S. Ryzhenkov and N. Vinnik, 250–83. Moscow: Moskovskiy obshchestvennyy nauchnyy fond.

March, James G., and Johan P. Olsen (1989) *Rediscovering Institutions: The Organizational Basis of Politics*. New York: Free Press.

Marková, Hana (2000) *Finance obcí, měst a krajů*. Prague: Orac.

Martinez-Vazquez, Jorge, and Jameson Boex (2001) 'Russia's Transition to a New Federalism.' Washington, DC: World Bank.

Matsuzato, Kimitaka (1999) 'Local Elites under Transition: County and City Politics in Russia 1985–1996.' *Europe-Asia Studies* 51, no. 8: 1367–400.

McAuley, Mary (1992) 'Politics, Economics, and Elite Realignment in Russia: A Regional Perspective.' *Soviet Economy* 8, no. 1: 46–88.

—— (1997) *Russia's Politics of Uncertainty*.: Cambridge University Press.

Meadcroft, John (2001) 'Political Recruitment and Local Representation: The Case of Liberal Democrat Councilors.' *Local Government Studies* 27, no. 1: 19–36.

Mendras, Marie (1998) 'L'état, L'argent, La Clientéle.' *La Revue Tocqueville/The Tocqueville Review* 1: 35–54.

—— (1999) 'How Regional Elites Preserve Their Power.' *Post-Soviet Affairs* 15, no. 4: 295–311.

Moyser, George, and Geraint Parry (1989) 'Councillors, Citizens and Agendas: Aspects of Local Decision-Making in Britain.' In *Local Politics and Participation in Britain and France*, edited by Albert Mabileau, George Moyser, Geraint Parry and Patrick Quantin, 157–77. Cambridge University Press.

Munteanu, Igor, and Victor Popa (eds) (2001) *Developing New Rules in the Old Environment*. Budapest: Open Society Institute.

Musil, Jiří (1992) 'Czechoslovakia in the Middle of Transition.' *Daedalus* 121: 175–95.

Nadvorníková, Dagmar (2002) 'Hospodaření rozpočtů krajů a obcí za rok 2001,' *Moderní obec* 8, no. 7 available at http://vyhledavani.ihned.cz (accessed 9 October 2002).

Nam, Chang Woon, Rüdiger Parsche and Bettina Reichl (2001) *Municipal Finance and Governance in Poland, the Slovak Republic, the Czech Republic and Hungary*. Munich: Ifo-Institut für Wirtschaftsforschung.

Newton, Kenneth (1976) *Second City Politics: Democratic Processes and Decision-Making in Birmingham*. Oxford: Clarendon Press.

North, Douglas (1990) *Institutions, Institutional Changes, and Economic Performance*. Cambridge University Press.

Oates, Wallace E. (1990) 'Decentralization of the Public Sector: An Overview.' In *Decentralization, Local Governments, and Markets: Towards a Post-Welfare Agenda*, edited by Robert J. Bennett, 43–58. Oxford University Press.

Offe, Claus (1996) 'Designing Institutions in East European Transitions.' In *The Theory of Institutional Design*, edited by Robert E. Goodin, 199–226. Cambridge University Press.

Orenstein, Mitchell (1998) 'A Genealogy of Communist Successor Parties in East-Central Europe and the Determinants of Their Success.' *East European Politics and Societies* 12, no. 3: 472–99.

Orttung, Robert W., Danielle N. Lussier and Anna Paretskaya (2000) *The Republics and Regions of the Russian Federation: A Guide to Politics, Policies, and Leaders*. Armonk, N.Y.: ME Sharpe.

Osborne, Stephen P., and Aniko Kaposvari (1998) 'Nongovernmental Organizations, Local Government and the Development of Social Services: Managing Social Needs in Postcommunist Hungary.' Budapest: Open Society Institute.

Ostrom, Elinor (1990) *Governing the Commons: The Evolution of Institutions for Collective Action*. Cambridge University Press.

Page, Edward C., and Michael J. Goldsmith (1987) 'Centre and Locality: Explaining Cross-National Variation.' In *Central and Local Government Relations: A Comparative Analysis of West European Unitary States*, edited by Edward C. Page and Michael J. Goldsmith, 156–68. London: Sage Publications.

Parrott, Bruce (1997) 'Perspectives on Postcommunist Democratization.' In *The Consolidation of Democracy in East-Central Europe*, edited by Karen Dawisha and Bruce Parrott, 1–39. Cambridge University Press.

Peterson, Paul E. (1981) *City Limits*. University of Chicago Press.

Petro, Nicolai (1995) *The Rebirth of Russian Democracy: An Interpretation of Political Culture*. Cambridge, Mass.: Harvard University Press.

———— (2004) *Crafting Democracy: How Novgorod Has Coped with Rapid Social Change*. New York: Cornell University Press, 2004.

Pigey, Juliana H., and Judit Kálmán (1999) 'Fiscal Decentralization and Local Government in Hungary 1989–1999.' Washington, DC: USAID.

Polsby, Nelson W. (1963) *Community Power and Political Theory*. New Haven: Yale University Press.

Przeworski, Adam (1991) *Democracy and the Market*. Cambridge University Press.

Putnam, Robert D. (1993) *Making Democracy Work: Civic Traditions in Modern Italy*. Princeton University Press.

———— (1995) 'Tuning in, Tuning Out: The Strange Disappearance of Social Capital in America,' *Political Science and Politics* 28, no. 4: 664–83.

Rechnitzer, János (2001) 'Cross-Border Co-Operations in Hungary in the 1990s.' In *Transformations in Hungary: Essays in Economy and Society*, edited by Peter Meusburger and Heike Jöns, 355–82. Heidelberg: Physica.

Regulski, Jerzy (2000) *Samorzad III Rzeczpospolitej: Koncepcje I Realizacja*. Warsaw.

Higgins, Richard G. (1989) Jr. 'Alternative Service Delivery in Local Government: Conceptual Issues and Current Trends.' *Research in Urban Policy* 3: 93–108.

Rose, Lawrence, Stanislav Buchta, György Gajduschek, Miroslaw Grochowski, and Ondrej Hubacek (1996) 'Political Culture and Citizen Involvement.' In *Local Democracy and the Processes of Transformation in East-Central Europe*, edited by Harald Baldersheim, Michal Illner, Audun Offerdal, Lawrence Rose and Pawel Swianiewicz, 43–104. Boulder: Westview Press.

Rose, Richard (1994a) 'Distrust as an Obstacle to the Civil Society.' *The Journal of Democracy* 5 (April).

———— (1994b) 'Postcommunism and the Problem of Trust.' *Journal of Democracy* 5, no. 3: 18–30.

———— (1997) 'Where Are Postcommunist Societies Going?' *Journal of Democracy* 8, no. 3: 92–108.

Sani, Giacomo, and Giovanni Sartori (1983) 'Polarization, Fragmentation and Competition in Western Democracies.' In *Western European Party Systems: Continuity and Change*, edited by Hans Daalder and Peter Mair, 307–40. London: Sage Publications.

Sartori, Giovanni (1976) *Parties and Party Systems: A Framework for Analysis*. Vol. 1. Cambridge University Press.

Schattschneider, E.E. (1960) *The Semi-Sovereign People: A Realist's View of Democracy in America*. New York: Holt, Rinehart and Winston.

Sevic, Zeljko (2003) 'Measuring Public Sector Performance in South East Europe: Addressing the Challenges of Democratic Transition.' In *Gauging Success: Performance Measurement in South Eastern Europe*, edited by Zeljko Sevic, 15–30. Budapest: Local Government and Public Service Reform Initiative.

Singer, Matthew M. (2004) 'Local Parties and Local Politics: Electoral Fragmentation and Municipal Budget Choices in Bolivia and Mexico.' Paper read at APSA, 2004, September 2–5, at Chicago, IL.

Smith, John William, and John S. Klemanski (1990) *The Urban Politics Dictionary*. Santa Barbara, Calif.: Abc-Clio.

Soós, Gábor, and Judit Kálmán (2002) 'Country Report: Hungary.' In *The State of Local Democracy in Central Europe*, edited by Gábor Soós, Gábor Tóka and Glen Wright. Budapest: Local Government and Public Service Reform Initiative.

Startsev, Yaroslav (1999) 'Gubernatorial Politics in Sverdlovsk Oblast.' *Post-Soviet Affairs* 15, no. 4: 336–61.

Stoker, Gerry (1996) 'Introduction: Normative Theories of Local Government and Democracy.' In *Rethinking Local Democracy*, edited by Desmond King and Gerry Stoker, 1–27. London: Macmillan.

Stone, Clarence N. (1980) 'Systemic Power in Community Decision Making: A Restatement of Stratification Theory.' *The American Political Science Review* 74: 978–90.

—— (1995) 'Political Leadership in Urban Politics.' In *Theories of Urban Politics*, edited by David Judge, Gerry Stoker and Harold Wolman, 96–116. London: Sage Publications.

Stoner-Weiss, Kathryn (1997) *Local Heroes: The Political Economy of Russian Regional Governance*. Princeton: Princeton University Press.

Swianiewicz, Pawel (2001) 'Institutional Performance of Local Government Administration in Poland.' In *Ten Years of Transition: Prospects and Challenges for the Future of Public Administration. Proceedings from the Eighth Annual Conference Held in Budapest, Hungary 13–15 April 2000*, edited by Jak Jabes, 162–86. Bratislava: NISPACEE.

Swianiewicz, Pawel, Wojciech Dziemanowicz, and Marta Mackiewicz (2000) *Sprawnosc Instytucjonalna Administracji Samorzadowej W Polsce: Zróznicowanie Regionalne*. Warsaw.

Swianiewicz, Pawel, Mikolaj Herbst and Julita Lukomska (2004) 'Local Governments and Economic Development: What Works and What Does Not?' Warsaw: Local Government Initiative/Open Society Institute, Budapest.

Szuks, Stefan (1998) *Democracy in the Head: A Comparative Analysis of Democratic Leadership Orientations among Local Elites in Three Phases of Democratisation*. Göteborg: Center for Public Sector Research, Göteborg University.

Szuly, Kinga (n.d.) 'The Role of Local Governments in the Hungarian Privatization Process: Some Aspects of Property Management and the Case of Gas Service Utility Shares,' www.ucc.ie/euroloc/student/Kinga_Szuly.doc (accessed 25 July 2003).

Tarrow, Sidney (1997) *Between Center and Periphery: Grassroots Politicians in Italy and France*. New Haven: Yale University Press.

Temesi, István (2000) 'Local Government in Hungary.' In *Decentralization: Experiments and Reforms*, edited by Tamás Horváth, 343–84. Budapest: Local Government and Public Service Reform Initiative.

Thelen, Peter (2002) 'Die Linke siegt bei den Oktober – Konmunalwahlen in Ungarn, Bericht and Bewertung durch den Leiter des Budapester Büros der Friedrich-Ebert-Stiftung, http://jestportal. Fes.de/pls/porta130/docs/folder/presse/beridute/ungarn/html (accessed 8 November 2002).

Tiebout, C.M. (1956) 'A Pure Theory of Local Expenditures.' *Journal of Political Economy* 64: 416–24.

Tocqueville, Alexis de (1994) 'Townships, Municipal Administration, State Government.' In *Democracy in America*, edited by J.P. Mayer. London: Fontana Press.

Tóka, Gábor (1999) 'Parties and Social Divisions in Hungary: A Common East Central European Pattern?' In *A Society Transformed: Hungary in Time-Space Perspective*, edited by Rudolf Andorka, Tamás Kolosi, Richard Rose and György Vukovich, 155–78. Budapest: CEU Press.

Tóka, Gábor (1996) 'Parties and Social Divisions: A Common East-Central European Pattern?' In *A Society Transformed: Hungary in Time-Space Perspective*, edited by Rudolf Andorka, Tamás Kolosi, Richard Rose and György Vukovich, 155–78. Budapest: Central European University Press.

Tokes, Rudolf L. (2000) 'Hungary: Elites and the Use and Abuse of Democratic Institutions.' In *Elites after State Socialism: Theories and Analysis*, edited by John Higley and György Lengyel, 71–85. Lanham: Rowman and Littlefield Publishers.

Vedral, Josef (2002) 'Schválená regulace obecní zadluženosti,' *Obec & finance 7*, no. 1, http://denik.obce.cz (accessed 7 October 2003).

Vodička, Karel (1997) 'Verwaltungsreform und Verwaltungsstrukturen in Tschechien nach 1990.' *Verwaltung 1*: 97–108.

Walder, Andrew G. (2003) 'Elite Opportunity in Transitional Economies,' *American Sociological Review 68*, no. 6: 899–916.

Warren, R., M.S. Rosentraub, and L.F. Weschler (1985) 'Urban Service Delivery and a Community Service Budget: Public Spending, Private Actions, and Coproduction.' In *Urban Innovations as Response to Urban Fiscal Strain*, edited by Terry Clark, Gerd Michael Hellstern and Guido Martinotti, 70–82. Berlin: Europäische Perspektiven.

Whitefield, Stephen (2005) 'Political Culture and Post-Communism' In *Political Culture and Post-Communism*, edited by S. Whitefield, 1–14. New York: Palgrave Macmillan.

Wollmann, Hellmut, and Natalia Butusova (2003) 'Local Self-Government in Russia: Precarious Trajectory between Power and Law.' In *Local Democracy in Post-Communist Europe*, edited by Harald Baldersheim, Michal Illner and Hellmut Wollmann, 211–40. Opladen: Leske + Budrich.

Wollmann, Hellmut, and Tomila Lankina (2003) 'Local Government in Poland and Hungary.' In *Local Democracy in Post-Communist Europe*, edited by Harald Baldersheim, Michal Illner and Hellmut Wollmann, 91–122.

Wolman, Harold (1990) 'Decentralization: What It Is and Why We Should Care.' In *Decentralization, Local Governments, and Markets: Towards a Post-Welfare Agenda*, 29–42. Oxford University Press.

Wong, Kenneth K. (1989) 'Toward a "Political Choice" Model in Local Policy Making.' *Research in Urban Policy 3*: 217–45.

Young, John F. (1994) 'Institutions, Elites, and Local Politics in Russia: The Case of Omsk.' In *Local Power and Post-Soviet Politics*, edited by Jeffrey W. Hahn and Theodore Friedgut. London: ME Sharpe.

Index